N E W
HOME PLANS
For 1996

Submit all Canadian
plan orders to:

The Garlinghouse Company
20 Cedar Street North
Kitchener, Ontario N2H 2WB

Canadian Orders Only: 1-800-561-4169
Fa
Custome

Library o

IS

GW00597453

TABLE OF CONTENTS

PLAN NO. 34043 REAR VIEW — PAGE 2

PLAN NO. 24319 REAR VIEW — PAGE 71

GARLINGHOUSE

Publisher James D. McNair III
Cover Design by Paula Mennone

ONE-LEVEL VICTORIAN

This convenient, one-level plan is perfect for the modern family with a taste for classic design. Traditional Victorian touches in this three-bedroom beauty include a romantic, railed porch and an intriguing breakfast tower just off the kitchen. But, the step-saving arrangement of the kitchen between the breakfast and formal dining rooms, the wide-open living room with sliders to a rear deck, and the handsome master suite with its skylit, compartmentalized bath make this a home you'll love today and long into the future. Notice the convenient laundry location on the bedroom hall.

Main area — 1,583 sq. ft.
Basement —
1,588 sq. ft.
Garage — 484 sq. ft.

Total living area:
1,583 sq. ft.

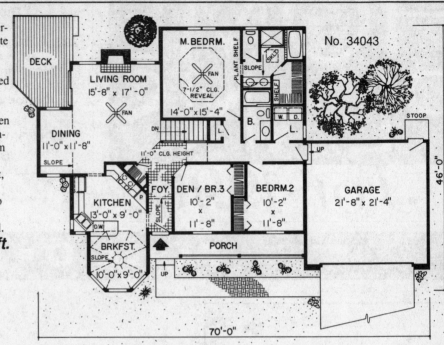

Refer to **Pricing Schedule B** on the order form for pricing information

An
EXCLUSIVE DESIGN
By Karl Kreeger

CLASSIC EXTERIOR, MODERN PLAN

This two-story brick home features the classic look of turn-of-the-century homes mixed with a contemporary floor plan. The bright two-story foyer is framed by an elegant dining room to the left and a den, for after hours work, on the right. The generous, island kitchen opens into a breakfast area surrounded by glass and perfect for reading the morning paper. The enticing master suite features a sitting area that makes the perfect getaway. Upstairs you'll enjoy a dramatic view of both the foyer and the family room below as you cross the bridge to any of the three additional bedrooms, all with walk-in closets and one with a private bath.

First floor — 2,385 sq. ft.
Second floor — 1,012 sq. ft.
Basement — 2,385 sq. ft.
Garage — 846 sq. ft.

Total living area:
3,397 sq. ft.

*This plan is not to be built within a 25 mile radius of Cedar Rapids, IA.

Refer to **Pricing Schedule F** on the order form for pricing information

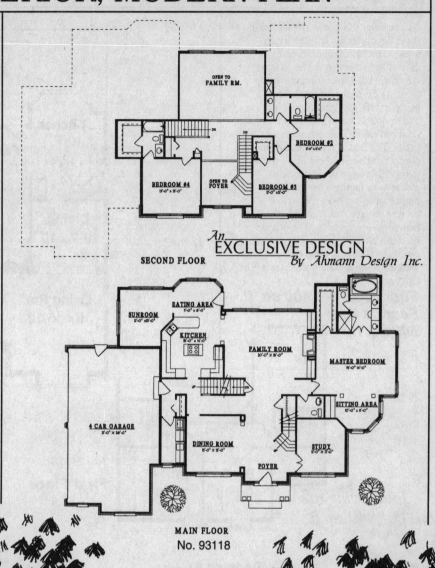

SECOND FLOOR

OPEN TO FAMILY RM.

BEDROOM #2

BEDROOM #4

OPEN TO FOYER

BEDROOM #3

An
EXCLUSIVE DESIGN
By Ahmann Design Inc.

EATING AREA

SUNROOM

KITCHEN

FAMILY ROOM

MASTER BEDROOM

4 CAR GARAGE

SITTING AREA

DINING ROOM

STUDY

FOYER

MAIN FLOOR
No. 93118

FIRST FLOOR MASTER SUITE

As you enter this home, the elevated foyer directs traffic into the living areas. The living room receives natural light through the large front window. The formal dining room is located next to the kitchen. The modern, efficient kitchen offers a corner double basin sink, bay area for informal eating and easy access to the patio. The family room has a fantastic corner fireplace to serve as its focal point. This large room is sure to please your family's needs. The master suite located on this floor insures privacy, since all the other bedrooms are upstairs. The private master bath has separate shower and oval tub. Bedroom three enjoys a walk-in closet and they all share a full hall bath.

First floor — 1,400 sq. ft.
Second floor — 540 sq. ft.

Total living area: 1,940 sq. ft.

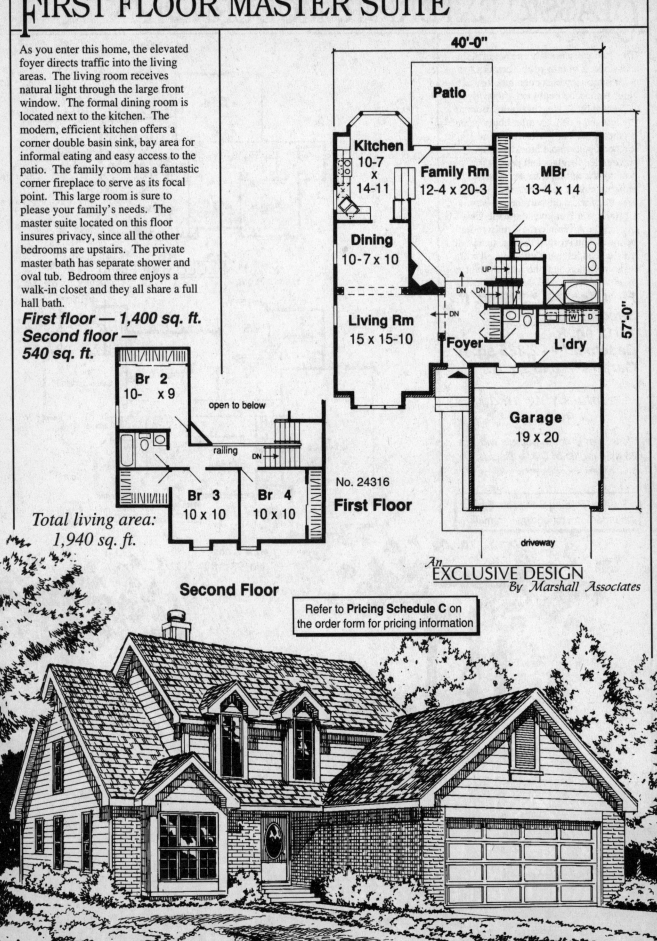

No. 24316
First Floor

Second Floor

An EXCLUSIVE DESIGN
By Marshall Associates

Refer to **Pricing Schedule C** on the order form for pricing information

B. LeBou

PERFECT FOR PARTIES

Does your family enjoy entertaining? Here's your home! This handsome, rambling beauty can handle a crowd of any size. Greet your guests in a beautiful foyer that opens to the cozy, bayed living room and elegant dining room with floor-to-ceiling windows. Show them the impressive two-story gallery and book-lined study, flooded with sunlight from atrium doors and clerestory windows. Or, gather around the fire in the vaulted family room. The bar connects to the efficient kitchen, just steps away from both nook and formal dining room. And, when the guests go home, you'll appreciate your luxurious first floor master suite and the cozy upstairs bedroom suites with adjoining sitting room.

First floor — 2,310 sq. ft.
Second floor — 866 sq. ft.
Garage — 679 sq. ft.

Total living area:
3,176 sq. ft.

Refer to **Pricing Schedule E** on the order form for pricing information

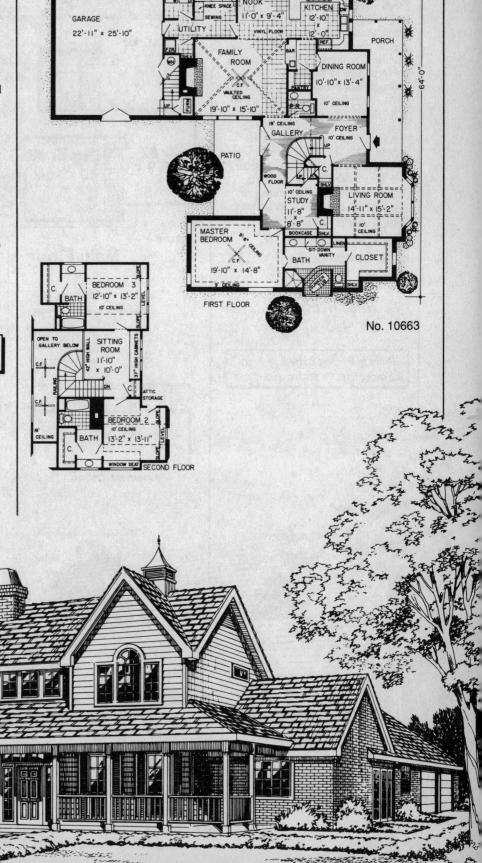

No. 10663

LARGE LIVING IN SMALL SPACES

Only 998 sq. ft., yet this house has the amenities that the 90's demand. The modern, efficient kitchen boasts a double sink, pantry, ample counter and cabinet space and convenient washer and dryer. The eating nook has easy access to the patio enabling you to expand your living space in the milder months. The corner fireplace becomes the focal point of the living room adding atmosphere and warmth to the room. The open layout of these rooms gives the appearance of spaciousness. You may enjoy your fireplace while making dinner, for the rooms blend together. The master bedroom enjoys its own bathroom, while the secondary bedrooms share a full hallway bath. The many features of this home give you the feeling of a much larger home.

Main area — 993 sq. ft.
Garage — 390 sq. ft.
Opt. basement —
987 sq. ft.

Total living area:
993 sq. ft.

Refer to **Pricing Schedule A** on
the order form for pricing information

48'-0"

39'-0"

Patio

Mst. Br
12-3 x 11-6

Living Rm
13 x 18-1

Nook
5-9 x 9

Kit.
6-9
x
9

Br #2
8-9
x
11-6

lin.

Den/Br #3
10 x 10-2

Foy

D W pan.

Garage
19-6 x 19-6

plant shelf

Main Floor

driveway
No. 24304

Kit
6-9
x
9

DN
pan.

Basement Option

An
EXCLUSIVE DESIGN
By Marshall Associates

FIREPLACE IN TWO ROOMS

This beautiful ranch design features an extra-large living room with plenty of formal dining space at the opposite end. Large wood burning fireplaces are found in both the living and family rooms. A mudroom, located off the kitchen, features a laundry area, half bath, and storage closet. The charming master bedroom has a full bath and plenty of closet space.

First floor — 1,878 sq. ft.
Garage — 538 sq. ft.

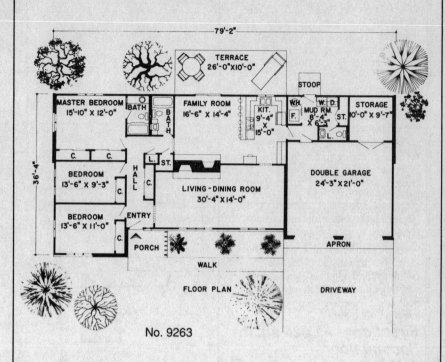

No. 9263

Total living area:
1,878 sq. ft.

Refer to **Pricing Schedule C** on the order form for pricing information

BIG COUNTRY HOME HAS CHARM

Covered porches, back and front, run the length of this quality country home, and complete the traditional exterior theme. A right turn off the formal entry leads to an elegant living room and unusual music alcove, complete with custom built-ins for audio equipment. The adjoining library features floor-to-ceiling built-in bookcases and a second fireplace. The country kitchen will rapidly become a favorite gathering spot, with a fireplace in the sitting/dining area, snack counter, and cooking layout designed for canning, baking, and gourmet meals. The back dining room has a wonderful view through the back porch to the yard beyond. Upstairs, you will have a hard time leaving this incredible master suite, with a combined dressing/bath suite with whirlpool that's as big as most folk's bedrooms. Two large bedrooms share a second full bath.

First floor — 2,026 sq. ft.
Second floor — 1,386 sq. ft.
Garage — 576 sq. ft.

Total living area: 3,412 sq. ft.

Refer to **Pricing Schedule F** on the order form for pricing information

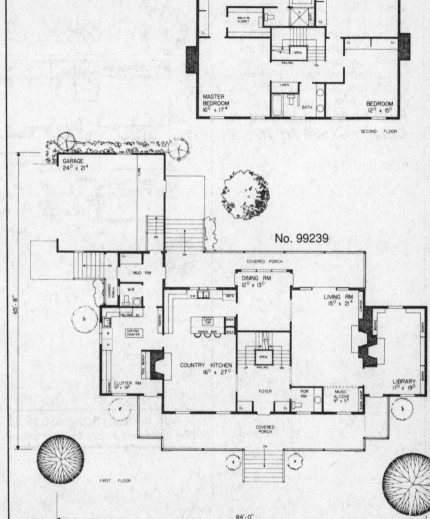

FRIENDLY COLONIAL

Casual living is the theme of this elegant Farmhouse Colonial. A beautiful circular stair ascends from the central foyer, flanked by the formal living and dining rooms. The informal family room, accessible from the foyer, captures the Early American style with exposed beams, wood paneling, and brick fireplace wall. A separate dinette opens to an efficient kitchen. Four bedrooms and a two-basin family bath, arranged around the central hall, occupy the second floor.

First floor — 1,099 sq. ft.
Second floor — 932 sq. ft.

Total living area: 2,031 sq. ft.

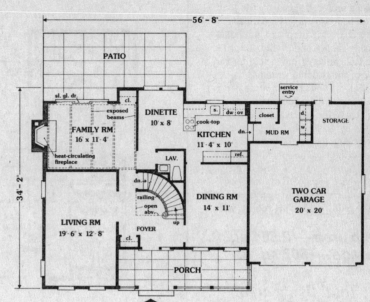

FIRST FLOOR PLAN

No. 90606

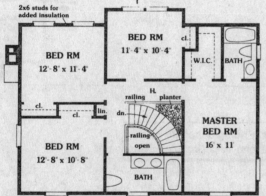

SECOND FLOOR PLAN

Refer to **Pricing Schedule C** on the order form for pricing information

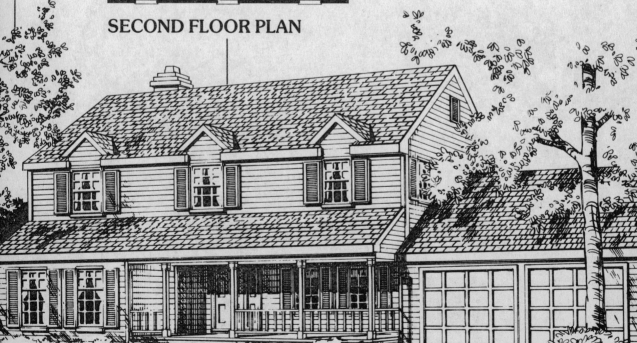

A SPECIAL SUITE FOR YOU

Create a secluded sanctuary for your master bedroom: a generous space with a charming fireplace, individual dressing rooms, and skylit bathing area. Relax away from the clutter and noise of the children's rooms, especially if you create a study or sewing room from bedroom two. You'll love the courtyard effect created by glassed-in living spaces overlooking the central covered patio with skylights. The sprawling charm of this house creates a sense of privacy everywhere you go. Extra touches, such as the wetbar and dual fireplaces for the family and living rooms, set this home apart.

Main area — 2,864 sq. ft.
Garage — 607 sq. ft.

Total living area:
2,864 sq. ft.

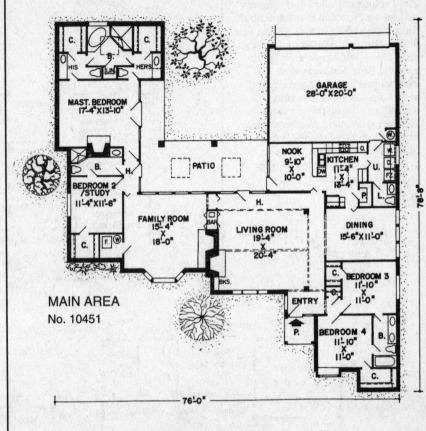

MAIN AREA
No. 10451

Refer to **Pricing Schedule E** on the order form for pricing information

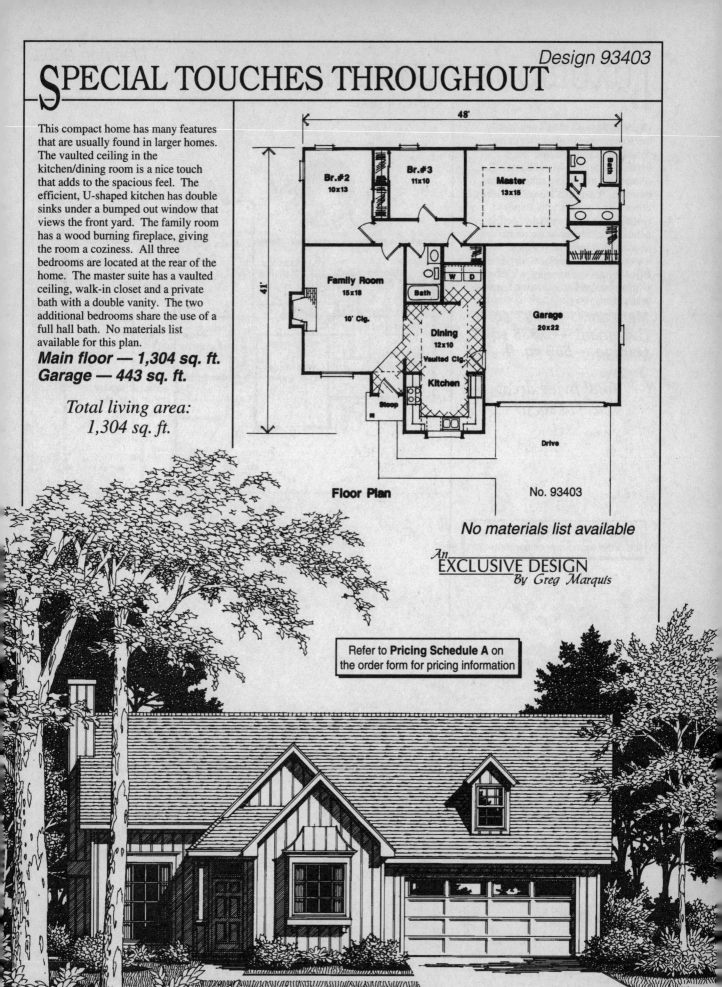

SPECIAL TOUCHES THROUGHOUT

This compact home has many features that are usually found in larger homes. The vaulted ceiling in the kitchen/dining room is a nice touch that adds to the spacious feel. The efficient, U-shaped kitchen has double sinks under a bumped out window that views the front yard. The family room has a wood burning fireplace, giving the room a coziness. All three bedrooms are located at the rear of the home. The master suite has a vaulted ceiling, walk-in closet and a private bath with a double vanity. The two additional bedrooms share the use of a full hall bath. No materials list available for this plan.

Main floor — 1,304 sq. ft.
Garage — 443 sq. ft.

Total living area:
1,304 sq. ft.

Floor Plan   No. 93403

No materials list available

An
EXCLUSIVE DESIGN
By Greg Marquis

Refer to **Pricing Schedule A** on the order form for pricing information

LUXURIOUS EXTERIOR

Graceful Spanish arches and stately brick suggests the right attention to detail that is found inside this expansive three bedroom home. The plush master bedroom suite, a prime example, boasts in a lounge, a walk-in closet and a private bath. Exposed rustic beams and a cathedral ceiling heighten the formal living room, and an unusually large family room savors a wood-burning fireplace. In addition to the formal dining room, a kitchen with dinette and access to the terrace is planned.

Main area — 2,333 sq. ft.
Basement — 2,333 sq. ft.
Garage — 559 sq. ft.

Total living area:
2,333 sq. ft.

Refer to **Pricing Schedule D** on the order form for pricing information

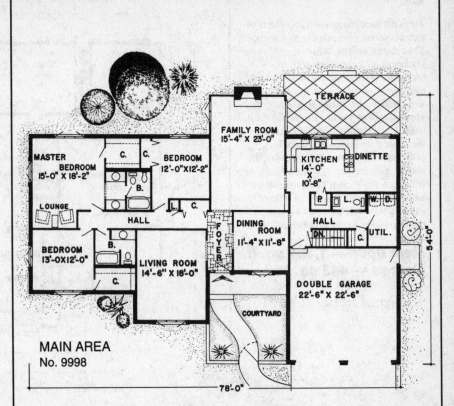

MAIN AREA
No. 9998

AN EARTH-SHELTERED HOME

As in all earth-sheltered homes, the living spaces are on the open side, for light and fire safety. The most prominent feature is the combined kitchen/living/dining room, with its semicircle of tall windows catching light from three sides. The kitchen counters, sitting at the hinge of two wall angles, make a lazy bend to create space for a media nook and pantry. A utility room with extra storage space fills the back corner of the house. The master suite is luxurious for a small home; besides the usual private bath, vanity, and walk-in closet, it also includes an oversized tub that looks out on the planting of a side patio.

Main floor — 1,482 sq. ft.
Garage — 564 sq. ft.
Width — 79'-0"
Depth — 50'-0"

Total living area:
1,482 sq. ft.

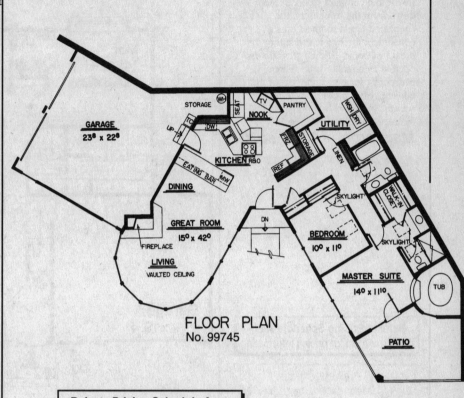

FLOOR PLAN
No. 99745

Refer to **Pricing Schedule A** on the order form for pricing information

HIGH IMPACT ANGLES

Lots of glass and soaring ceilings give this house a spacious, contemporary flavor in a compact space. A step down from the front entry, the fireplaced Great room adjoins a convenient kitchen with a sunny breakfast nook. Sliding glass doors open to an angular deck. Three bedrooms, located at the rear of the house to offer protection from street sounds, include a luxurious, vaulted master suite with private bath.

Main area — 1,368 sq. ft.

Total living area: 1,368 sq. ft.

Refer to **Pricing Schedule A** on the order form for pricing information

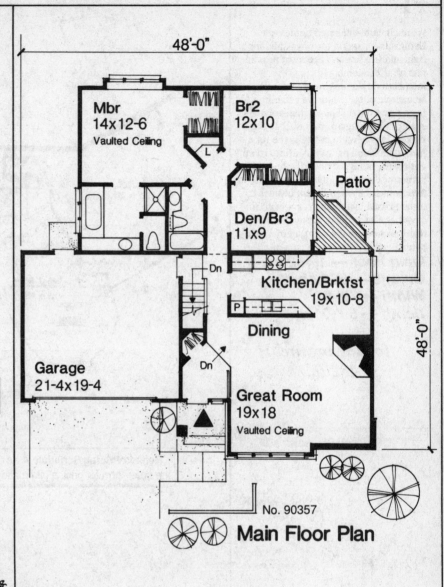

48'-0"

48'-0"

Mbr 14x12-6 Vaulted Ceiling

Br2 12x10

Patio

Den/Br3 11x9

Dn

Kitchen/Brkfst 19x10-8

Dining

Dn

Garage 21-4x19-4

Great Room 19x18 Vaulted Ceiling

No. 90357

Main Floor Plan

FAMILY LIVING ON ONE LEVEL

Design 91027

Arches adorn exterior and interior spaces in this four-bedroom beauty. Look at the graceful openings between the sunken living and dining rooms just off the foyer and the massive half-round window and curved entryway facing the street. Walk past the den to family areas at the rear of the house, centering around the convenient island kitchen. An open plan keeps the cook from getting lonely while the kids are gathered around the fireplace or doing homework at the handy desk. French doors unite the master bedroom with the backyard. At the end of a long day, the private spa is a plus you'll really appreciate. Please specify a basement or crawl space foundation when ordering this plan.

Main area — 2,174 sq. ft.
Garage — 2-car

Total living area:
2,174 sq. ft.

Refer to **Pricing Schedule C** on the order form for pricing information

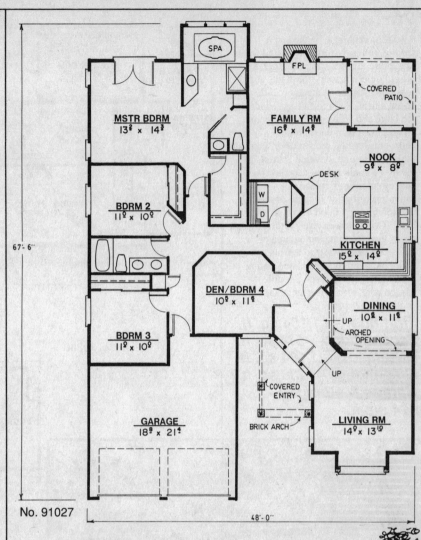

No. 91027

CAPE COD PASSIVE SOLAR

A solar greenhouse on the south employs energy storage rods and water to capture the sun's warmth, thereby providing a sanctuary for plants and supplying a good percentage of the house's heat. Other southern windows are large and triple glazed for energy efficiency. From one of the bedrooms, on the second floor, you can look out through louvered shutters to the living room below, accented by a heat circulating fireplace and a cathedral ceiling with three dormer windows which flood the room with light. On the lower level, sliding glass doors lead from the sitting area of the master bedroom suite to a private patio. Also on this level are a dining room, kitchen, mudroom, double garage with a large storage area, and another larger patio.

First floor — 1,164 sq. ft.
Second floor — 574 sq. ft.
Basement — 1,164 sq. ft.
Greenhouse — 238 sq. ft.
Garage & storage — 574 sq. ft.

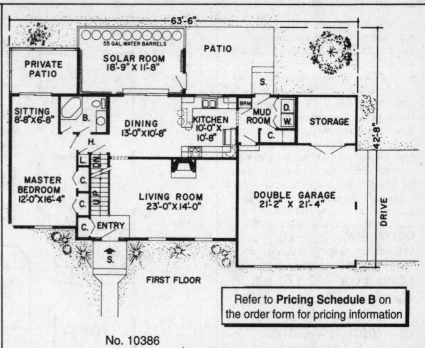

FIRST FLOOR

No. 10386

Refer to **Pricing Schedule B** on the order form for pricing information

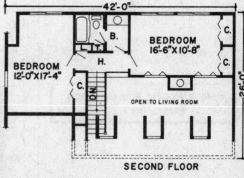

SECOND FLOOR

Total living area:
1,738 sq. ft.

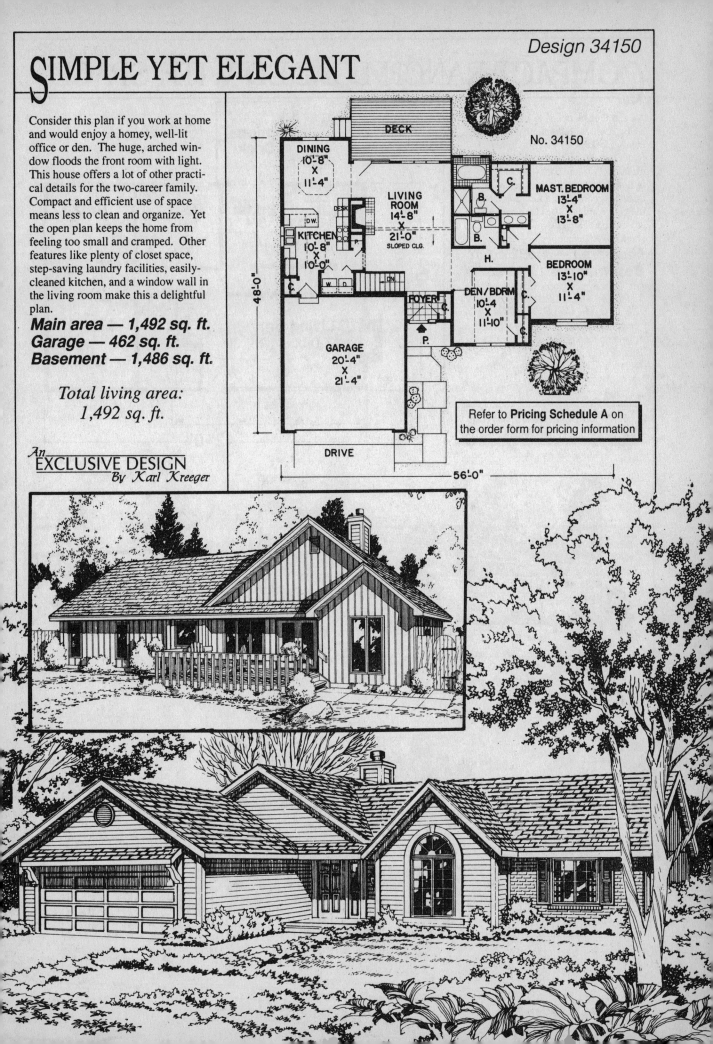

SIMPLE YET ELEGANT

Consider this plan if you work at home and would enjoy a homey, well-lit office or den. The huge, arched window floods the front room with light. This house offers a lot of other practical details for the two-career family. Compact and efficient use of space means less to clean and organize. Yet the open plan keeps the home from feeling too small and cramped. Other features like plenty of closet space, step-saving laundry facilities, easily-cleaned kitchen, and a window wall in the living room make this a delightful plan.

Main area — 1,492 sq. ft.
Garage — 462 sq. ft.
Basement — 1,486 sq. ft.

Total living area:
1,492 sq. ft.

An
EXCLUSIVE DESIGN
By *Karl Kreeger*

No. 34150

DECK

DINING
10'-8"
X
11'-4"

LIVING
ROOM
14'-8"
X
21'-0"
SLOPED CLG.

DESK

DW.

KITCHEN
10'-8"
X
10'-0"

MAST. BEDROOM
13'-4"
X
13'-8"

B.

C.

B.

H.

BEDROOM
13'-10"
X
11'-4"

W D

DN

FOYER

DEN / BDRM
10'-4"
X
11'-10"

C.

C.

P.

48'-0"

GARAGE
20'-4"
X
21'-4"

P.

DRIVE

56'-0"

Refer to **Pricing Schedule A** on the order form for pricing information

Design 34328

COMPACT RANCH LOADED WITH SPACE

A central entry opens to a spacious living room with ample windows and a handy closet nearby. The kitchen features a dining area with sliding glass doors to the backyard and optional deck. A hallway separates three bedrooms and a full bath from the active areas. The laundry facilities are tucked behind double doors for slab/crawlspace options.

Main area — 1,092 sq. ft.
Basement — 1,092 sq. ft.

Total living area:
1,092 sq. ft.

Refer to **Pricing Schedule A** on the order form for pricing information

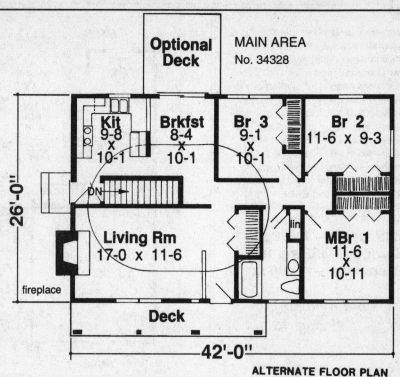

Optional Deck

MAIN AREA
No. 34328

Kit 9-8 x 10-1

Brkfst 8-4 x 10-1

Br 3 9-1 x 10-1

Br 2 11-6 x 9-3

DN

Living Rm 17-0 x 11-6

lin

MBr 1 11-6 x 10-11

fireplace

Deck

26'-0"

42'-0"

ALTERNATE FLOOR PLAN for Crawl Space

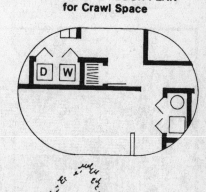

D W

COLUMNED PORCH SHELTERS ENTRANCE

Enter either through the columned porch entrance or the garage. The garage entrance adds the mudroom effect, keeping soiled shoes from the rest of the house. Half walls with columns, accent the entrance into the formal living room. The formal dining room directly accesses the living room for ease in entertaining. An efficient kitchen layout makes food preparation a breeze. The cooktop island doubles as an eating bar. The breakfast bay provides a bright, sunny place for the family to start the day. The family room is sunken and incorporates a handsome fireplace and built-in shelves. All the sleeping quarters are located on the second floor as well as two full baths and the utility room. No materials list available for this plan.

First floor — 1,378 sq. ft.
Second floor —
1,270 sq. ft.

Total living area:
2,648 sq. ft.

No materials list available

44'-0"

56'-0"

- Future Gazebo
- **Brkfst** 10 x 7-6
- **Deck**
- **Family** 13 x 16-8
- island
- **Kit** 16 x 14-6
- **Dining** 11-6 x 13
- DN
- built-in
- balcony
- DN
- UP
- built-in
- bench
- 8" columns on 1/2 wall
- **Living** 11 x 14-4
- **Foyer**
- **Garage** 21-8 x 21-8
- No. 24589
- **First Floor**

An **EXCLUSIVE DESIGN**
By Britt J. Willis

Refer to **Pricing Schedule E** on the order form for pricing information

- whirlpool tub
- **Mstr Br** 16 x 13
- **Br 2** 11-6 x 13
- **Br 4** 13-6 x 11
- DN
- attic
- shelves
- shelves
- **Util.**
- D W
- open to below
- **Br 3** 11-8 x 12-8
- **Second Floor**

AFFORDABLE BEAUTY

Simple clean lines make this home affordable to build, without sacrificing beauty. The tiled entry advances into the living room, which features a gas fireplace that adjoins the dining room. An efficient U-shaped kitchen is separated from the dining room by a breakfast bar. Sliding glass doors add light and give access from the dining room to the rear deck. The master suite includes ample closet space and a private bath with a shower. A full bath in the hallway serves the two additional bedrooms. One of the bedrooms is crowned by a vaulted ceiling. No materials list available for this plan.

Main floor — 1,250 sq. ft.

Total living area: 1,250 sq. ft.

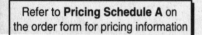

MAIN AREA
No. 93906

Refer to **Pricing Schedule A** on the order form for pricing information

No materials list available

STUNNING IMPRESSIONS

Gather the family around you while you prepare supper in your sunny, well-equipped kitchen. The adjoining glass-walled dinette makes this a cheerful, expansive area for happy family hours. The brick wall surrounding the fireplace in the adjacent family room adds atmosphere and helps store the heat of the crackling fire. Formal areas are just off the foyer. The bow window makes the living room seem even larger than its generous size. Up that sweeping stairway, there are enough bedrooms to give everyone a room. And, double sinks in the front bath will make mornings so convenient, you'll wonder how you ever lived without them.

First floor — 1,119 sq. ft.
Second floor — 837 sq. ft.
Basement — 1,080 sq. ft.

Total living area:
1,956 sq. ft.

Refer to **Pricing Schedule C** on the order form for pricing information

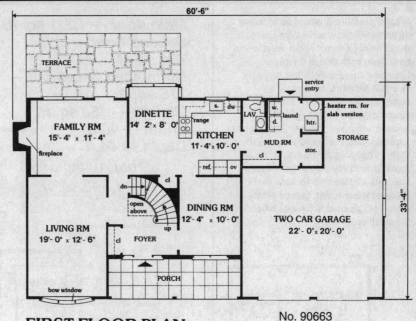

FIRST FLOOR PLAN

No. 90663

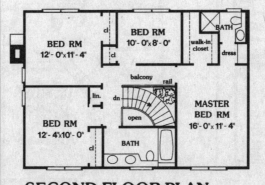

SECOND FLOOR PLAN

Design 90924

FRENCH DOORS LEAD TO STUDY

What a pleasure it would be to move into a new house, settle down, and never need to worry about what might have been included in the plan. Choosing this Tudor house will give you that pleasure, because it's complete in every way. The brick and stucco exterior is highlighted by beautiful window shapes. The angular, vaulted living room and a dining room with its own covered sundeck are set apart from everyday traffic. With a spacious kitchen overlooking the sunken family room, there's plenty of room for informal activities, whatever the weather.

Main floor — 1,211 sq. ft.
Second floor — 734 sq. ft.
Unfinished basement — 716 sq. ft.
Garage — 452 sq. ft.
Width — 46 ft.
Depth — 44 ft.

Total living area: 1,945 sq. ft.

Refer to **Pricing Schedule C** on the order form for pricing information

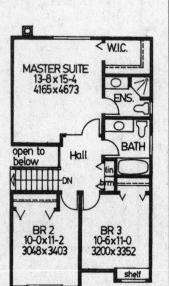

SECOND FLOOR PLAN

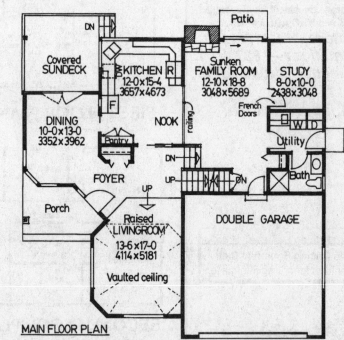

MAIN FLOOR PLAN

An
EXCLUSIVE DESIGN
By Westhome Planners. Ltd.

No. 90924

Little Charmer with Side Patio

This versatile design will fit a variety of building situations. The large covered front entry courtyard as an option, could have a gate placed in line with the master bedroom wall to increase security. There is also an entrance from the garage into a big utility room, which is placed conveniently just off the kitchen. A roomy kitchen includes a breakfast nook for informal dining, which looks out onto the private side patio. Nearby, the formal dining room combines with the living room to yield a good-sized area for formal entertaining. By adjusting window locations in the living room you can tailor-make this home to suit your lot.

Main area — 1,412 sq. ft.
Garage — 365 sq. ft.
Width — 39'-0"
Depth — 60'-0"

Total living area:
1,412 sq. ft.

Refer to **Pricing Schedule A** on the order form for pricing information

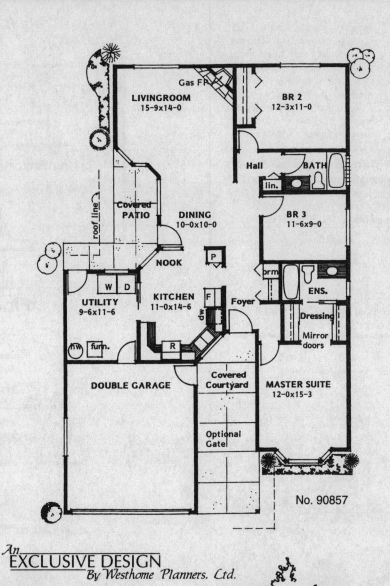

LIVINGROOM
15-9x14-0

Gas FP.

BR 2
12-3x11-0

Hall

BATH

lin.

Covered PATIO

DINING
10-0x10-0

BR 3
11-6x9-0

roof line

NOOK

P

orm

ENS.

W   D

KITCHEN
11-0x14-6

F

Foyer

Dressing

UTILITY
9-6x11-6

dw

Mirror doors

hw   furn.

R

Covered Courtyard

MASTER SUITE
12-0x15-3

DOUBLE GARAGE

Optional Gate

No. 90857

An
EXCLUSIVE DESIGN
By Westhome Planners, Ltd.

Design 34353

RANCH HAS CONTEMPORARY FLAVOR

The L-shaped living and dining room arrangement is enhanced by bump-out windows, a fireplace and sliders to the backyard. The adjoining compact, galley-style kitchen easily serves the dining room and the rear entry is an added convenience. A hallway leads to the sleeping wing where there are three bedrooms and one and three-quarters baths.

Main area — 1,268 sq. ft.
Basement — 1,248 sq. ft.

Total living area:
1,268 sq. ft.

Refer to **Pricing Schedule A** on the order form for pricing information

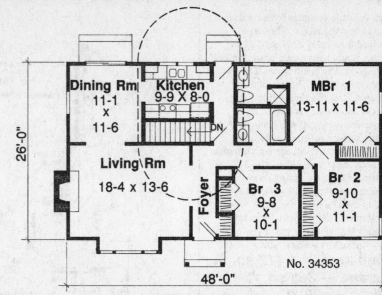

Floor Plan

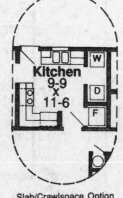

Slab/Crawlspace Option

EXPANDABLE HOME

An efficient kitchen adjoins the dining room that has sliders to the patio. The extra-large living room gives a wide-open feeling to all who enter. Two bedrooms and a full bath complete the first floor. On the second floor, you'll find the spacious master suite with a room-sized walk-in closet and master bath. The other bedroom and full bath can be used to accommodate visiting guests. This plan is available with a slab, crawl or basement foundation option. Please specify when ordering.

First floor — 957 sq. ft.
Second floor — 800 sq. ft.

Total living area: 1,757 sq. ft.

Refer to **Pricing Schedule B** on the order form for pricing information

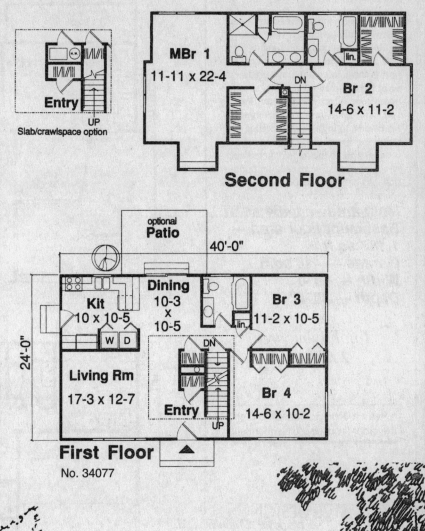

Entry
UP
Slab/crawlspace option

Second Floor

MBr 1
11-11 x 22-4

Br 2
14-6 x 11-2

lin.

DN

optional **Patio**

40'-0"

24'-0"

Kit
10 x 10-5

Dining
10-3
x
10-5

lin.

Br 3
11-2 x 10-5

W   D

Living Rm
17-3 x 12-7

DN

Entry
UP

Br 4
14-6 x 10-2

First Floor

No. 34077

GRADE-LEVEL-ENTRY HOME

Looking for a grade-level-entry house that is a little different? Here is a multi-featured design with many desirable items. Entry from the double carport is through an attractive grade-level foyer, up an open staircase to the main floor. Once on the main floor, you will notice the attractive corner fireplace and high-vaulted ceiling of the living room. The entire living area is accessible to the large covered deck which provides for an excellent relationship between indoor-outdoor living spaces.

Main area — 1,464 sq. ft.
Basement floor area — 1,187 sq.ft.
Garage — 418 sq.ft.
Width — 48'-0"
Depth — 39'-0"

Total living area: 2,651 sq. ft.

Refer to **Pricing Schedule C** on the order form for pricing information

An **EXCLUSIVE DESIGN** *By Westhome Planners, Ltd.*

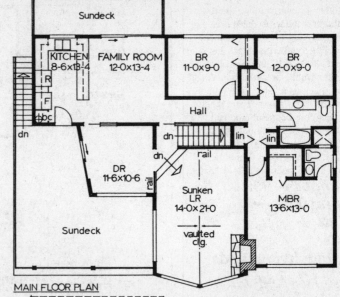

MAIN FLOOR PLAN

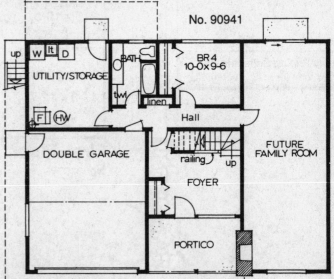

BASEMENT FLOOR PLAN

A-FRAME FOR YEAR-ROUND LIVING

If you have a hillside lot, this open design may be just what you've been looking for. With three bedrooms, it's a perfect plan for your growing family. The roomy foyer opens to a hallway that leads to the kitchen, bedrooms, and a dramatic, vaulted living room with a massive fireplace. A wrap-around sundeck gives you lots of outdoor living space. And, upstairs, there's a special retreat — a luxurious master suite complete with its own private deck.

Main floor — 1,238 sq. ft.
Loft — 464 sq. ft.
Basement — 1,175 sq. ft.
Width — 34'-0"
Depth — 56'-0"

Total living area:
1,702 sq. ft.

Refer to **Pricing Schedule B** on the order form for pricing information

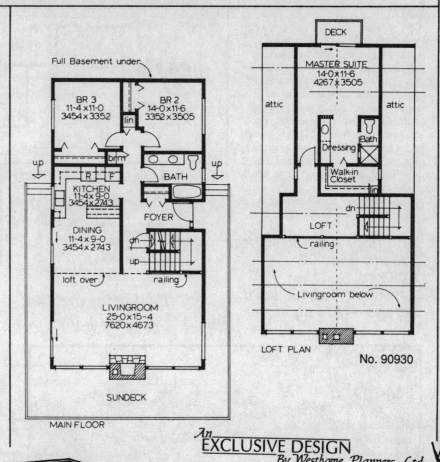

MAIN FLOOR

LOFT PLAN

No. 90930

An EXCLUSIVE DESIGN
By Westhome Planners, Ltd.

Design 10500

CONTEMPORARY FEATURES

Lots of living is packed into this well organized design. The expansive Great room is accented by a massive fireplace and a beamed, cathedral ceiling. The kitchen and breakfast area includes a charming and efficient angled cooking center, while the formal dining room is convenient, yet protected from noise. Indulge yourself in the master suite with its luxurious 5-piece bath, including a raised tile tub. Three bedrooms and a loft, which opens onto the foyer, are located on the second floor. Each bedroom has a walk-in closet and direct access to a full bath.

First floor — 2,188 sq. ft.
Second floor — 1,083 sq. ft.
Basement — 2,188 sq. ft.
Garage — 576 sq. ft.

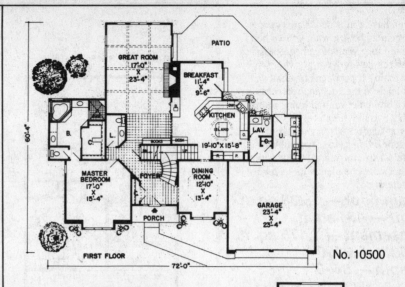

No. 10500

Total living area: 3,271 sq. ft.

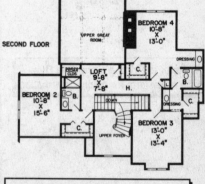

Refer to **Pricing Schedule F** on the order form for pricing information

An
EXCLUSIVE DESIGN
By Karl Kreeger

CREATIVE USE OF FLOOR SPACE

This splendid, contemporary home makes creative use of a unique floor plan. From the imposing front with large windows and stunning stucco exterior, to the dramatic coved ceilings and angular rooms, it's a dream come true. Luxuriate in the spa in the master suite or enjoy views from magnificent windows in the family and living rooms, dining nook and master bedroom.

Main floor — 1,173 sq. ft.
Upper floor — 823 sq. ft.
Bonus room —
204 sq. ft.
Garage — 2-car

Total living area:
1,996 sq. ft.

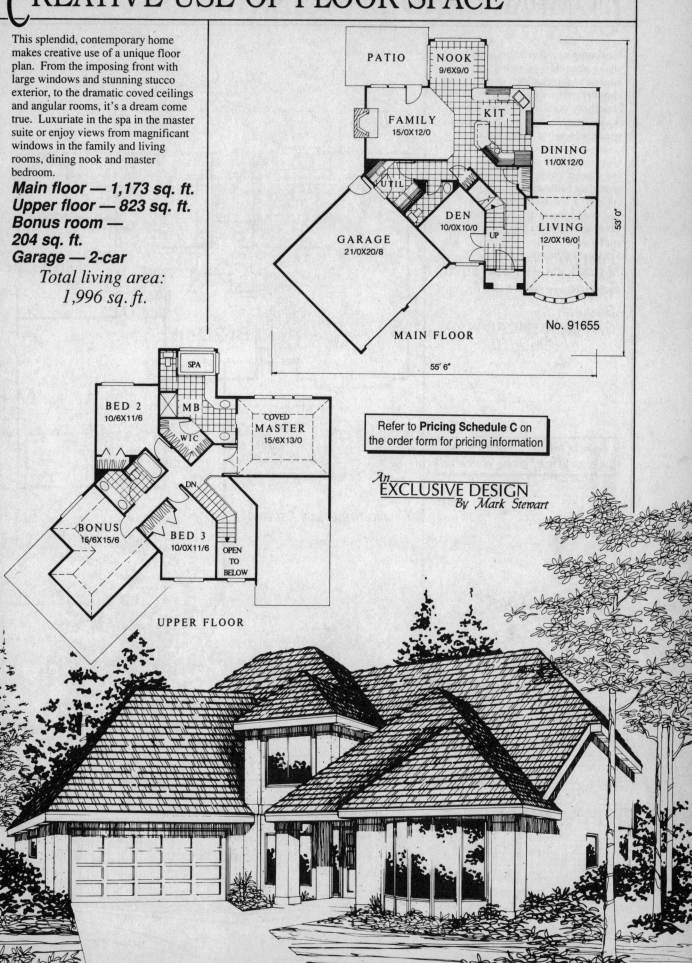

PATIO

NOOK
9/6X9/0

FAMILY
15/0X12/0

KIT

DINING
11/0X12/0

UTIL

DEN
10/0X10/0

UP

LIVING
12/0X16/0

GARAGE
21/0X20/8

53' 0"

MAIN FLOOR

No. 91655

55' 6"

SPA

BED 2
10/6X11/6

MB

WIC

COVED
MASTER
15/6X13/0

DN

BONUS
15/6X15/6

BED 3
10/0X11/6

OPEN
TO
BELOW

UPPER FLOOR

Refer to **Pricing Schedule C** on the order form for pricing information

An
EXCLUSIVE DESIGN
By Mark Stewart

COMPACT AND EFFICIENT

This compact and efficient home has all the amenities you would find in a larger home, including a covered porch and skylight over the dining area. It is actually an economical home to build. A tiled entry leads to the living room, which is equipped with a vaulted ceiling and a fireplace. The large kitchen has an abundance of cabinets and counter space. There are two secondary bedrooms, one of these could be a den, that share a full bath. The master suite has a large walk-in closet and a private shower with a pocket door closure. No materials list available for this plan.

Main floor — 1,390 sq. ft.
Garage — 440 sq. ft.

Total living area:
1,390 sq. ft.

Refer to **Pricing Schedule A** on the order form for pricing information

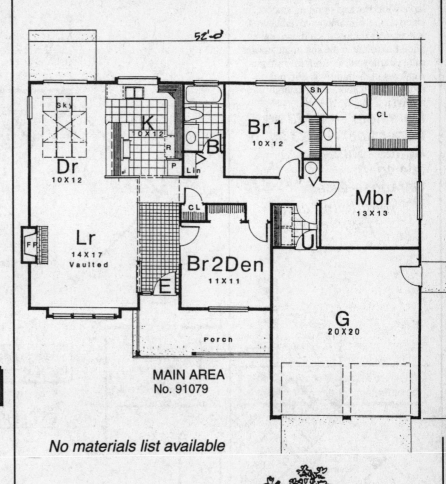

MAIN AREA
No. 91079

No materials list available

A LOT OF HOUSE IN A SMALL PACKAGE

The modern, efficient kitchen layout of this home is a plus; it is conveniently located off the family room, perfect for entertaining. The island and nook make preparing meals and keeping up with the family conversation at the end of the day easy. The formal dining room runs smoothly into the living room. The master bedroom features a walk-in closet and master bath room. Three other bedrooms, plus a bonus room, are also found on the second floor. This Frank Lloyd Wright inspired contemporary has it all. No materials list available for this plan.

First floor — 1,028 sq. ft.
Second floor — 1,043 sq. ft.
Bonus room — 244 sq. ft.
Garage — 390 sq. ft.

Total living area: 2,071 sq. ft.

Refer to **Pricing Schedule C** on the order form for pricing information

No materials list available

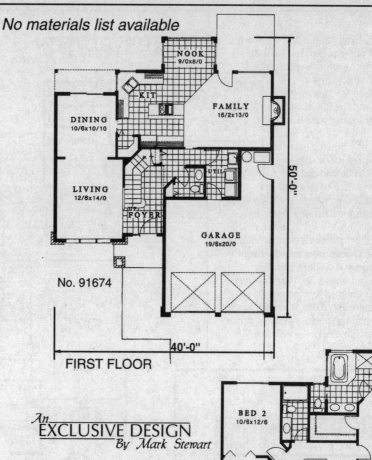

No. 91674

50'-0"

40'-0"

FIRST FLOOR

An EXCLUSIVE DESIGN *By Mark Stewart*

SECOND FLOOR

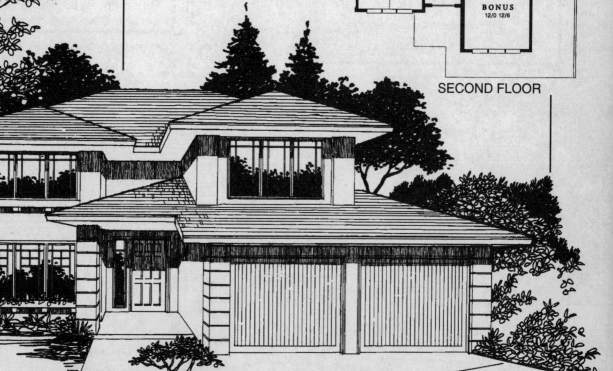

LUXURY IS ALWAYS POPULAR

Here's a stately home that's a treasure chest of popular features, including a sunken great room, a spectacular breakfast nook, and a bridge-like balcony on the 2nd floor. The luxurious, 1st floor master suite is a marvel, with two huge walk-in closets, a 5-piece bath, and a sitting room with bay window. The 2nd and 3rd bedrooms each have a walk-in closet and private bath. The great room features a bar, fireplace, and built-in cabinets for TV and stereo, all crowned by a sloping, beamed ceiling. Both the dining room and the foyer have cathedral ceilings and are overlooked by the 2nd floor balcony. A fully equipped kitchen enjoys a sweeping view of the patio and opens to the stunning nook. All in all, this is a fabulous and impressive home.

An **EXCLUSIVE DESIGN**
By Karl Kreeger

First floor — 2,579 sq. ft.
Second floor — 997 sq. ft.
Basement — 2,579 sq. ft.
Garage & Storage — 1,001 sq. ft.

Total living area: 3,576 sq. ft.

Refer to **Pricing Schedule F** on the order form for pricing information

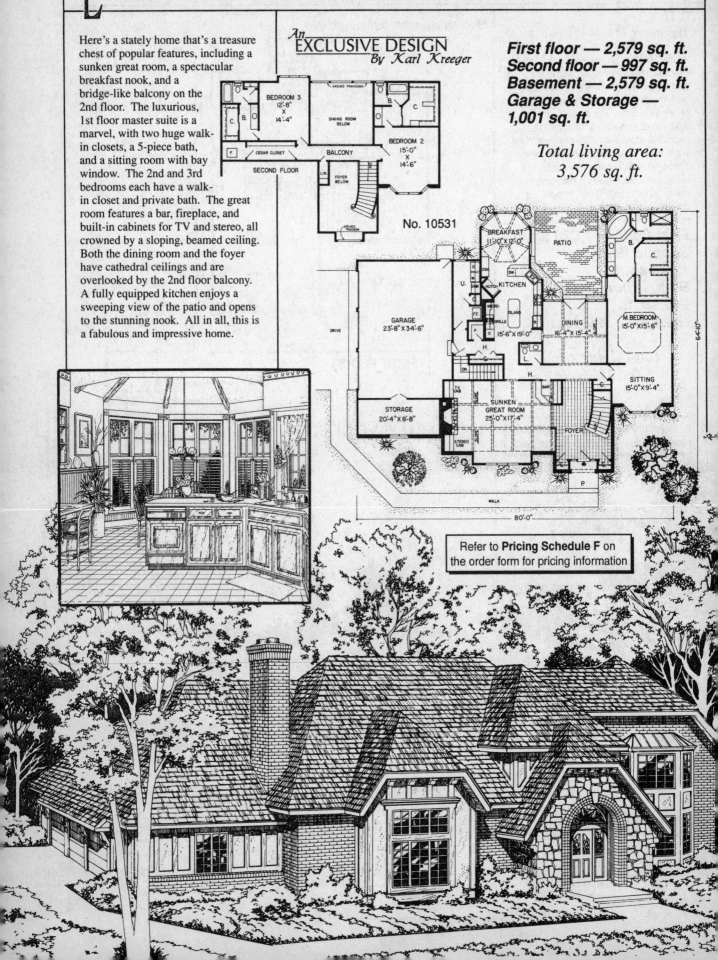

SPECIAL ROOMS HIGHLIGHTED

Design 10492

Refer to **Pricing Schedule F** on the order form for pricing information

With a special television room plus a family room and an upstairs sitting room, there's plenty of opportunity for everyone in the family to enjoy personal activities and pursuits. The well-designed kitchen adjoins the formal dining room and also has its own dining nook with lots of windows for sunny family breakfasts and lunches. Both the living room and family room open onto patios for indoor-outdoor entertaining. The second floor sitting room, complete with fireplace and warm hearth, adjoins the spacious master suite with its six-piece bath complete with Roman tub and oversized, walk-in closet. Two smaller bedrooms flank a walk-through bath to complete the second floor of this roomy, family home.

First floor — 2,409 sq. ft.
Second floor — 2,032 sq. ft.
Garage — 690 sq. ft.

Total living area: 4,441 sq. ft.

No.10492

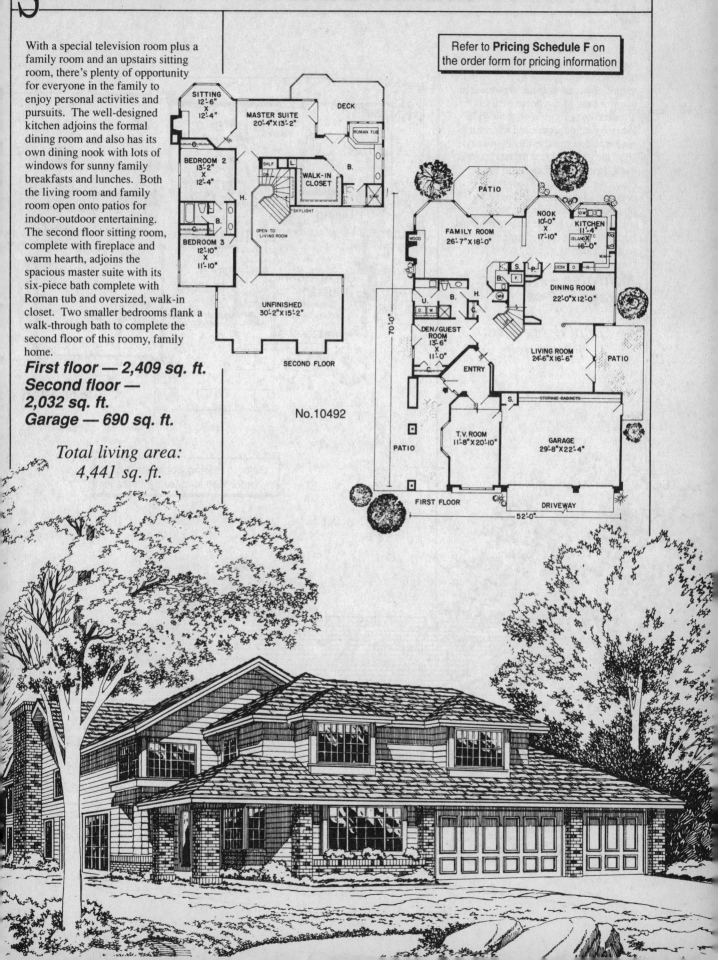

Design 90360

DETAILED RANCH DESIGN

Stylish houses, to suit the higher design expectations of the sophisticated first-time and move-up buyers, need to present a lot of visible values. Starting with the very modern exterior look of this home with its arcaded living room sash, through its interior vaulted spaces and interesting master bedroom suite, this house says "buy me". Foundation offsets are kept to the front where they count for character; simple main roof frames over main house body and master bedroom are cantilevered. Note, too, the easy option of eliminating the third bedroom closet and opening this room to the kitchen as a family room plus two bedroom home.

Main area — 1,283 sq. ft.
Garage — 2-car

Total living area:
1,283 sq. ft.

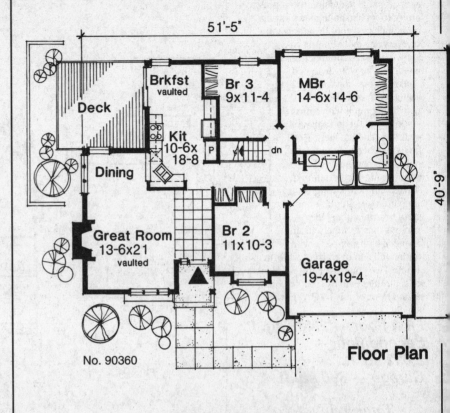

Floor Plan

No. 90360

51'-5"

40'-9"

Deck

Brkfst
vaulted

Br 3
9x11-4

MBr
14-6x14-6

Kit
10-6x
18-8

Dining

dn

Great Room
13-6x21
vaulted

Br 2
11x10-3

Garage
19-4x19-4

Refer to **Pricing Schedule A** on the order form for pricing information

Balcony Overlooks Living Room

Smaller houses are getting better all the time, not only in their exterior character and scale, but in their use of spacial volumes and interior finish materials. Here a modest two-story gains importance, impact, and perceived value from the sweeping roof lines that make it look larger than it really is. Guests will be impressed by the impact of the vaulted ceiling in the living room up to the balcony hall above, the easy flow of traffic, and abundant space in the kitchen and dining areas. Note too, the luxurious master suite with a window seat bay, walk-in closet, dressing area, and private shower.

Main floor — 674 sq. ft.
Upper floor — 677 sq. ft.
Garage—2-car

Total living area:
1,351 sq. ft.

Refer to **Pricing Schedule A** on the order form for pricing information

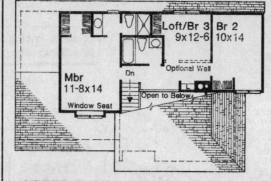

UPPER FLOOR PLAN

Loft/Br 3 9x12-6
Br 2 10x14
Mbr 11-8x14
Window Seat
Optional Wall
Dn
Open to Below

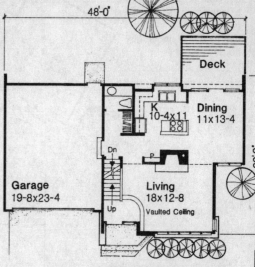

MAIN FLOOR PLAN
No. 90356

48'-0"
30'-2"
Deck
K 10-4x11
Dining 11x13-4
Garage 19-8x23-4
Dn
Up
Living 18x12-8
Vaulted Ceiling

PLAN HAS UNIQUE GREAT ROOM

Design 10380

Expanses of glass and rugged exposed beams dominate the front of this design's six-sided living center, creating a contemporary look that would be outstanding in any setting. Angled service and sleeping wings flow to the right and left, creating unusual shaped rooms and leaving nooks and crannies for storage. Spiral stairs just inside the tiled entry rise to a loft overlooking the Great room. All rooms have sloped ceilings with R-38 insulation while sidewalls call for R-24. Living and dining possibilities are expanded by use of the rear patio and deck. A full basement lies under the house.

Refer to **Pricing Schedule D** on the order form for pricing information

No. 10380

First floor — 2,199 sq. ft .
Loft — 336 sq. ft.
Garage — 611 sq. ft.
Basement — 2,199 sq. ft.
Total living area:
2,535 sq. ft.

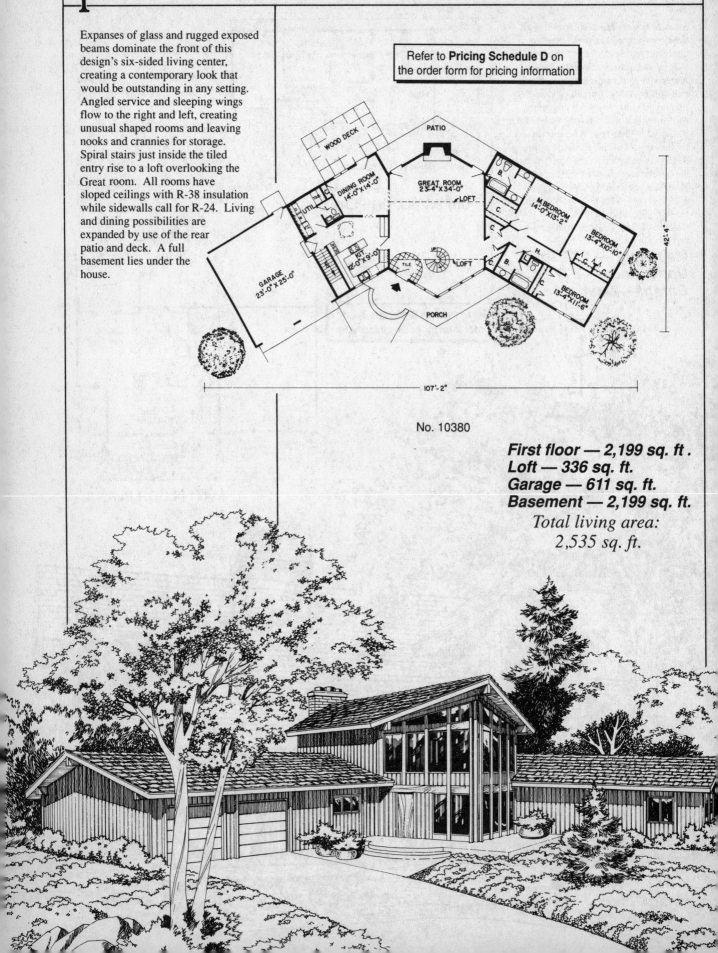

CATHEDRAL CEILING ACCENTS

This rustic-contemporary modified A-Frame design combines a high cathedral ceiling over a sunken living room with a large studio over the two rear bedrooms. The isolated master suite features a walk-in closet and compartmentalized bath with double vanity and linen closet. The two rear bedrooms include ample closet space and share a unique bath-and-a-half arrangement. On one side of the U-shaped kitchen and breakfast nook is the formal dining room which is separated from the entry by the planter. On the other side is a utility room which can be entered from either the kitchen or garage. The exterior features a massive stone chimney, large glass areas and a combination of vertical wood siding and stone. This plan is available with a basement, slab or crawl space foundation. Please specify when ordering.

First floor — 2,213 sq. ft.
Second floor — 260 sq. ft.
Basement — 2,213 sq. ft.
Garage — 422 sq. ft.
Total living area: 2,473 sq. ft.

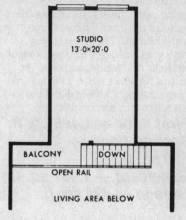

STUDIO
13-0×20-0

BALCONY   DOWN
OPEN RAIL

LIVING AREA BELOW

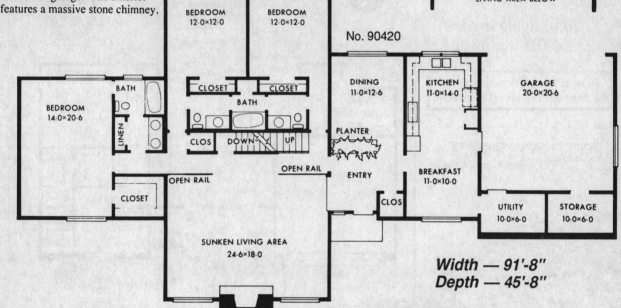

No. 90420

BEDROOM 12-0×12-0

BEDROOM 12-0×12-0

BATH

CLOSET   CLOSET

BATH

BEDROOM 14-0×20-6

LINEN

CLOS   DOWN   UP

DINING 11-0×12-6

KITCHEN 11-0×14-0

GARAGE 20-0×20-6

PLANTER

OPEN RAIL   OPEN RAIL

CLOSET   ENTRY

BREAKFAST 11-0×10-0

SUNKEN LIVING AREA 24-6×18-0

CLOS

UTILITY 10-0×6-0   STORAGE 10-0×6-0

Width — 91'-8"
Depth — 45'-8"

Refer to **Pricing Schedule D** on the order form for pricing information

L. M. GINN

Design 34049

INTERESTING BEDROOM TOWER

Sloping ceilings and open spaces characterize this four-bedroom home. The dining room off the foyer adjoins the breakfast room and the convenient island kitchen. The beamed living room is crowned by a balcony overlook that links the upstairs bedrooms. The vaulted first-floor master suite features a private deck, a walk-in closet and a full bath with a double vanity.

First floor — 1,496 sq. ft.
Second floor — 520 sq. ft.
Basement — 1,487 sq. ft.
Garage — 424 sq. ft.

Total living area: 2,016 sq. ft.

Refer to **Pricing Schedule C** on the order form for pricing information

An **EXCLUSIVE DESIGN** *By Karl Kreeger*

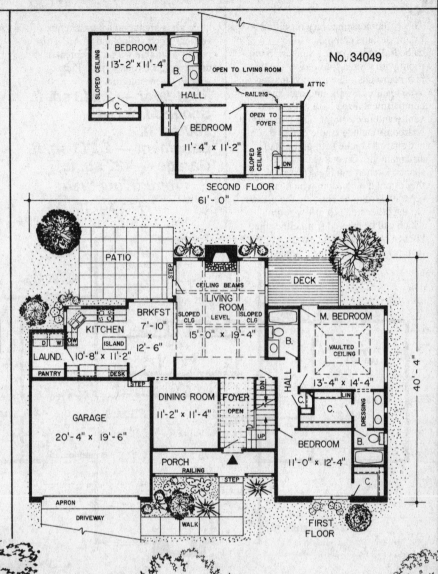

INVITING WRAP-AROUND PORCH

A warm and inviting welcome is the feeling brought home by the wrap-around porch in this elevation. A skylight illuminates the entry area. The Great room features a corner gas fireplace and includes two skylights overhead. Flowing directly from the Great room, the dining room receives natural light from sliding glass doors to a rear deck and a skylight. The well-appointed, U-shaped kitchen includes another skylight and a breakfast bar separating it from the dining room. The bedrooms are clustered to the right of the home. A luxurious master bath and a private deck highlight the master suite. Two additional bedrooms share use of the full bath in the hallway, and receive light from the dormers, acting like clerestory windows above. No materials list available for this plan.

Main floor — 1,716 sq. ft.
Width — 72'-0"
Depth — 46'-0"

Total living area:
1,716 sq. ft.

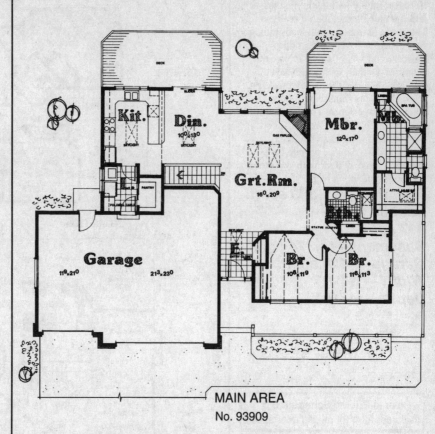

MAIN AREA
No. 93909

No materials list available

Refer to **Pricing Schedule B** on the order form for pricing information

STATELY MANOR

Here is a stately looking home that appears much larger than it really is. The grand entrance porch leads into a very spacious foyer with an open staircase and lots of angles. Note the beautiful kitchen with a full-bayed wall that includes the roomy breakfast nook. Meal preparation will be a delightful experience. The family room enjoys a fireplace and wetbar for cozy entertaining. The master suite, a retreat with its 5-piece private bath, shares the second floor with two other bedrooms and a hall bath.

First floor — 1,383 sq. ft.
Second floor — 997 sq. ft.
Basement — 1,374 sq. ft.
Garage — 420 sq. ft.
Width — 54'-0"
Depth — 47'-0"

Total living area: 2,380 sq. ft.

Refer to **Pricing Schedule D** on the order form for pricing information

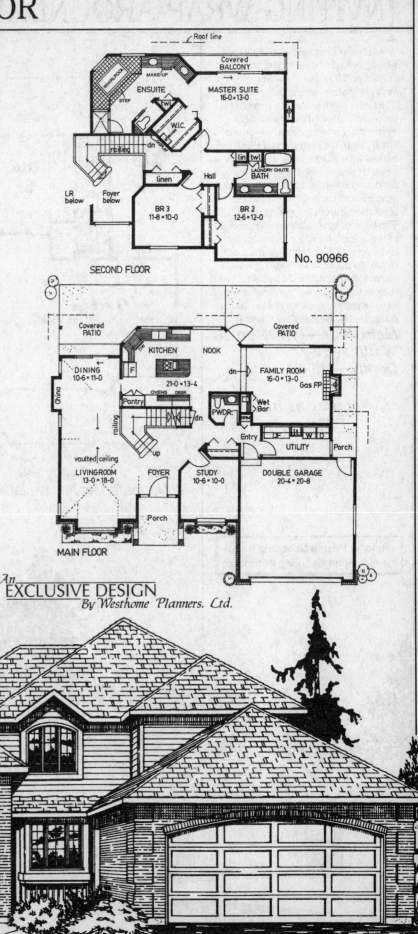

No. 90966

SECOND FLOOR

MAIN FLOOR

An EXCLUSIVE DESIGN *By Westhome Planners, Ltd.*

OPTIONS UNLIMITED

Plan for the future in this three-bedroom, basement-entry beauty. The ground floor offers unlimited options for your growing family. Use the practical plan suggested to finish this level, or have fun with your own ideas. Walk up the open staircase to the distinctive main floor, which possesses many charming amenities. The fireplaced living room, which features a bay window seat, adjoins the formal dining room in a spacious, L-shaped arrangement. The covered deck affords protected outdoor dining, rain or shine. And the galley kitchen opens to the family room and bayed nook overlooking the sundeck. Three bedrooms and two full baths complete the main floor of this special, sunny home.

Main area — 1,490 sq. ft.
Garage — 2-car

Total living area:
1,490 sq. ft.

Refer to **Pricing Schedule A** on the order form for pricing information

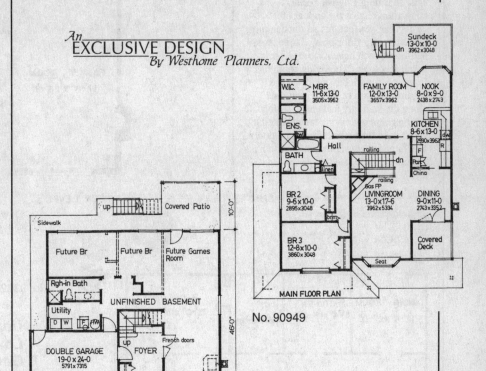

An
EXCLUSIVE DESIGN
By Westhome Planners, Ltd.

MAIN FLOOR PLAN

No. 90949

BASEMENT FLOOR PLAN

A STATELY HOME

This charming English Tudor adaptation retains the appeal of yesteryear, yet features an outstanding contemporary floor plan. Three large bedrooms each have a closet over seven feet long. The living room has a fireplace, square bay window, and ornamental iron railing which runs along the stairway and entry. A formal dining room opens onto an elevated wood deck through sliding glass doors. The huge family room, which also has a fireplace, is located on the lower level.

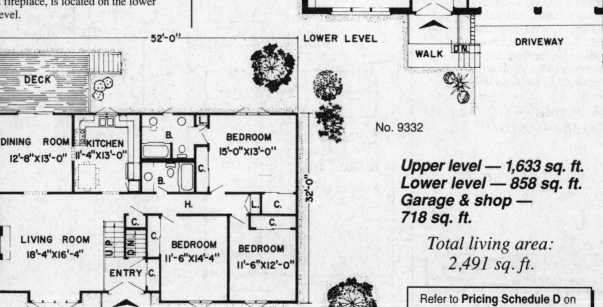

No. 9332

Upper level — 1,633 sq. ft.
Lower level — 858 sq. ft.
Garage & shop —
718 sq. ft.

Total living area:
2,491 sq. ft.

Refer to **Pricing Schedule D** on the order form for pricing information

OCTAGONAL FEATURED ROOMS

The luxurious master suite of this uniquely designed, three bedroom home is secluded on an upper floor. It is linked to the stairway by a balcony which overlooks the first floor family room and central hall. Additionally it features a full wall of double closets, a sloped ceiling and a private fireplace. The octagonal, five-piece bath also features a sloped ceiling. The octagonal treatment is carried out in the first floor nook which adjoins the kitchen and in the arrangement of the casement windows in the living room. The family room boasts a corner fireplace and has its own sloped ceiling. Two additional bedrooms, each with a large closet, a four-piece bath, and a conveniently located laundry room complete this unusual and inviting home.

First floor — 1,704 sq. ft.
Second floor — 561 sq. ft.
Garage — 439 sq. ft.
Total living area: 2,265 sq. ft.

Refer to **Pricing Schedule D** on the order form for pricing information

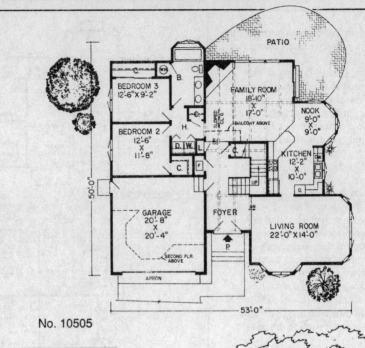

No. 10505

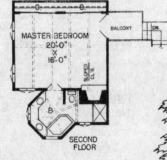

ATTRACTIVE TUDOR STYLE

Design 99605

This English Tudor home portrays the image of a country estate. Besides an attractive exterior and a good functioning plan, it is abound with features such as the decorative circular stair and the curved corners in the foyer; the sunken living room, a regal dining room terminating in a circular bay, a family room with a fireplace, a large pantry closet in the fully equipped kitchen, a lounging porch and a separate dining porch, and a spacious powder room privately located. The second floor features a sitting area which can be used as a library, a master suite consisting of a huge bedroom with large walk-in closets, a study which can be used as a studio, office or retreat room, a bathroom with an oversized whirlpool tub, stall shower and towel closet. The other bedrooms are good size. This house truly lends itself to gracious living.

First floor — 1,352 sq. ft.
Second floor — 1,416 sq. ft.
Garage — 2-car

Total living area: 2,768 sq. ft.

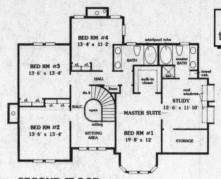

SECOND FLOOR

Refer to **Pricing Schedule E** on the order form for pricing information

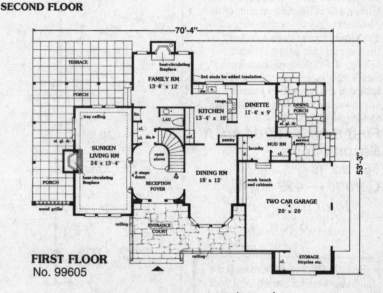

FIRST FLOOR
No. 99605

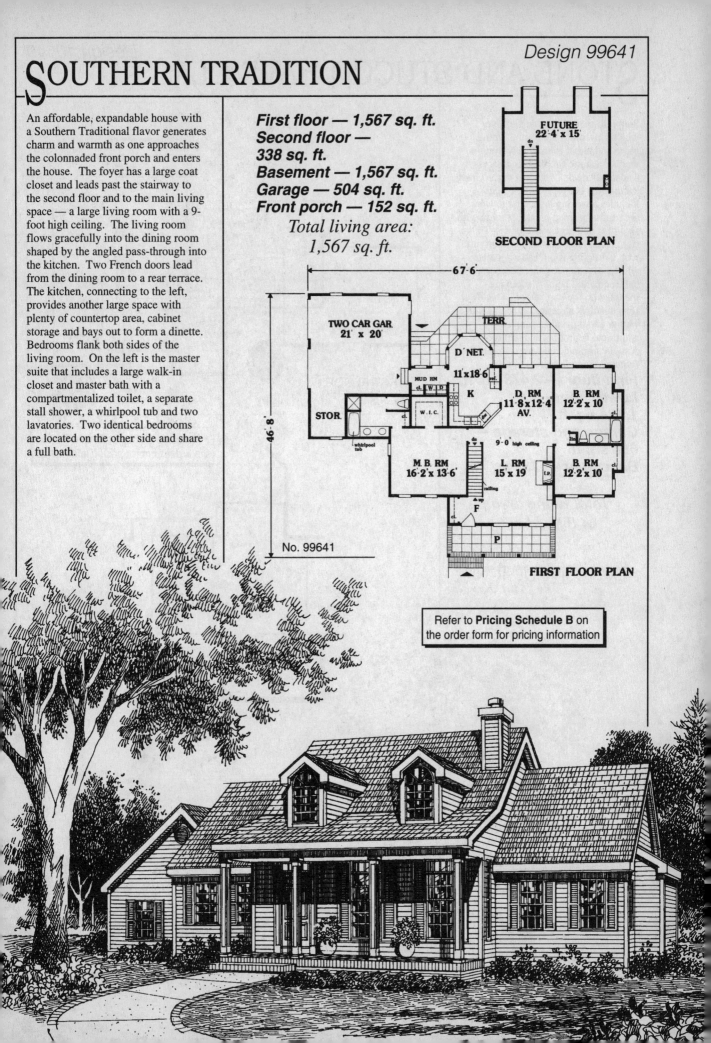

SOUTHERN TRADITION

An affordable, expandable house with a Southern Traditional flavor generates charm and warmth as one approaches the colonnaded front porch and enters the house. The foyer has a large coat closet and leads past the stairway to the second floor and to the main living space — a large living room with a 9-foot high ceiling. The living room flows gracefully into the dining room shaped by the angled pass-through into the kitchen. Two French doors lead from the dining room to a rear terrace. The kitchen, connecting to the left, provides another large space with plenty of countertop area, cabinet storage and bays out to form a dinette. Bedrooms flank both sides of the living room. On the left is the master suite that includes a large walk-in closet and master bath with a compartmentalized toilet, a separate stall shower, a whirlpool tub and two lavatories. Two identical bedrooms are located on the other side and share a full bath.

First floor — 1,567 sq. ft.
Second floor —
338 sq. ft.
Basement — 1,567 sq. ft.
Garage — 504 sq. ft.
Front porch — 152 sq. ft.

Total living area:
1,567 sq. ft.

FUTURE
22'-4" x 15'

SECOND FLOOR PLAN

67'-6"

46'-8"

TWO CAR GAR.
21' x 20'

TERR.

D' NET.
11' x 18'-6"

MUD RM
cl. W D

STOR.

K

W.I.C.

D. RM
11'-8" x 12'-4"
AV.

B. RM
12'-2" x 10'

whirlpool tub

9'-0" high ceiling

M. B. RM
16'-2" x 13'-6"

dn

L. RM
15' x 19'

l.p.

B. RM
12'-2" x 10'

railing

up

F

P

No. 99641

FIRST FLOOR PLAN

Refer to **Pricing Schedule B** on the order form for pricing information

STONE AND STUCCO HAVE CLASS

Step into the large, majestic foyer which flows into the formal dining room and Great room that features a wetbar, a stone fireplace and access to a spacious deck. Adjacent to the Great room is the dream kitchen which includes a writing area, a large work area and a beamed breakfast room with skylights and access to a patio. To the right is the huge master bedroom suite with a dressing room and a separate whirlpool bath. Another bedroom, bathroom, and laundry room are included on the main floor. The lower floor features a recreation room, with a wetbar and a fireplace, and two additional bedrooms and bathrooms. A two-car garage and a separate hobby room give ample storage space.

First floor — 2,473 sq. ft.
Lower floor —
1,624 sq. ft.
Garage and storage —
686 sq. ft.
Basement — 732 sq. ft.

Total living area:
4,097 sq. ft.

An
EXCLUSIVE DESIGN
By Karl Kreeger

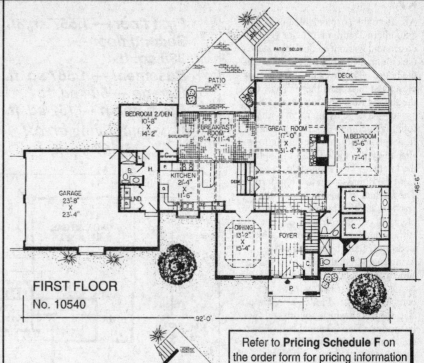

FIRST FLOOR
No. 10540

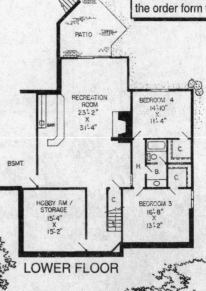

LOWER FLOOR

Refer to **Pricing Schedule F** on the order form for pricing information

CLASSIC SUNCATCHER

Plenty of glass and open spaces highlight this spectacular design which is finished in easy-to-care-for stucco. The cozy family room features a wood-burning fireplace for those cool evenings...and you will enjoy the convenience of the kitchen/nook area so close at hand. Upstairs, the master bedroom has a 5-piece compartmentalized bath complete with garden tub. Two other bedrooms and a bath share the upper floor.

First floor — 1,359 sq. ft.
Second floor —
863 sq. ft.
Basement — 1,347 sq. ft.
Garage — 441 sq. ft.
Width — 42'-0"
Depth — 59'-0"

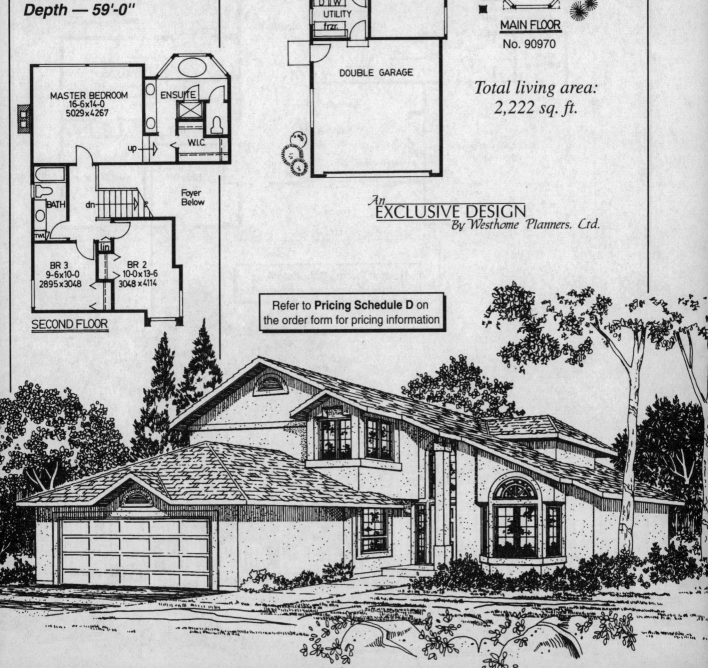

MAIN FLOOR
No. 90970

Total living area:
2,222 sq. ft.

An
EXCLUSIVE DESIGN
By Westhome Planners, Ltd.

Refer to **Pricing Schedule D** on the order form for pricing information

MASTER BEDROOM
16-6 x 14-0
5029 x 4267

ENSUITE

W.I.C.

BATH

Foyer
Below

BR 3
9-6 x 10-0
2895 x 3048

BR 2
10-0 x 13-6
3048 x 4114

SECOND FLOOR

PATIO

NOOK

FAMILY ROOM
16-6 x 16-0
5029 x 4876

KITCHEN
13-0 x 15-6
3962 x 4724

DINING
11-0 x 12-6
3352 x 3810

WOOD BOX

wet bar

BATH

BR/STUDY
11-6 x 13-6
3505 x 4114

UTILITY

frzr.

Optional vaulted clg.

LIVINGROOM
14-6 x 16-0
4419 x 4876

FOYER

DOUBLE GARAGE

AFFORDABLE ENERGY-SAVER

This attractive ranch, which possesses many features only available in larger homes, is the perfect choice for the budget-conscious family looking for a touch of luxury. Look at the wide-open arrangement of the living and dining rooms, bathed in light from skylights overhead and large expanses of front and rear-facing glass. A heat circulating fireplace helps lower your energy bills. Enjoy your morning coffee in the greenhouse setting of the dinette bay off the kitchen. Or, on a summer morning, the terrace off the dining room is a nice place to spread out the Sunday paper. In the bedroom wing off the foyer lie three bedrooms, served by two full baths. Look at the private deck complete with hot tub off the master suite.

Main area — 1,393 sq. ft.
Basement — 1,393 sq. ft.
Garage/laundry — 542 sq. ft.
Front porch — 195 sq. ft.
Total living area: 1,393 sq. ft.

Refer to **Pricing Schedule A** on the order form for pricing information

UNIQUE TRIANGULAR ENTRANCE

Design 99614

The gracious and spacious central foyer sets the tone for this luxurious 3 bedroom ranch home. The featured triangular ceiling of the entrance porch extends into the foyer. Recalling this triangular form are the bedroom bays. Other features include the large glazed bay the full width of the living room; the dinette which has a six sided shape, four sides of which are glazed; three floor to ceiling glass panels are at the rear of the family room, one of which slides and gives access to the huge rear terrace; an angled kitchen counter acts as a snack bar convenient to the family room; high sloping ceiling in living and family rooms. In addition, the master bathroom is equipped with two basins, a shower stall, a whirlpool tub and a towel closet. The hall bathroom also has two basins and natural light.

Main area — 2,282 sq. ft.
Laundry/mudroom — 114 sq. ft.
Garage — 509 sq. ft.
Basement — 2,136 sq. ft.

Total living area:
2,396 sq. ft.

Refer to **Pricing Schedule D** on the order form for pricing information

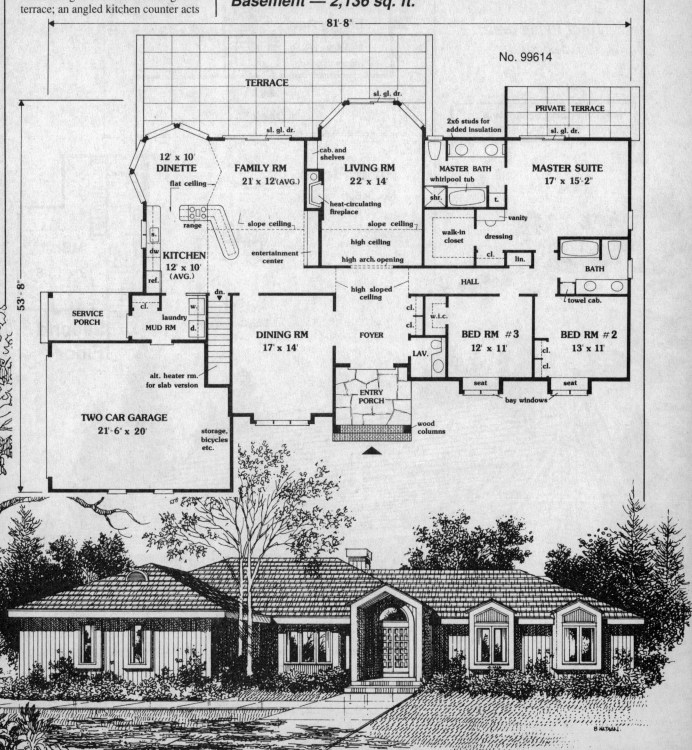

B. NATHAN.

Design 34600

RUSTIC EXTERIOR; COMPLETE HOME

Although rustic in appearance, the interior of this cabin is quiet, modern and comfortable. Small in overall size, it still contains three bedrooms and two baths in addition to a large, two-story living room with exposed beams. As a hunting/fishing lodge or mountain retreat, this compares well.

First floor — 1,013 sq. ft.
Second floor —
315 sq.ft.
Basement — 1,013 sq. ft.

Total living area:
1,328 sq. ft.

Refer to **Pricing Schedule A** on the order form for pricing information

38'-0"

36'-0"

Kitchen
17-4 x 10-8

Br 2
12 x 10-4

lin.

DN

Br 3
12 x 13

Living Rm
19-4 x 16-8
beamed ceiling

slope

UP

Deck

slope

First Floor
No. 34600

Slab/Crawlspace Option

DN

lin.

MBr 1
12 x 13-8

Second Floor

COMPACT DREAM HOUSE

Does your building lot have a small buildable area? Here's a compact Cape that can fit in the smallest space, and still fulfill the dreams of your growing family. The central entry is flanked by a cozy study and a sunny, formal living room with windows on two sides. Two fireplaces help with the heating bills, adding a friendly glow to active areas. Eat in the formal dining room, or in the huge country kitchen, which features a triple window with built-in seating and a beamed ceiling. Three bedrooms share the second floor with two full baths. You'll love the cheerful atmosphere upstairs, achieved by generous windows and a full dormer overlooking the backyard.

First floor — 1,020 sq. ft.
Second floor — 777 sq. ft.

Total living area:
1,797 sq. ft.

No. 90245

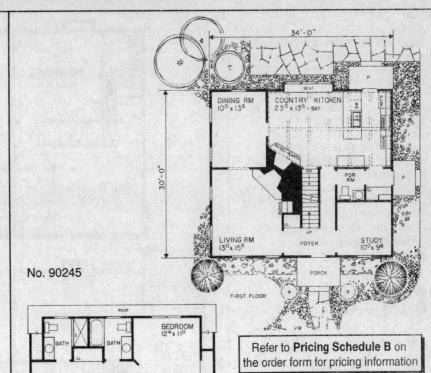

FIRST FLOOR

SECOND FLOOR

Refer to **Pricing Schedule B** on the order form for pricing information

GRACIOUS LIVING

This 1,120 square foot per unit duplex was designed for gracious living with the dining room conveniently located between the living room and kitchen. The handy serving bar between the dining room and kitchen can serve as either a serving or breakfast bar. The washer and dryer are conveniently located off the kitchen for easy servicing. On the main floor, the open stair rail visually increases the size of the living room. The patio/deck is partially covered for protection of those summer showers. Walk-in closets, always a plus, are featured in each ample-sized bedroom.

Main unit area — 1,120 sq. ft.
Width — 54'-0"
Depth — 43'-0"

Total living area: 1,120 sq. ft.

Refer to **Pricing Schedule A** on the order form for pricing information

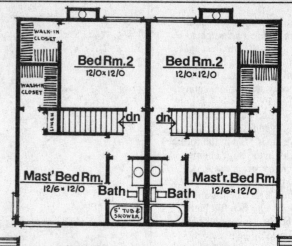

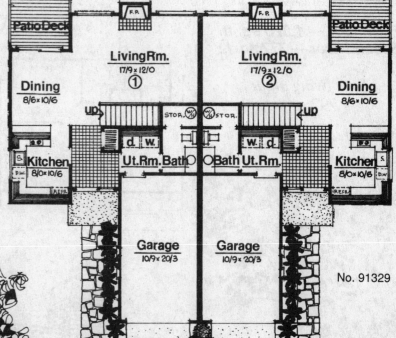

No. 91329

SPLIT ENTRY WITH TRADITIONAL LINES

On the main level of this home an open layout creates a feeling of spaciousness in the living room, dining room and kitchen. A gas fireplace, sliding glass doors to the rear deck and a breakfast bar are just a few of the highlights of this great living space. A master bedroom and a secondary bedroom share the full bath in the hall. The lower level features a spacious family room, two more bedrooms and a full bath. No materials list available for this plan.

Main level — 968 sq. ft.
Lower level — 968 sq. ft.

Total living area:
1,936 sq. ft.

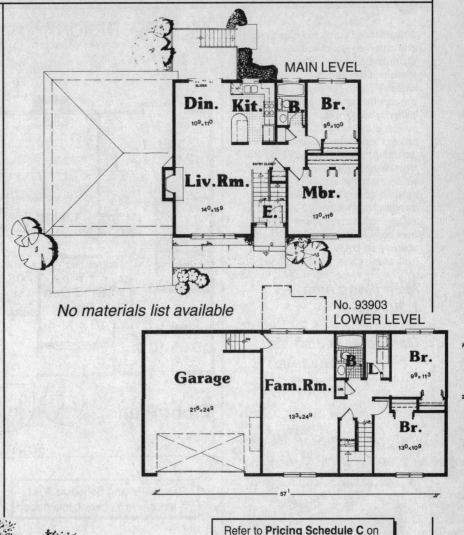

MAIN LEVEL

No materials list available

No. 93903
LOWER LEVEL

Refer to **Pricing Schedule C** on the order form for pricing information

DELIGHTFUL DOLL HOUSE

Design 20161

With its railed porch and gingerbread trim, this convenient ranch looks like a Victorian doll house. But there's lots of room in this compact, three-bedroom plan. The foyer, tucked between the two-car garage and bedroom wing, opens to a spacious, fireplaced living room. Soaring ceilings and an open arrangement with the adjoining dining room add to the airy feeling in this sunny space. The kitchen, steps away, offers easy, over-the-counter service at mealtime. And there's a large pantry just across from the adjacent laundry room. The two front bedrooms share a full bath. The master suite boasts its own private bath, plus a closet-lined wall and decorative touches that make it special.

**Main living area —
1,307 sq. ft.
Basement — 1,298 sq. ft.
Garage — 462 sq. ft.**

*Total living area:
1,307 sq. ft.*

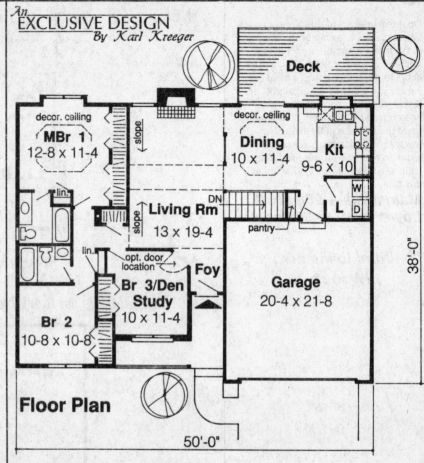

An **EXCLUSIVE DESIGN**
By Karl Kreeger

Floor Plan

Deck

decor. ceiling

MBr 1
12-8 x 11-4

slope

decor. ceiling

Dining
10 x 11-4

Kit
9-6 x 10

lin.

slope

Living Rm
13 x 19-4

DN

pantry

W
L
D

lin.

opt. door location

Br 3/Den Study
10 x 11-4

Foy

Garage
20-4 x 21-8

Br 2
10-8 x 10-8

38'-0"

50'-0"

No. 20161

Refer to **Pricing Schedule A** on the order form for pricing information

ATTRACTIVE FLOOR PLAN

Keep dry during the rainy season under the covered porch entryway of this gorgeous home. A foyer separates the dining room, with a decorative ceiling, from the breakfast area and kitchen. Off the kitchen, conveniently located, is the laundry room. The living room features a vaulted beamed ceiling and fireplace. Located between the living room and two bedrooms, both with large closets, is a full bath. On the other side of the living room is the master bedroom. The master bedroom not only has a decorative ceiling, but also a skylight above the entrance of its private bath. The double-vanitied bathroom features a large walk-in closet. For those who enjoy outdoor living, an optional deck is offered, accessible through sliding glass doors off of this wonderful master bedroom. Please indicate slab,

An EXCLUSIVE DESIGN
By Karl Kreeger

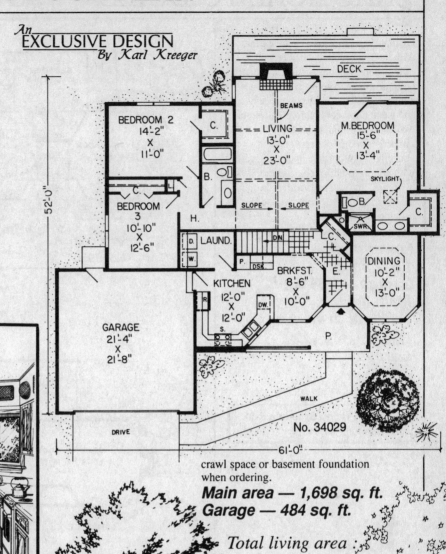

crawl space or basement foundation when ordering.
Main area — 1,698 sq. ft.
Garage — 484 sq. ft.

Total living area :
1,698 sq. ft.

Refer to **Pricing Schedule B** on the order form for pricing information

PRACTICAL TO BUILD

Distinctive as this home may appear, with its deck-encircled hexagonal living room, its construction is actually quite practical. The main level houses the living room with exposed beams and a cathedral ceiling, four bedrooms, two baths, a dining room and a kitchen. On the lower level, an enormous family room opens to a patio with a built-in barbecue. Another bedroom, den and bath with a shower are detailed. Boat storage is also provided on this level.

First floor — 1,672 sq. ft.
Lower floor —
1,672 sq. ft.
Garage — 484 sq. ft.

Total living area:
3,344 sq. ft.

Refer to **Pricing Schedule F** on the order form for pricing information

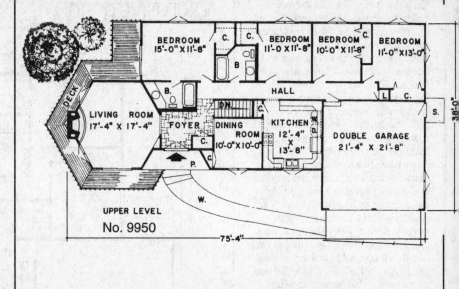

UPPER LEVEL
No. 9950

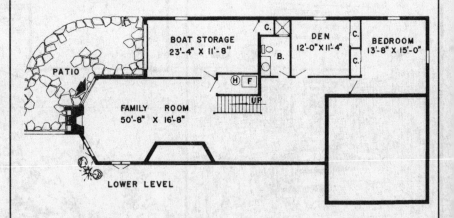

LOWER LEVEL

RANCH PROVIDES GREAT FLOOR PLAN

This great ranch features a front porch to sit and admire your view. A large living room and dining room flow together into one open space perfect for entertaining. The laundry room, which doubles as a mudroom, is off the kitchen and a back door entrance gives easy access to the outside. A master suite includes a private bathroom and the three additional bedrooms share a bathroom. A double-car garage is included in this plan.

Main area — 1,527 sq. ft.
Basement — 1,344 sq. ft.
Garage — 425 sq. ft.

Total living area:
1,527 sq. ft.

Refer to **Pricing Schedule B** on the order form for pricing information

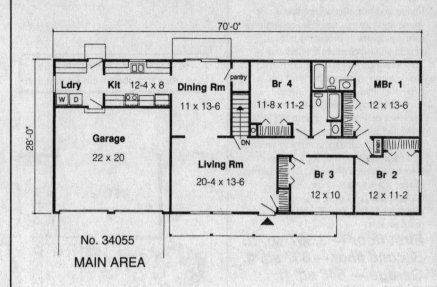

No. 34055
MAIN AREA

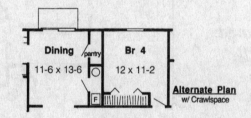

Alternate Plan
w/ Crawlspace

KITCHEN IS GOURMET'S HEAVEN

Design 10417

Inside and out, this design speaks of space and luxury. Outside, cedarshake roofing contrasts nicely with brick veneer to complement arched and leaded windows and false dormers. Double entry doors usher you into a two-story entrance with staircase curving gently to second level rooms. Ten-foot ceilings throughout the lower level and nine-foot ceilings upstairs add to the spaciousness already created by large rooms. And, look at these kitchen features — 60 sq. ft. of counter space, a 5 x 6 step-saving island cooking range, a desk area, a windowed eating nook, and nearby patio access.

First floor — 3,307 sq. ft.
Second floor — 837 sq. ft.
Garage — 646 sq. ft.
Porch and patios —
382 sq. ft.

Total living area:
4,144 sq. ft.

Refer to **Pricing Schedule F** on the order form for pricing information

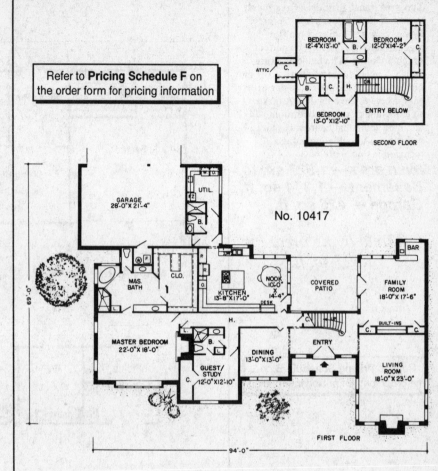

MULTIPLE LEVELS ENLARGE PLAN

Behind double doors, just off the two-story foyer, the den in this exciting home will give you a quiet place to work or greet clients. And, the charming living room with adjoining dining room is a great place to entertain. The huge island kitchen can handle a crowd of any size. Watch your guests arrive from the window seat in the sitting room of your master suite, a cozy spot with a fireplace and built-in bookcase. Skylights brighten the bedroom, walk-in closet, and both upstairs baths without compromising your privacy. And, on busy mornings when everyone's in a hurry, you're sure to appreciate the double vanities. This plan is available with a crawl space foundation only.

Main floor — 1,831 sq. ft.
Upper floor — 1,269 sq. ft.
Width — 61'-0"
Depth — 53'-0"

Total living area: 3,100 sq. ft.

Refer to **Pricing Schedule E** on the order form for pricing information

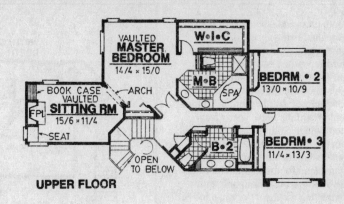

UPPER FLOOR

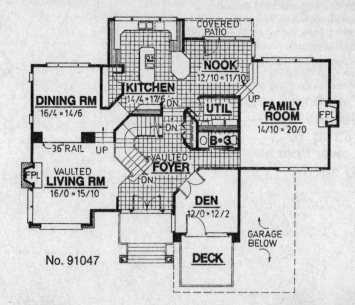

No. 91047

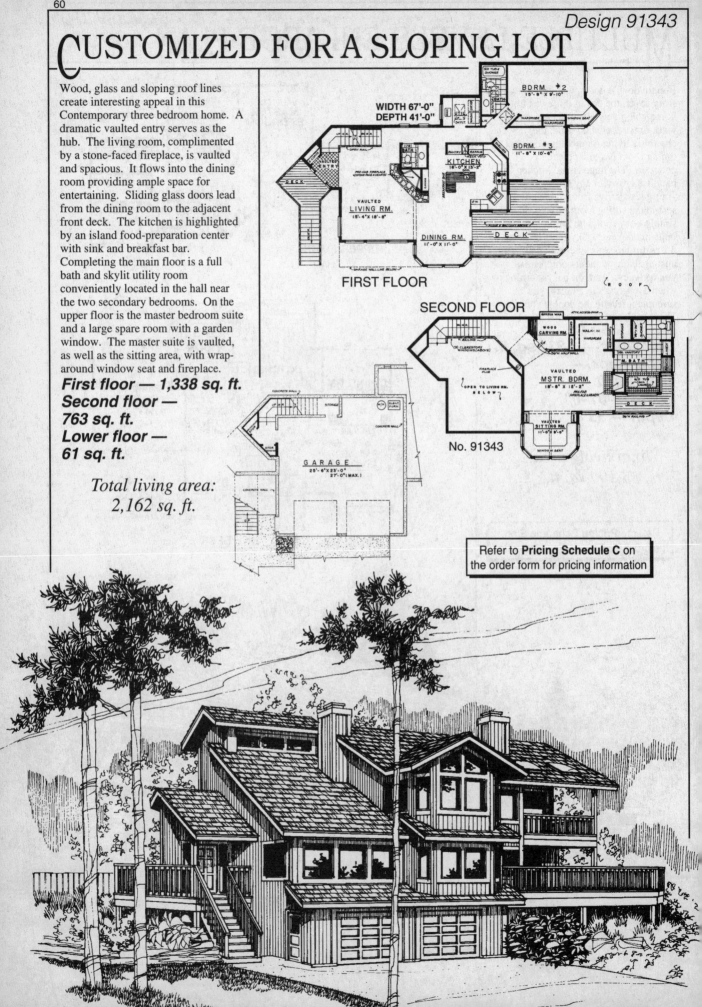

Design 91343

CUSTOMIZED FOR A SLOPING LOT

Wood, glass and sloping roof lines create interesting appeal in this Contemporary three bedroom home. A dramatic vaulted entry serves as the hub. The living room, complimented by a stone-faced fireplace, is vaulted and spacious. It flows into the dining room providing ample space for entertaining. Sliding glass doors lead from the dining room to the adjacent front deck. The kitchen is highlighted by an island food-preparation center with sink and breakfast bar. Completing the main floor is a full bath and skylit utility room conveniently located in the hall near the two secondary bedrooms. On the upper floor is the master bedroom suite and a large spare room with a garden window. The master suite is vaulted, as well as the sitting area, with wrap-around window seat and fireplace.

First floor — 1,338 sq. ft.
Second floor — 763 sq. ft.
Lower floor — 61 sq. ft.

Total living area: 2,162 sq. ft.

WIDTH 67'-0"
DEPTH 41'-0"

FIRST FLOOR

SECOND FLOOR

No. 91343

Refer to **Pricing Schedule C** on the order form for pricing information

COUNTRY-STYLE FOR TODAY

No doubt about it, this plan, with its wide wrap-around porch, matches the nostalgic image of a farmhouse. However, except for the living room, which can't help but remind us of an old-fashioned parlor with its double doors, this house is thoroughly modern. High-ceilinged and bright, the kitchen, nook, family room and dining room have a free-flowing layout and the area opens onto a wide deck. The first thing you see, upon entering the home, is the polished wood of a graceful open stairwell. At the second floor landing, it forms an open bridge. Two bedrooms are tucked away on the second floor with a full bath. The kitchen contains both a huge butcher-block work island and another long eating bar island. It also features a large walk-in pantry and built-in desk. The master suite has a spa and a huge walk-in closet as well as a shower, double vanities and its own access to the deck.

First floor — 1,785 sq. ft.
Second floor —
621 sq. ft.

Total living area:
2,406 sq. ft.

Refer to **Pricing Schedule D** on the order form for pricing information

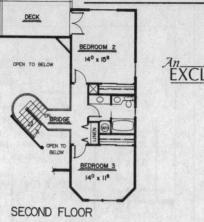

SECOND FLOOR

An
EXCLUSIVE DESIGN
By Landmark Designs, Inc.

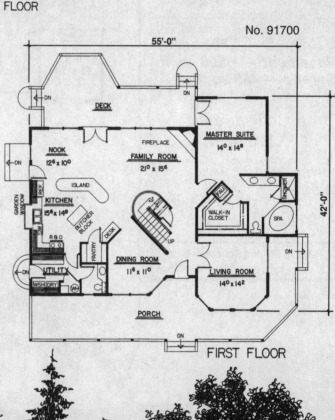

No. 91700

FIRST FLOOR

ONE LEVEL LIVING

An open plan gives this home spaciousness despite its modest square footage. The large Great room opens fully to the dining room, both with high ceilings of 11-1/2 feet. These rooms then open up to a stunning and efficient kitchen equipped with a dinette. A skylight enhances the natural light in the Great room. The luxurious master suite is privately located and separated from the other two bedrooms. It includes a dressing area, with a huge walk-in closet, and a sizeable linear closet. The laundry is conveniently located between the two additional bedrooms in a wide hallway.

Main area — 1,506 sq. ft.
Basement — 1,506 sq. ft.
Garage — 455 sq. ft.

Total living area:
1,506 sq. ft.

Refer to **Pricing Schedule B** on
the order form for pricing information

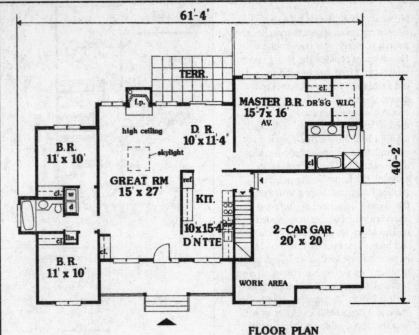

61'-4"

40'-2"

TERR.

f.p.

high ceiling

D. R.
10' x 11'-4"

MASTER B.R. DR'S'G W.I.C.
15'-7 x 16'
AV.

B. R.
11' x 10'

skylight

GREAT RM
15' x 27'

ref

KIT.

cl.

2-CAR GAR.
20' x 20'

w
d

10'x15'-4"
D'N'TTE

dw

cl.

lin.

B. R.
11' x 10'

cl.

WORK AREA

FLOOR PLAN
No. 99651

COUNTRY CHARMER WITH STYLE

What family wouldn't be comfortable in this functional, yet elegant home? This home features a nice-sized living room for entertaining, as well as a large open family room for living. The bayed breakfast nook unites with the kitchen through a unique, angled serving bar. The sunny kitchen boasts corner windows. The separate bayed dining room, with elegant details like a coffered ceiling, makes this home a winner. The bedroom wing occupies the second floor. The added charm of bay and dormer windows in the large bedrooms make this home a decorator's delight. The master bedroom, separated from the other bedrooms, features a large bathroom with a whirlpool tub, a double vanity, and a large efficient walk-in closet. The second story landing is unique with it's central loft which opens to the first floor, adding interest and volume to the house. No materials list available for this plan.

Main floor — 1,252 sq. ft.
Upper floor — 1,007 sq. ft.
Basement — 1,226 sq. ft.
Garage — 861 sq. ft.
Width — 60'-0"
Depth — 47'-0"

Total living area: 2,259 sq. ft.

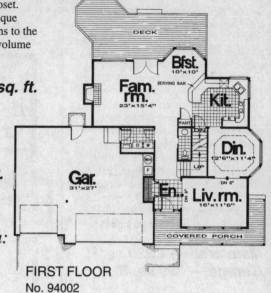

FIRST FLOOR
No. 94002

An
EXCLUSIVE DESIGN By
CRANE DESIGN inc.

Refer to **Pricing Schedule D** on the order form for pricing information

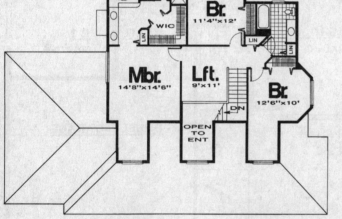

SECOND FLOOR
No materials list available

ARCHED LIVING ROOM WINDOW

Look at this great design, two good-sized bedrooms and a family room in only 1,220 sq. ft. Open-planning is the secret, combination rooms and good sight lines enhance the spacious feeling of this already roomy plan. There is plenty of counter space in the kitchen, and the eating nook is a bright start to any day. There is easy access to the patio area for outdoor dining. This area is warmed by a corner gas fireplace that also makes the family room a cozy place to be. The master suite is complete with walk-in closet and it's own bath. The living room and dining area flow into each other. The utility area is roomy enough for a freezer.

Main area — 1,220 sq. ft.
Garage — 399 sq. ft.

Total living area:
1,220 sq. ft.

Refer to **Pricing Schedule A** on the order form for pricing information

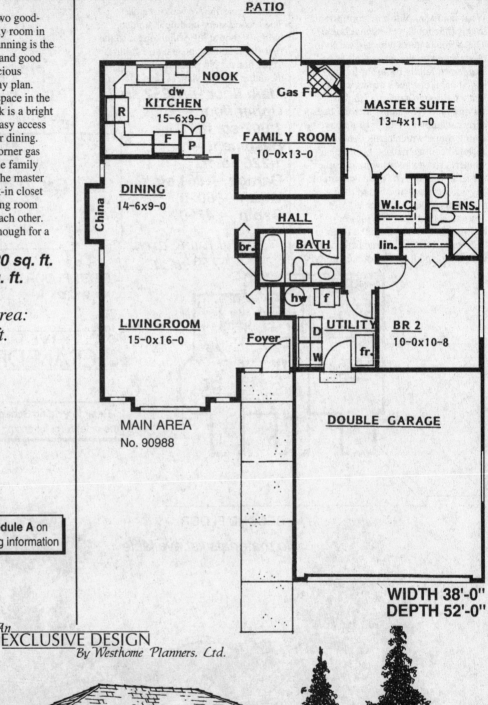

MAIN AREA
No. 90988

WIDTH 38'-0"
DEPTH 52'-0"

An
EXCLUSIVE DESIGN
By Westhome Planners, Ltd.

FOR THE YOUNG AT HEART

For the move-down buyers on-the-go or the family on-the-grow, this three bedroom home has all the right features. The home draws its look from the nostalgic elements of older Traditional homes. It has half-round transom and gable details, divided light windows, a covered entry porch and bay windows. The interior features a vaulted Great room with a fireplace, a transom window, and a vaulted kitchen with a breakfast area and sliders to the deck. The master suite has its own bath.

Main area — 1,307 sq. ft.
Garage — 2-car

Total living area:
1,307 sq. ft

Refer to **Pricing Schedule A** on the order form for pricing information

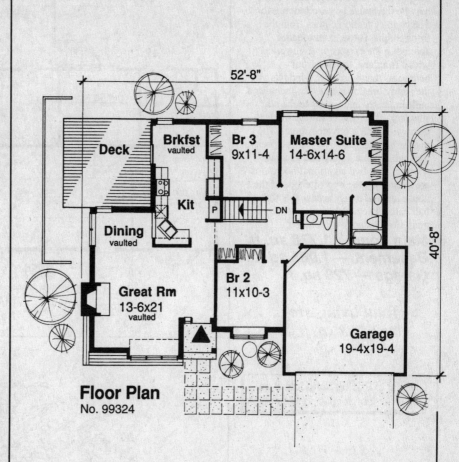

52'-8"

40'-8"

Deck

Brkfst
vaulted

Br 3
9x11-4

Master Suite
14-6x14-6

Kit

P

DN

Dining
vaulted

Great Rm
13-6x21
vaulted

Br 2
11x10-3

Garage
19-4x19-4

Floor Plan
No. 99324

Design 93261

Terrific Front Porch

If you are looking for a country type home with a few extra touches, this may be the house you are looking for. The country feeling comes from the front porch. Those extra touches abound in the expansive living area with a fireplace, the two front bedrooms that enjoy bay windows and the sunny breakfast area that includes a built-in pantry and access to the rear sun deck. The master suite provides the owner with a private retreat. The master bath includes a walk-in closet, oval tub, double vanity and separate shower. The two additional bedrooms are located on the opposite side of the house and have easy access to a full hall bath. The added convenience of a main floor laundry is included.

Main floor — 1,778 sq. ft.
Basement — 1,008 sq. ft.
Garage — 728 sq. ft.

Total living area:
1,778 sq. ft.

Refer to **Pricing Schedule B** on the order form for pricing information

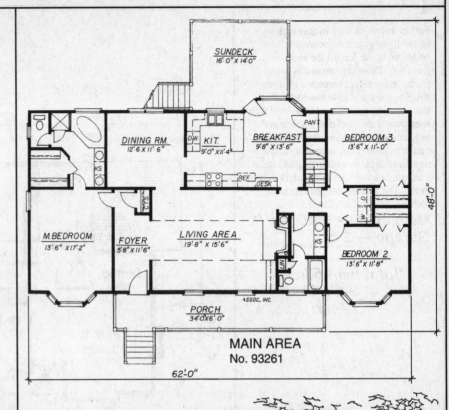

An
EXCLUSIVE DESIGN
By Jannis Vann & Associates, Inc.

CLASSIC FEATURES

Design 90691

Return to the classics in this carefree ranch. The portico is echoed inside, where columns divide the entry foyer from the dramatic, fireplaced living room. You'll find service and dining areas at the rear of the house, overlooking the terrace. Skylights, a spectacular bow window in the dining room, and sliding glass doors in the country kitchen combine with an open arrangement for an outdoor feeling. The nearby laundry/mudroom features two-way access to the garage and the covered side porch. Three bedrooms are tucked away from active areas. A hall bath serves the rear bedrooms, but the master suite boasts a private bath with relaxing whirlpool tub.

Main area — 1,530 sq. ft.
Basement — 1,434 sq. ft.
Garage — 2-car

Total living area:
1,530 sq. ft.

Refer to **Pricing Schedule B** on the order form for pricing information

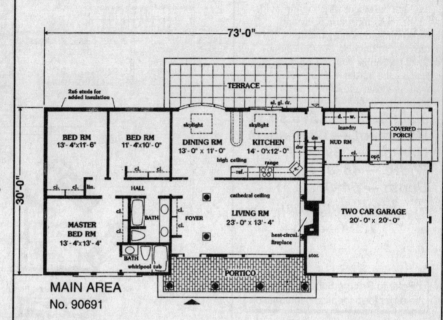

MAIN AREA
No. 90691

Design 90983

ATTRACTIVE ROOF LINES

Unusual roof lines, which are both varied and balanced, are a feature of this hillside home. An open floor plan is shared by the sunken living room, dining and kitchen areas. An open staircase leads to the unfinished daylight basement which will provide ample room for future bedrooms, bathroom and laundry facilities. To the right of the plan, are three good-sized bedrooms with lots of closet space....the master suite has a big walk-in closet and its own bath featuring a double shower.

Main floor — 1,396 sq. ft.
Basement — 1,396 sq. ft.
Garage — 389 sq. ft.
Width — 48'-0"
Depth — 54'-0"

Total living area: 1,396 sq. ft.

Refer to **Pricing Schedule A** on the order form for pricing information

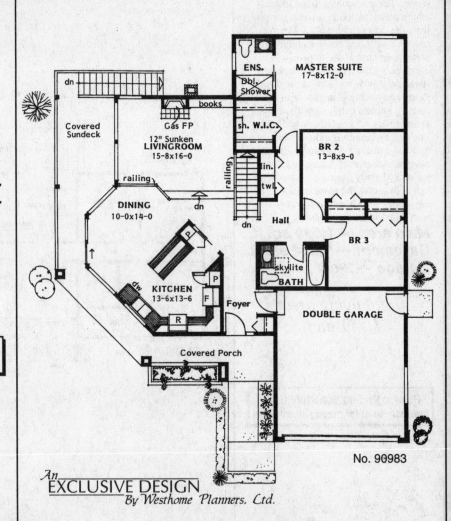

No. 90983

An
EXCLUSIVE DESIGN
By Westhome Planners. Ltd.

SUNNY SPLIT-LEVEL DESIGN

Here's a unique approach to the split-level home. A central, glass-walled foyer creates a brilliant impression on all who enter. Walk down to the fireplaced family room, double garage with workbench, a very private bedroom, full bath and utility area. Main living areas are situated for comfort and convenience. In the bedroom wing to the right of the open staircase, a skylit hall bath serves the two front bedrooms. The master suite enjoys a backyard view and private bath with mirrored dressing room. Active areas possess a wonderful, open atmosphere accented by a huge bay window in the living room, sliders in the dining room and informal nook that flanks the kitchen. The sundeck is a great dining option when the weathers' nice.

Main floor — 1,473 sq. ft.
Basement floor — 791 sq. ft.
Garage — 2-car

Total living area: 2,264 sq. ft.

Refer to **Pricing Schedule D** on the order form for pricing information

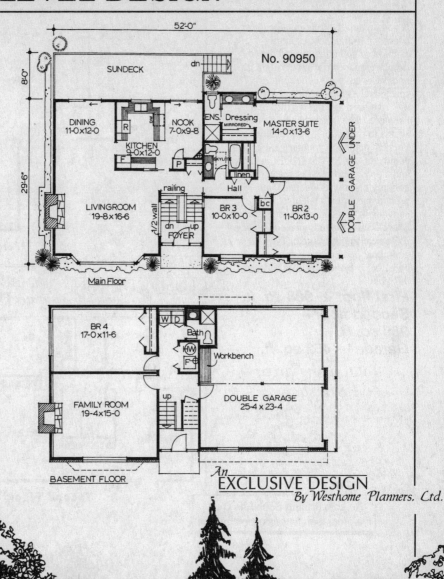

An **EXCLUSIVE DESIGN**
By Westhome Planners, Ltd.

PLAN MAKES FOR EASY LIVING

If you dream of sitting outside on a country porch on a hot summer's evening or gathering around the cozy fireplace on a cold winter's night, this house is what you're looking for. The spacious living room enjoys a view of the front yard and the warmth of the fireplace. The family room has direct access to the patio. The efficient kitchen includes a counter/eating bar peninsula, double sinks, built-in pantry and a broom closet. The master suite not only has a walk-in closet and private master bath but also a convenient, built-in audio/video center. There is an efficiently placed laundry room near the bedrooms. Two additional bedrooms share a full hall bath. No materials list available for this plan.

First floor — 908 sq. ft.
Second floor — 908 sq. ft.
Garage — 462 sq. ft.

Total living area:
1,816 sq. ft.

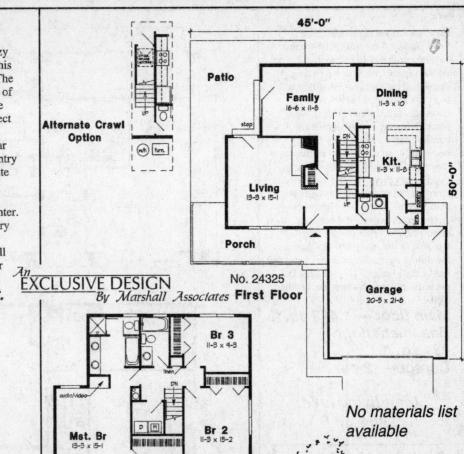

An
EXCLUSIVE DESIGN
By Marshall *Associates*

No. 24325
First Floor

Second Floor

No materials list available

Refer to **Pricing Schedule C** on the order form for pricing information

HOME WITH MANY VIEWS

This home is a vacation haven with views from every room, whether it is situated on a lake or a mountaintop. The main floor features a living room and dining room split by a fireplace. The kitchen flows into the dining room and is gracefully separated by a bar. There is a bedroom and a full bath on the main floor. The second floor has a bedroom or library loft, with clerestory windows, which opens above the living room. The master bedroom and bath are also on the top floor. The lower floor has a large recreation room with a whirlpool tub and a bar, a laundry room and a garage. This home has large decks and windows on one entire side.

Main floor — 728 sq. ft.
Upper floor — 573 sq. ft.
Lower floor — 379 sq. ft.
Garage — 240 sq. ft.

Total living area:
1,680 sq. ft.

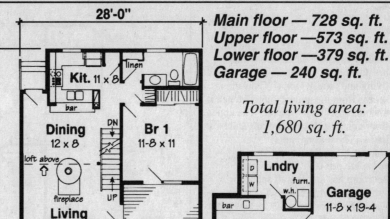

28'-0"
32'-0"

Kit. 11 x 8
linen
bar
Dining 12 x 8
DN
Br 1 11-8 x 11
loft above
fireplace
UP
Living 15 x 15
Deck

Main Floor
No. 24319

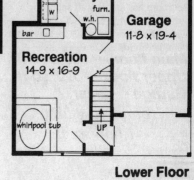

Lndry
D W
furn.
w.h.
Garage 11-8 x 19-4
bar
Recreation 14-9 x 16-9
whirlpool tub
UP

Lower Floor

An
EXCLUSIVE DESIGN
By Marshall Associates

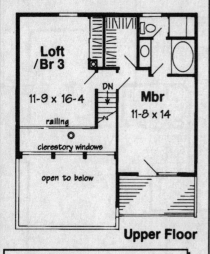

Loft /Br 3
11-9 x 16-4
DN
Mbr 11-8 x 14
railing
clerestory windows
open to below

Upper Floor

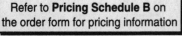

Refer to **Pricing Schedule B** on the order form for pricing information

Design 91348

UNIQUELY ANGLED HALLWAY

Not often found in 909 sq. ft. on the main floor, are a dining room plus breakfast nook as well as ample sized living and family rooms. Convenient access from the garage to the kitchen is a working woman's dream. The upper floor contains three bedrooms and two baths. The master bath is compartmentalized to provide complete privacy. The master bedroom has ample wall space for furniture arrangements. A walk-in wardrobe is conveniently located to the bath, bedroom and dressing area.

Main floor — 909 sq. ft.
Upper floor — 727 sq.ft.
Garage — 2-car

Total living area:
1,636 sq. ft.

Refer to **Pricing Schedule B** on the order form for pricing information

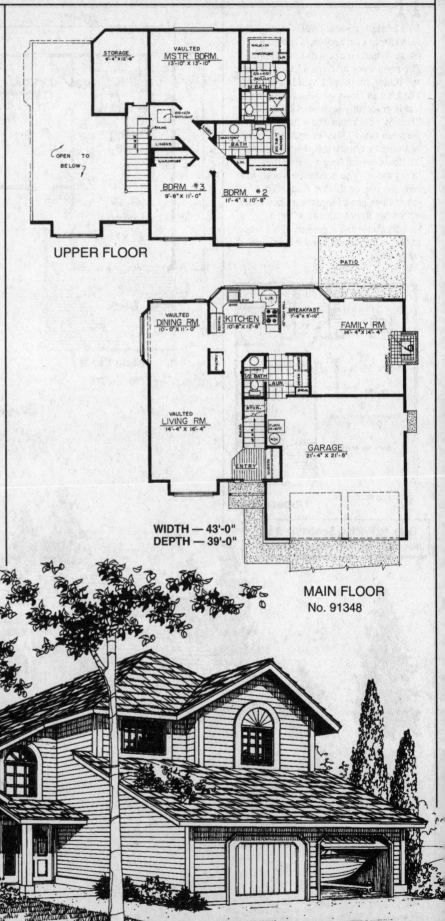

UPPER FLOOR

WIDTH — 43'-0"
DEPTH — 39'-0"

MAIN FLOOR
No. 91348

IMPRESSIVE FOYER WITH COLUMNS

Arched, multi-paned windows and an elegant brick design that looks much larger than its square footage indicates, are just a few of the features of this plan. The impressive foyer with columns features a sky-bridge above the family room. The parlor and dining rooms are designed to provide an elegant entertaining area. The island kitchen is enhanced by the convenience to both the breakfast nook and the formal dining room. The master suite with its privacy on the first floor has a first class bath and a retreat. Take notice of the library, which features a wood mantel fireplace and window seats. Upstairs, two large bedrooms have window seats and share another bath.

First floor — 2,024 sq. ft.
Second floor — 874 sq. ft.
Garage — 648 sq. ft.

Total living area:
2,898 sq. ft.

FIRST FLOOR PLAN

No. 92126

Shop

Dbl. Garage
23-4 x 23-4

Patio

Util.

M. Bath

Kitchen

Nook

WALK-IN CLOS.

Master Bedroom
15 x 15-8

Family Rm.
14 x 18

VAULTED CLO.

Porte-Cochere

74'

Retreat
10-8 x 8

Dining
14-6 x 10-6

BUTLERY

NICHE

POW. Rm.

COAT

Foyer

NICHE

UP

Parlor
13 x 14-6

Porch

70'

SECOND FLOOR PLAN

SEAT

Bedroom
12-8 x 11-8

WARDROBE

LIN.

Bedroom
12-8 x 10-6

OPEN TO BELOW

SEAT

Library
12-6 x 14

DESK

WARDROBE

BALCONY

Bath

DN.

SEAT

OPEN TO BELOW

Refer to **Pricing Schedule E** on the order form for pricing information

FOR THE FAMILY ON THE GO

Today's lifestyle needs convenience, without sacrificing style. The designer kept this in mind in designing this home. The spacious entry is graced on one side by an arched opening into the living room and on the other side by French doors into the den. The living room is accented by a focal point fireplace and a camphered ceiling. An arched opening joins the living room to the dining room, which is crowned by an elegant coffered ceiling. An island, built-in pantry and breakfast nook are featured in the kitchen. The large family room includes a second fireplace. The master suite is equipped with a lavish bath with a skylight. Two additional bedrooms are served by a full bath in the hallway. No materials list available for this plan.

First floor — 1,219 sq. ft.
Second floor — 803 sq. ft.

Total living area:
2,022 sq. ft.

Refer to **Pricing Schedule C** on the order form for pricing information

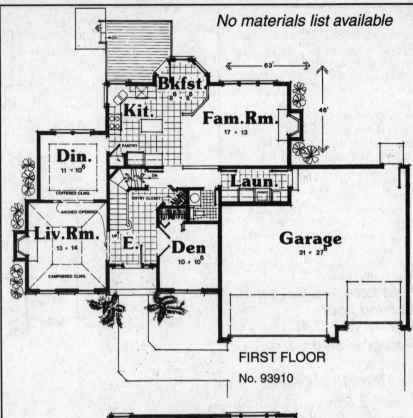

No materials list available

FIRST FLOOR

No. 93910

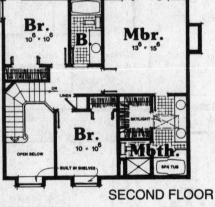

SECOND FLOOR

EYE-CATCHING ELEVATION

This elevation uses beautiful brick work surrounding the entry. Inside, the foyer area takes you through an arched entrance into the living room, accented by the front window with a window seat and a second arched opening into the dining room. A camphered ceiling adds elegance to the formal dining room, which has direct access from the kitchen. The well-appointed kitchen features a work island/eating bar and a built-in pantry. A bright breakfast nook accommodates informal meals. The family room, open to both the nook and kitchen, includes a gas fireplace; visible from the kitchen and nook areas. A master suite with a raised sitting area and two additional bedrooms, with private access to a full bath, completes the second floor. No materials list available for this plan.

First floor — 1,498 sq. ft.
Second floor — 1,227 sq. ft.
Basement — 1,484 sq. ft.

Total living area: 2,725 sq. ft.

Refer to **Pricing Schedule E** on the order form for pricing information

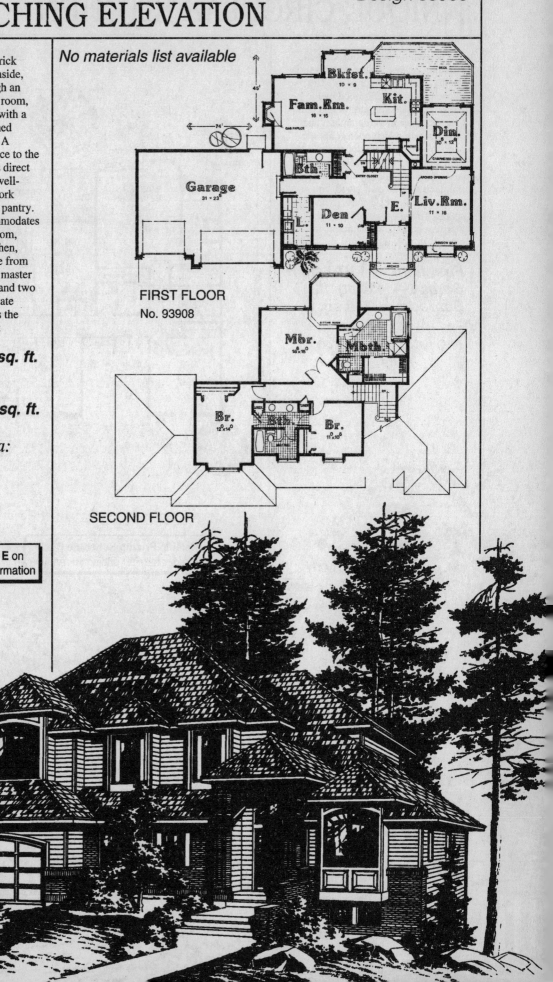

No materials list available

FIRST FLOOR
No. 93908

SECOND FLOOR

UNIQUE CIRCULAR KITCHEN

Design 10514

The unusual design of this kitchen provides the centerpiece for this thoroughly delightful floor plan. The kitchen is further enhanced by the tiled hallways which surround it and delineate the adjacent living areas. The dining room, which opens onto the patio with large glass doors, includes both a built-in hutch and a display case. The large family room has a fireplace with its own wood storage and provides direct access to the sunspace. The master bedroom suite has a private patio, a bay window, five-piece bath, separate vanity and a large, walk-in closet.

First floor — 1,870 sq. ft.
Garage — 434 sq. ft.
Sunroom — 110 sq. ft.

Total living area:
1,980 sq. ft.

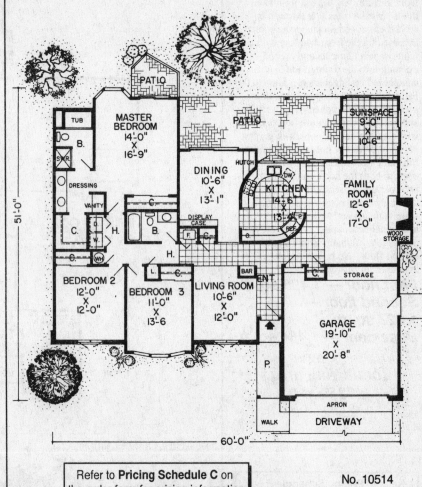

Refer to **Pricing Schedule C** on the order form for pricing information

No. 10514

SUNKEN LIVING ROOM FEATURED

No materials list available

This house is unique in many ways, from its staircase, sunken living and dining rooms, to its private second floor deck. The two-story foyer includes two spacious entry closets. Double doors provide entry into the den which is highlighted by a bay window. The kitchen has a large walk-in pantry, a wrap-around counter including a breakfast bar, an island and a phone desk. A skylight brightens the secondary bathroom, which is located next to the broom and linen closets. The executive master bath includes a wrap-around vanity, a spa tub, a shower and a room-size walk-in closet. A lovely touch to the master suite is the privacy deck. No materials list available for this plan.

First floor — 1,618 sq. ft.
Second floor —
1,087 sq. ft.
Width — 69'-0"
Depth — 48'-0"

Total living area:
2,705 sq. ft.

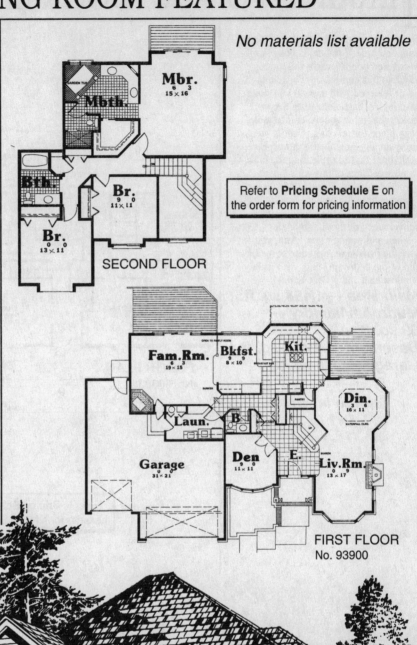

Refer to **Pricing Schedule E** on the order form for pricing information

SECOND FLOOR

FIRST FLOOR
No. 93900

TERRACE FOR OUTDOOR LIVING

Here's a charming Ranch that is loaded with amenities for today's busy family. A covered porch lends a welcoming touch to this compact, yet spacious home adorned with a wood and stone exterior. A heat circulating fireplace makes the living room a comfortable, cozy place for relaxing. Family areas enjoy an airy greenhouse atmosphere, with three skylights piercing the high, sloping ceilings of this wide-open space. A glass wall and sliders to the terrace add to the outdoor feeling. You'll appreciate the pass-over convenience of the side-by-side kitchen and dining room. And, you'll love the private master suite at the far end of the bedroom wing, with its bay window seat and private bath.

Main area — 1,498 sq. ft.
Mudroom/laundry — 69 sq. ft.
Basement — 1,413 sq. ft.
Garage — 490 sq. ft.

Total living area:
1,567 sq. ft.

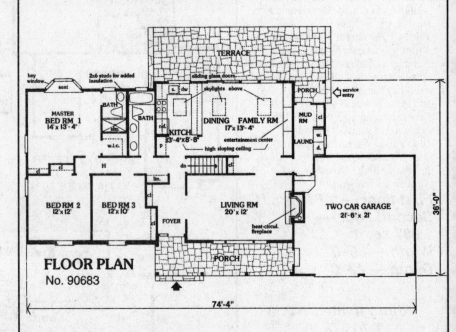

FLOOR PLAN
No. 90683

Refer to **Pricing Schedule B** on the order form for pricing information

UNITY DISTINGUISHES PLAN

Are you a sun worshipper? A rear orientation and a huge, wrap-around deck make this one-level home an outdoor lover's dream. Stepping into the entry, you're afforded a panoramic view of active areas, from the exciting vaulted living room to the angular kitchen overlooking the cheerful breakfast nook. Columns divide the living and dining rooms. Half-walls separate the kitchen and breakfast room. The result is a sunny celebration of open space not often found in a one-level home. Bedrooms feature special window treatments and interesting angles. A full bath serves the two front bedrooms, but the luxurious master suite boasts its own private, skylit bath with double vanities, as well as a generous walk-in closet.

Main area — 1,630 sq. ft.
Garage — 2-car

Total living area:
1,630 sq. ft.

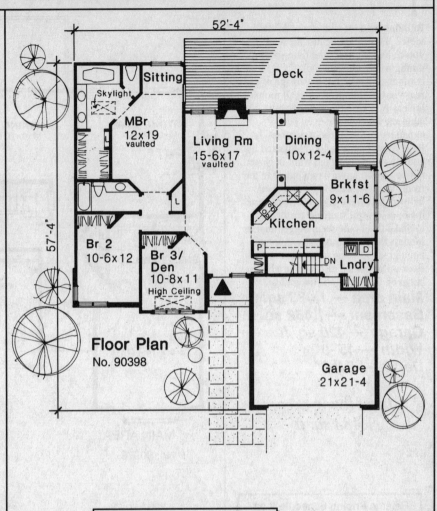

Floor Plan
No. 90398

Refer to **Pricing Schedule B** on the order form for pricing information

TRADITIONAL STYLING

Building on a lot with a spectacular view? This might be just the plan you're looking for. The living room, dining room, kitchen/nook combination take full advantage of a rear view building site, and all rooms are easily accessible to a spacious sundeck which could even be expanded in size if room permits. A large master suite is complemented by equally roomy bath and walk-in closet, notice the attractive bay window to the front. A good-sized foyer and open hallway provide a good traffic pattern, the open central staircase really helps to make this home seem bigger than its modest floor area suggests. Another popular step-saving feature is the main floor utility which also acts as a buffer between the house and the garage.

Main area — 1,483 sq. ft.
Basement — 1,462 sq. ft.
Garage — 420 sq. ft.
Width — 45'-0"
Depth — 54'-0"

Total living area:
1,483 sq. ft.

Refer to **Pricing Schedule A** on the order form for pricing information

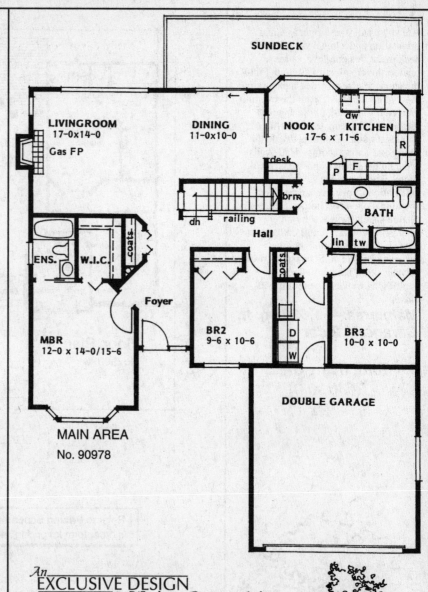

LIVINGROOM 17-0x14-0 Gas FP
DINING 11-0x10-0
NOOK
KITCHEN 17-6 x 11-6
BATH
ENS.
W.I.C.
coats
Hall
Foyer
MBR 12-0 x 14-0/15-6
BR2 9-6 x 10-6
BR3 10-0 x 10-0
DOUBLE GARAGE
SUNDECK

MAIN AREA
No. 90978

An EXCLUSIVE DESIGN
By Westhome Planners, Ltd.

NEAT AND TIDY PLAN

This compact house has plenty of closets and storage areas where you can stow away the gear you usually need on vacation. The utility room is also larger than most and opens directly outside. There's no excuse for anyone to track snow or mud in. Sliding glass doors lead from the two-story living room and dining room onto a paved patio. Tucked into a corner, the kitchen is both out of the way and convenient. A handsome stone fireplace adds a functional and decorative element to both the interior and exterior of the home. A downstairs bedroom will sleep either children or guests. Beyond the railed loft, a master suite with a full bath and walk-in closet provides the owner of this home with every comfort. Please specify basement or crawl space foundation when ordering.

Main floor — 952 sq. ft.
Upper floor — 297 sq. ft.

Total living area:
1,249 sq. ft.

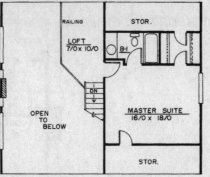

UPPER FLOOR

Refer to **Pricing Schedule A** on the order form for pricing information

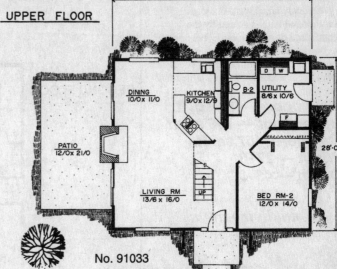

No. 91033

MAIN FLOOR

CHARMING AND COMPACT

This home is a sure winner for those who are looking for that unique house with all the extras, and have a smaller budget to work with. The covered porch leads you into the great room that opens into another covered porch towards the rear of the house. A separate dining room adjoins the efficient kitchen and laundry area which leads to the garage. The second floor consists of three bedrooms. The master suite, with the added details of a window seat, houses a full bath and a generously sized walk-in closet. Another full bath is shared by the second and third bedrooms. All of this is compacted into an affordable 1,400 square foot home with loads of street appeal. No materials list available for this plan.

Main floor — 694 sq. ft.
Upper floor — 706 sq. ft.
Garage — 457 sq. ft.
Width — 37'-0"
Depth — 43'-0"

Total living area:
1,400 sq. ft.

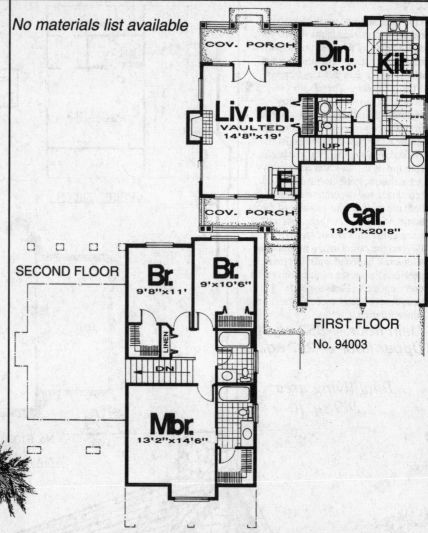

No materials list available

COV. PORCH
Din. 10'x10'
Kit.
Liv. rm. VAULTED 14'8"x19'
UP
COV. PORCH
Gar. 19'4"x20'8"

FIRST FLOOR
No. 94003

SECOND FLOOR
Br. 9'8"x11'
Br. 9'x10'6"
LINEN
DN
Mbr. 13'2"x14'6"

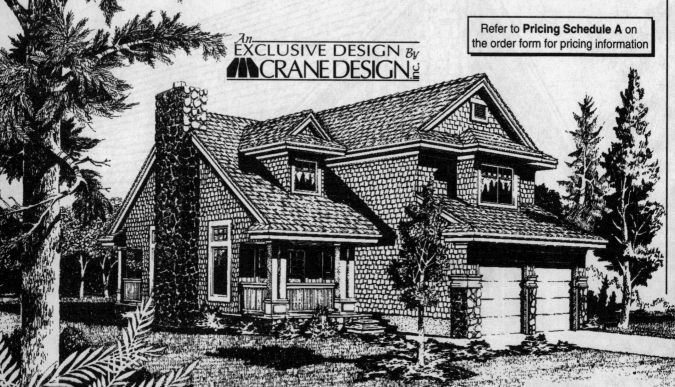

An EXCLUSIVE DESIGN *By* CRANE DESIGN inc.

Refer to **Pricing Schedule A** on the order form for pricing information

PORCH PROVIDES WELCOME

A charming angled covered porch welcomes you to this home trimmed with masonry. The spacious two-story entry, which repeats the same exterior angle, invites you to the well laid out main level of the home. A generously sized living room with a bay window and vaulted ceilings opens into the dining room. Find another bay window here, making entertaining easy with access to the kitchen. An open family area conveys warmth and style. The efficient kitchen with corner windows features a large walk-in pantry for extra storage and a convenient eating bar. An easy, open, staircase with a beautiful window detail leads you to the four spacious second story bedrooms. The master suite features a large master bath complete with a whirlpool tub, a double vanity and a large walk-in closet. No materials list available for this plan.

Main floor — 1,202 sq. ft.
Upper floor —
1,050 sq. ft.
Garage — 572 sq. ft.
Width — 61'-0"
Depth — 42'-0"

Total living area:
2,252 sq. ft.

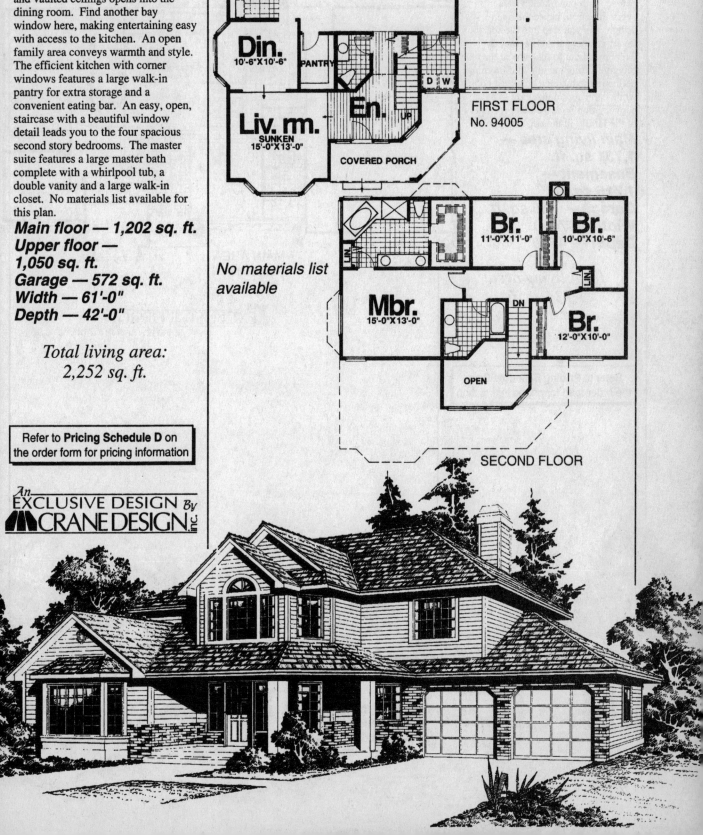

Bfst.

Fam. rm.
16'-0"X15'-0"

Kit

Gar.
21'-6"X24'-0"

PATIO

WOODSTOVE

Din.
10'-6"X10'-6"

PANTRY

D W

Liv. rm.
SUNKEN
15'-0"X13'-0"

En.

UP

COVERED PORCH

FIRST FLOOR
No. 94005

No materials list available

Br.
11'-0"X11'-0"

Br.
10'-0"X10'-6"

LIN

LIN

Mbr.
15'-0"X13'-0"

DN

Br.
12'-0"X10'-0"

OPEN

SECOND FLOOR

Refer to **Pricing Schedule D** on the order form for pricing information

An
EXCLUSIVE DESIGN *By*
CRANE DESIGN *inc.*

Design 90986

SURROUNDED WITH SUNSHINE

Here's a cheerful rancher, characterized by lots of windows and an airy plan. The Italian styling of the exterior is today's hottest look, and the theme is carried indoors with tile and columns. This home was originally designed to sit on the edge of a golf course, with panoramic vistas in every direction, hence the open design. As you step into the spacious foyer, your eye travels across the Great room out to the view at the rear. Imagine sitting having your morning coffee in the turreted breakfast nook, while carrying on in happy conversation with the other members of the family in the adjacent kitchen.

**Main living area —
1,731 sq. ft.
Basement —
1,715 sq. ft.
Garage — 888 sq. ft.
Width — 74'-0"
Depth — 45'-0"**

*Total living area:
1,731 sq. ft.*

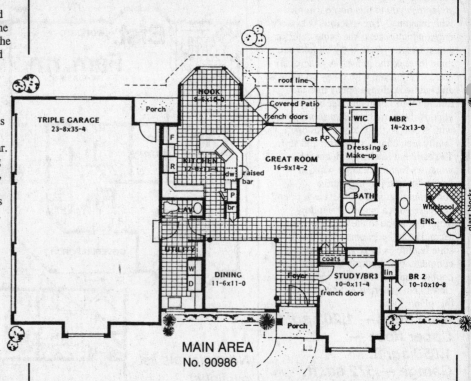

MAIN AREA
No. 90986

An
EXCLUSIVE DESIGN
By Westhome Planners, Ltd.

Refer to **Pricing Schedule B** on
the order form for pricing information

COMPACT DESIGN OFFERS BIGGER LOOK

The move-up market is demanding more than the basics: more in appearance, more in space, and more in quality equipment. This plan is designed to appeal to those who want the look of a bigger house with traditional details within a contemporary compact form.

First floor — 817 sq. ft.

Second floor — 699 sq. ft.

Garage — 2-car

Total living area: 1,516 sq. ft.

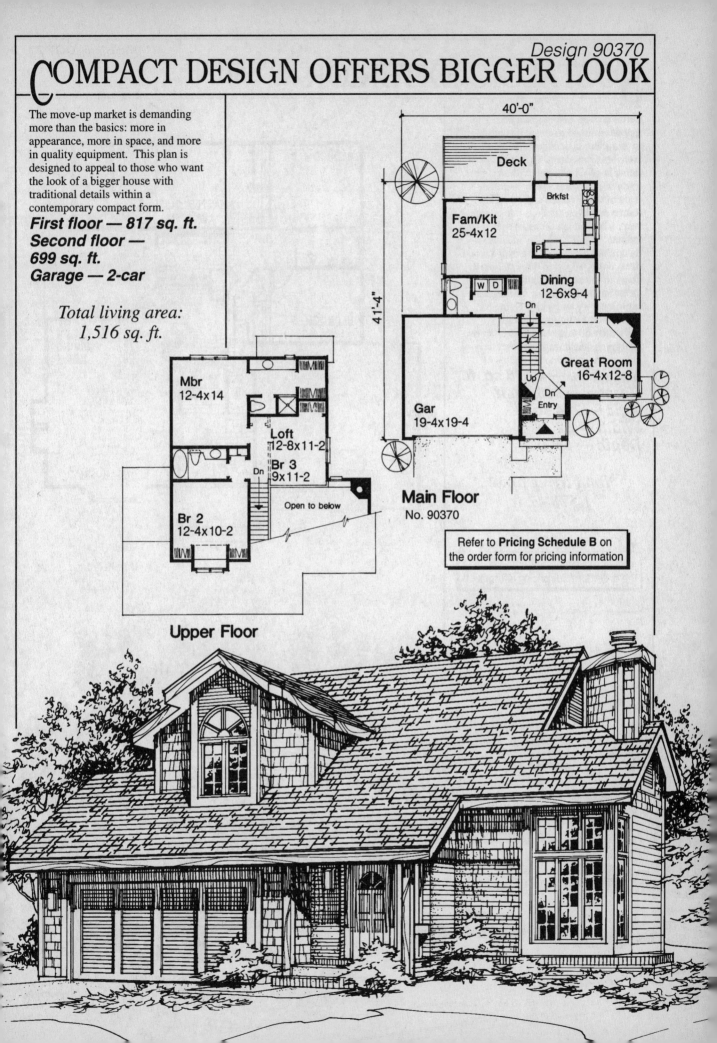

Mbr
12-4x14

Loft
12-8x11-2

Br 3
9x11-2

Br 2
12-4x10-2

Dn

Open to below

Upper Floor

40'-0"

41'-4"

Deck

Brkfst

Fam/Kit
25-4x12

P

Dining
12-6x9-4

W D

Dn

Great Room
16-4x12-8

Up

Dn
Entry

Gar
19-4x19-4

Main Floor
No. 90370

Refer to **Pricing Schedule B** on the order form for pricing information

NOSTALGIC EXTERIOR

Cedar shakes, gables and a brick facade combine to create this nostalgic exterior, but inside the home is completely modern. The entry opens into a huge Great room with skylights, a bay window and a wide hearth in front of the fireplace and wood box. Range and oven are built into a large work island in the center of the kitchen. A wide window in front of the kitchen sink looks out over a wood deck, easily accessed through French doors in the adjacent dining area. Other amenities include a triangular step-in pantry and a long eating bar. The master bedroom, although physically no larger than the other two bedrooms, has a walk-in closet, private bath and access onto the deck.

Main area — 1,578 sq. ft.
Garage — 658 sq. ft.
Attic — 724 sq. ft.
Width — 52'-0"
Depth — 56'-0"

Total living area:
1,578 sq. ft.

Refer to **Pricing Schedule B** on the order form for pricing information

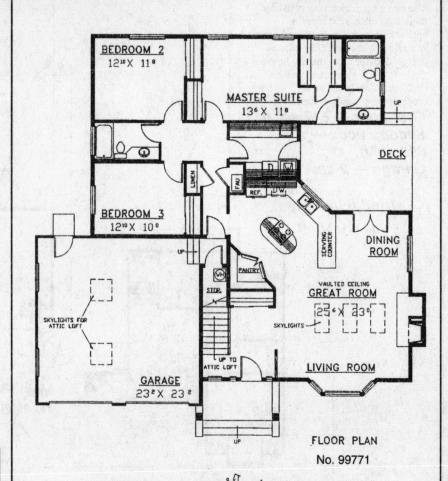

FLOOR PLAN

No. 99771

NEW ENGLAND CHARM

Refer to **Pricing Schedule B** on the order form for pricing information

The New England charm and warmth are expressed in this three bedroom Ranch house. It is basically divided into four parts: formal area, informal area, bedroom wing and service area. Featured are the master bedroom with its bath, the kitchen and the flowing spaces of living and dining rooms in the rear and the kitchen and family room/dinette in front. Each room is well defined. The combination of spaces fit well and give an impression of largeness. The spacious master bedroom has a dressing alcove off of it, and is adjacent to the other bedroom. It is equipped with a huge walk-in closet plus a linear one. Extras in the bathroom are two basins, shower stall and a 5'-6" whirlpool bathtub. The fully equipped kitchen is separated from the family room by a counter and high cabinets.

Terminating the family room is a pleasant bay suitable for a dinette table. Adjacent to the two-car garage is the service area, comprising a porch, family closet, laundry and lavatory.

Main living area — 1,686 sq. ft.
Basement — 1,609 sq. ft.
Garage and storage — 430 sq. ft.

Total living area: 1,686 sq. ft.

FLOOR PLAN
No. 99643

Floor plan labels

74'-4"
41'-4"

TERR.
fence

D. R. 10' x 12'
L. R. 18 x 14'

SERVICE PORCH
MUD RM
cl. D W
up
STORAGE
dn.
up
ref.
ptry
K. 10' x 14'
dw
low wall
FAM. RM 12'-8" x 15'
D'N'TTE
P.

TWO CAR GAR. 20' x 19'

M. B. R. 15 x 16'
shr.
whirlpool tub
t.v.
dress'g
W.I.C.
cl.
lin.
cl.
cl.
H.
B. R. 10' x 10'
cl.
cl.
B. R. 13' x 12'

FRONT PORCH ADDS A COUNTRY TOUCH

A large front porch is always an old-fashioned welcome to any home. This cape provides such a welcome. Once inside the home, the vaulted ceiling and grand fireplace of the living room add to the character of this house. The efficient kitchen has a double sink and a peninsula counter that may double as an eating bar. A laundry center is conveniently located in the full bath. Two of the three bedrooms are located on the first floor. The second floor provides the privacy the master suite deserves. Sloping ceilings, a walk-in closet and a private master bath give the owner of this home a private retreat on the second floor.

First floor — 1,007 sq. ft.
Second floor — 408 sq. ft.
Basement — 1,007 sq. ft.

Total living area:
1,415 sq. ft.

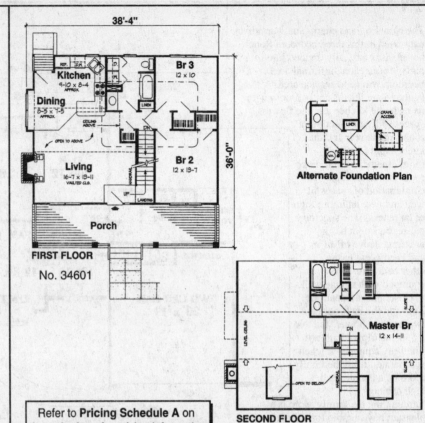

Alternate Foundation Plan

FIRST FLOOR

No. 34601

SECOND FLOOR

Refer to **Pricing Schedule A** on the order form for pricing information

DRAMATIC RANCH

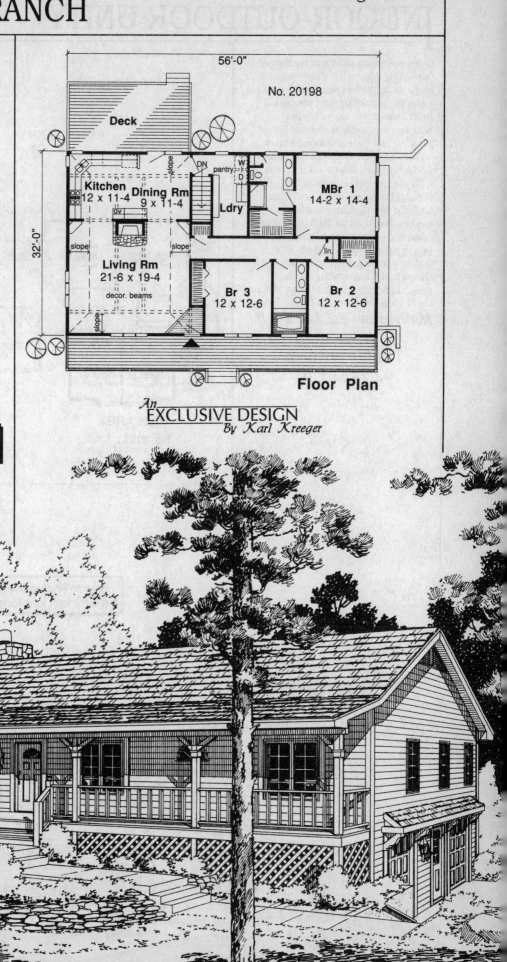

Design 20198

The exterior of this ranch home is all wood with interesting lines. It is more than a ranch home, it has an expansive feeling to drive up to. The large living area has a stone fireplace and decorative beams. The kitchen and dining room lead to an outside deck. The laundry room has a large pantry and is off the eating area. The master bedroom has a wonderful bathroom with a huge walk-in closet. In the front of the house there are two additional bedrooms with a bathroom. This house offers one-floor living and has nice big rooms.

**Main living area —
1,792 sq. ft.
Basement — 864 sq. ft.
Garage — 928 sq. ft.**

*Total living area:
1,792 sq. ft.*

Refer to **Pricing Schedule B** on the order form for pricing information

56'-0"

No. 20198

Deck

Kitchen 12 x 11-4

Dining Rm 9 x 11-4

pantry

W D

Ldry

DN

MBr 1 14-2 x 14-4

lin.

32'-0"

slope · slope · slope · slope

ov

Living Rm 21-6 x 19-4

decor. beams

Br 3 12 x 12-6

Br 2 12 x 12-6

Floor Plan

An EXCLUSIVE DESIGN *By Karl Kreeger*

INDOOR-OUTDOOR UNITY

One-level living has never been more interesting than in this three-bedroom home with attached three-car garage. From the protected entry, the central foyer leads down the hall to the bedroom wing, into the formal living areas, or into the sun-washed library. At the end of the bedroom hall, you'll find a luxurious master suite, complete with spa and a private deck. Straight ahead, glass walls and an open plan unite the formal dining and sunken living rooms with the backyard. The adjoining island kitchen, nook, and family room continue the outdoor feeling with expansive windows and sliders to the surrounding covered patio. Please specify basement, slab or crawl space foundation when ordering.

Main area — 2,242 sq. ft.

Total living area: 2,242 sq. ft.

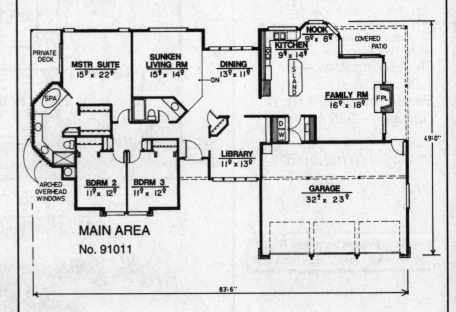

MAIN AREA

No. 91011

Refer to **Pricing Schedule D** on the order form for pricing information

GREEK REVIVAL

The large front entrance porch with its pediment and columns, although classical in style, presents a farmhouse quality. The 11 foot ceiling height for the foyer and 25 foot long living room, the focal point of which is a stunning, brick-faced, heat-circulating fireplace flanked by cabinetry and shelves, give a spacious feeling throughout. The formal dining room with a bayed window, connects to the living room and kitchen and overlooks a large rear terrace. The private bedroom wing, separately zoned from the main active living spaces, contains three bedrooms and two baths. One bath with two basins and a whirlpool tub serves the master bedroom while the other is shared by the other two bedrooms. The master bath has sliding glass doors which connect to a private terrace.

Main area — 1,460 sq. ft.
Lndry/mudroom —
68 sq. ft.
Garage & storage —
494 sq. ft.
Basement — 1,367 sq. ft.

Total living area:
1,528 sq. ft.

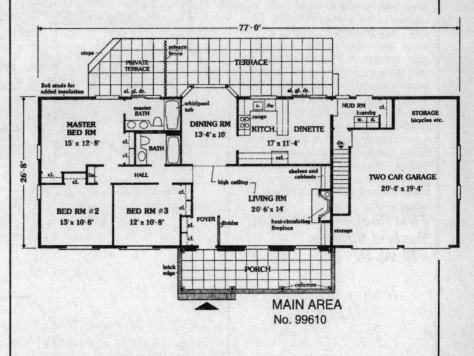

MAIN AREA
No. 99610

Refer to **Pricing Schedule B** on
the order form for pricing information

ENJOY THE VIEWS

Sitting in the sunken, circular living room of this elegant family home, you'll feel like you're outdoors even when you're not. Windows on four sides combine with a vaulted clerestory for a wide-open feeling you'll love year-round. When it's warm, throw open the windows, or relax on the deck. But, when there's a chill in the air, back-to-back fireplaces keep the atmosphere toasty in the living room and adjoining Great room. Even the convenient kitchen, with its bay dining nook, enjoys a backyard view. Do you sew? You'll love this roomy spot just steps away from the kitchen. Bump-out and bay windows give the three upstairs bedrooms a cheerful atmosphere as well as cozy sitting nooks.

**First floor — 1,439 sq. ft.
Second floor —
873 sq. ft.**

*Total living area:
2,312 sq. ft.*

Refer to **Pricing Schedule D** on the order form for pricing information

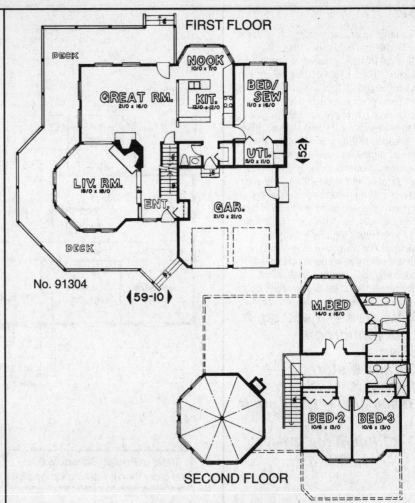

FIRST FLOOR

DECK

NOOK
10/0 x 7/0

GREAT RM.
21/0 x 16/0

KIT.
12/0 x 12/0

BED/
SEW
11/0 x 16/0

UTI.
5/0 x 11/0

52

LIV. RM.
18/0 x 18/0

ENT.

GAR.
21/0 x 21/0

DECK

No. 91304

59-10

M.BED
14/0 x 16/0

BED-2
10/6 x 13/0

BED-3
10/6 x 13/0

SECOND FLOOR

CONTEMPORARY WITH ELEGANCE

An impressive varied roof line sparks curb appeal for this contemporary home. The formal areas are located to the front while the family living area is to the rear. A warm fireplace accents the living room. The dining room easily accesses the kitchen. An island work area, built-in desk and a walk-in pantry highlight the kitchen. Columns define the entrance into the family room, which is equipped with a second fireplace flanked by built-in shelves. The first floor master suite has a private location. Three additional bedrooms, on the second floor, are served by a full hall bath. No materials list available for this plan.

First floor — 1,860 sq. ft.
Second floor — 803 sq. ft.

Total living area: 2,663 sq. ft.

An
EXCLUSIVE DESIGN
By Britt J. Willis

Refer to **Pricing Schedule E** on the order form for pricing information

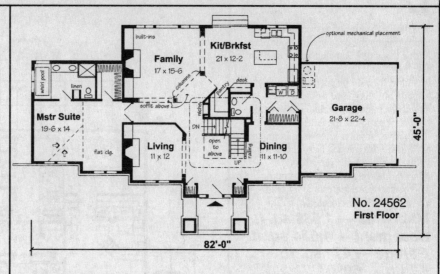

No. 24562
First Floor

No materials list available

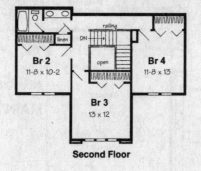

Second Floor

LET THE SUN SHINE IN

A striking Contemporary exterior compliments the exceptional floor plan in this attractive Ranch home zoned for area function. Designed to sit on a level lot, it could be adapted to a hillside building site. Some of the amenities include a secluded, covered breakfast patio off the family room, a distinctive, angular kitchen, a fireplace complete with a wood box, and a vaulted ceiling with clerestory windows in the sunken living room. The master suite features a 3/4 bath and a big walk-in closet.

Main area — 1,589 sq. ft.
Basement — 1,534 sq. ft.
Garage — 474 sq. ft.
Width — 60'-0"
Depth — 56'-0"

Total living area:
1,589 sq. ft.

Refer to **Pricing Schedule B** on the order form for pricing information

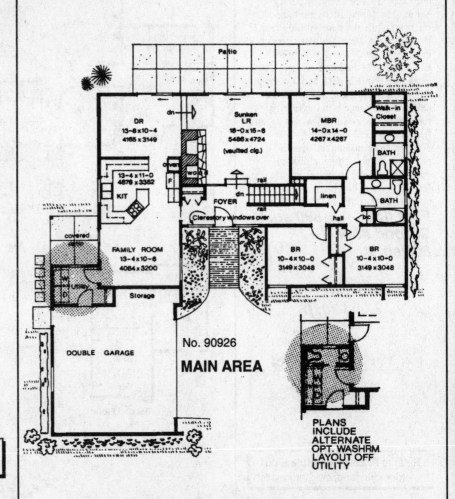

No. 90926
MAIN AREA

PLANS INCLUDE ALTERNATE OPT. WASHRM. LAYOUT OFF UTILITY

An
EXCLUSIVE DESIGN
By Westhome Planners, Ltd.

ATTRACTIVE VACATION RETREAT

Soaring windows and a wrap-around deck create an attractive exterior for this vacation retreat. The interior shows off vaulted ceilings and a spacious Great room concept. A captivating view, through the tower bay windows, is featured in this home's efficient kitchen. The Great room combines the living and dining rooms; each with French doors exiting to the deck. The entire upper floor contains a vaulted master bedroom and adjoining bath. No materials list available for this plan.

First floor — 1,329 sq. ft.
**Second floor —
342 sq. ft.**
Garage — 885 sq. ft.
Deck — 461 sq. ft.

*Total living area:
1,671 sq. ft.*

Refer to **Pricing Schedule B** on the order form for pricing information

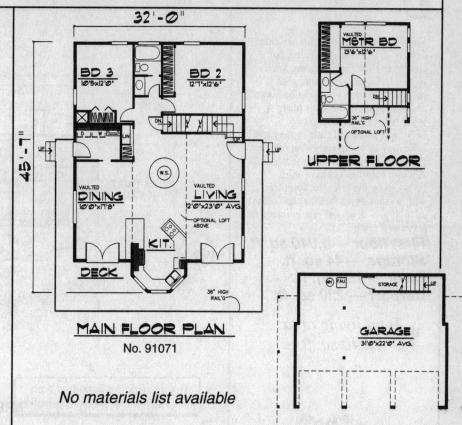

MAIN FLOOR PLAN

No. 91071

No materials list available

UPPER FLOOR

LOWER FLOOR

DESIGN FEATURES SIX SIDES

Simple lines flow from this six-sided design. It's affordably scaled, but sizable enough for a growing family. Active living areas are snuggled centrally between two quiet bedroom and bath areas in the floor plan. A small hallway, leading to two bedrooms and a full bath on the right side, may be completely shut off from the living room, providing seclusion. Another bath lies behind a third bedroom on the left side, complete with washer-dryer facilities and close enough to a stoop and rear entrance to serve as a mudroom.

First floor — 1,040 sq. ft.
Storage — 44 sq. ft.
Deck — 258 sq. ft.
Carport — 230 sq. ft.

Total living area:
1,040 sq. ft.

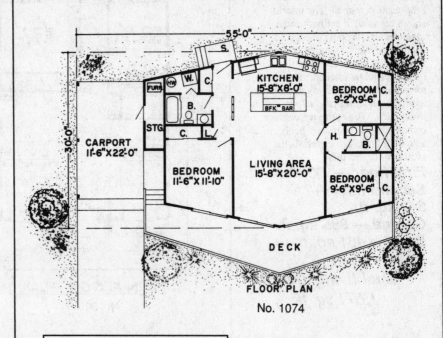

FLOOR PLAN
No. 1074

Refer to **Pricing Schedule A** on the order form for pricing information

VACATION RETREAT

A long central hallway divides formal from informal areas, assuring privacy for the two bedrooms located in the rear. Also located along the central portion of the design are a utility room and a neighboring bath. The furnace, water heater and washer-dryer units are housed in the utility room. An open living-dining room area with exposed beams, sloping ceilings and optional fireplace occupies the front. Two pairs of sliding glass doors access the large deck from this area. The house may also be entered from the carport on the right or the deck on the left.

First floor — 1,024 sq. ft.
Carport & storage — 387 sq. ft.
Deck — 411 sq. ft.

Total living area: 1,024 sq. ft.

Refer to **Pricing Schedule A** on the order form for pricing information

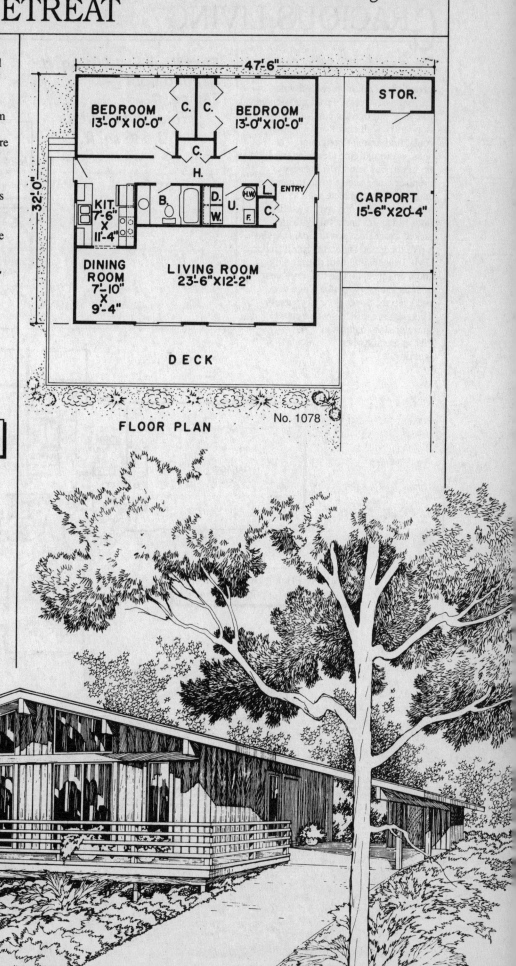

47'-6"

STOR.

BEDROOM
13'-0" X 10'-0"

C. C.

BEDROOM
13'-0" X 10'-0"

C.

CARPORT
15'-6" X 20'-4"

32'-0"

H.

KIT.
7'-6"
X
11'-4"

B.

D.
W.

U.

HW

L.

ENTRY

F.

C.

DINING
ROOM
7'-10"
X
9'-4"

LIVING ROOM
23'-6" X 12'-2"

DECK

FLOOR PLAN

No. 1078

Design 91023

GRACIOUS LIVING

Choose any beautiful site for this magnificent home. You'll want to take advantage of all the views provided by the impressive plan. From the moment you walk through the circular, two-story entry with clerestory windows, you'll find drama throughout. The open, exciting living areas feature skylights, bay windows, massive fireplaces, and access to an expansive outdoor deck, complete with a romantic gazebo and spa. Two first-floor bedrooms and a full bath are tucked away from active areas. At the top of the grand staircase, you'll find a skylit master suite with double sinks and a private spa. Use the room next door as a nursery, or use it as a den, and keep the upper floor to yourself. This plan is available with a crawl space or slab foundation. Please specify when ordering.

First floor — 1,901 sq. ft.
Second floor —
785 sq. ft.

Total living area:
2,686 sq. ft.

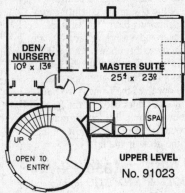

UPPER LEVEL
No. 91023

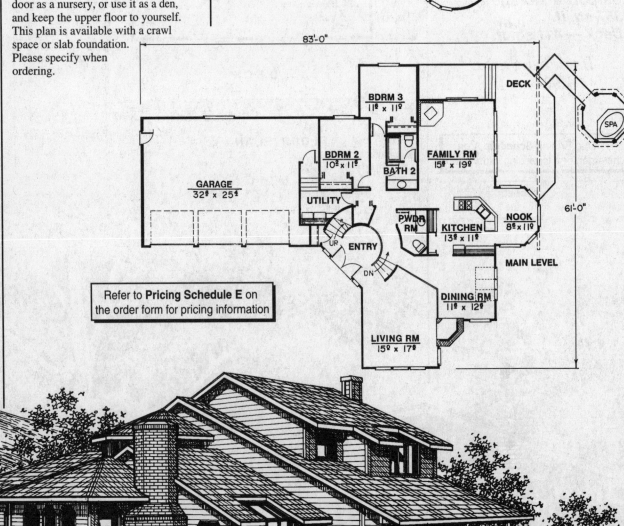

Refer to **Pricing Schedule E** on the order form for pricing information

REAR VIEW

INVITING PORCH WELCOMES GUESTS

Your guests may never want to leave your country ranch with its wrap-around covered porch. Inside, the cozy feeling continues throughout the house. The open plan of the family room, nook and island kitchen encourages conversation with friends gathered around the old-fashioned hearth. For more formal entertaining, there's an intimate dining room and angular, glass-walled living room. Thanks to the ingenious placement of the garage, the bedroom wing is sure to be a quiet retreat at day's end. This plan is available with a crawl space foundation only.

Main area — 1,850 sq. ft.

*Total living area:
1,850 sq. ft.*

Refer to **Pricing Schedule C** on the order form for pricing information

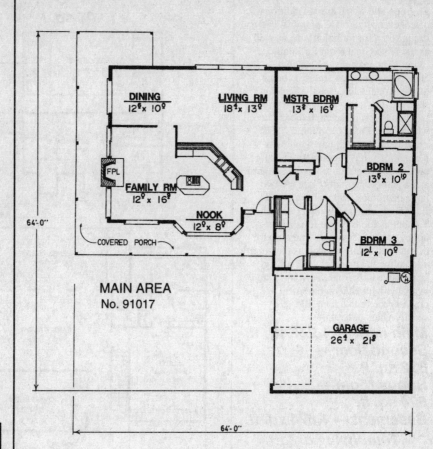

DINING
12⁶ x 10⁹

LIVING RM
18⁴ x 13⁹

MSTR BDRM
13⁸ x 16⁹

FPL

FAMILY RM
12⁹ x 16⁹

NOOK
12⁹ x 8⁹

BDRM 2
13⁸ x 10¹⁰

BDRM 3
12¹ x 10⁹

COVERED PORCH

64'-0"

MAIN AREA
No. 91017

GARAGE
26⁴ x 21⁸

64'-0"

TRADITIONAL THAT HAS IT ALL

This one-and-a-half story Traditional offers everything. The plan features a living room for formal affairs, as well as the large Great room for family living. The master suite has two closets, and the bath features corner tub with dual vanities and a separate shower. The large dining room with a bay window is adjacent to the kitchen, which has all major appliances. The breakfast room with bay window is perfect for sunny mornings. The large utility room features space for a freezer and a pantry. Upstairs there are two large bedrooms with walk-in closets. Each bedroom has it's own full bath. The bonus room can be finished as hobby room, office, etc. The mixture of rock and siding, as well as the porch and dormers, give this house a very impressive look from the front. Plan is available with either a basement or crawl space foundation. Please specify when ordering.

Main floor — 1,927 sq. ft.
**Second floor —
832 sq. ft.**
**Bonus room —
624 sq. ft.**
Basement — 1,674 sq. ft.

*Total living area:
2,759 sq. ft.*

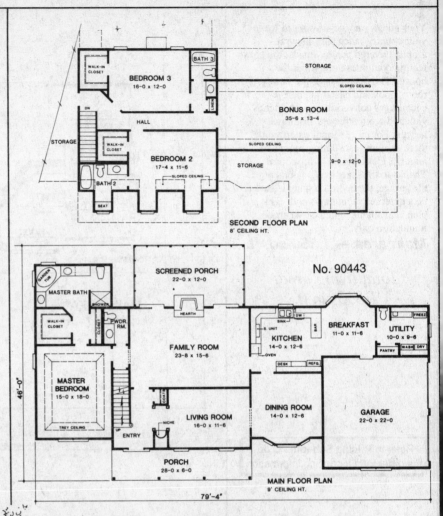

No. 90443

Refer to **Pricing Schedule E** on the order form for pricing information

ROMANCE PERSONIFIED

Here's a stately Victorian that will reflect your excellent taste and accommodate your family in comfort. A sprawling, wrap-around porch leads to a central foyer flanked by formal living and dining rooms. Informal areas overlook the backyard, including the fireplaced family room lined with bookcases, the sunny breakfast bay, and the adjoining country kitchen. Store your extra groceries in the large pantry on the way to the laundry room. The expansive master suite upstairs, which spans the width of the house, features built-in shelves, loads of closet space, and a private bath with every amenity. A hall bath serves the other two bedrooms tucked into the gables at the front of the house. This plan can be built with a basement or crawl space foundation. Please specify when ordering.

First floor — 1,366 sq. ft.
Second floor — 1,196 sq. ft.
Basement — 1,250 sq. ft.
Garage — 484 sq. ft.

Total living area:
2,562 sq. ft.

Refer to **Pricing Schedule D** on the order form for pricing information

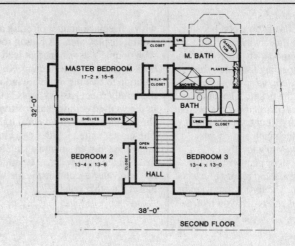

SECOND FLOOR

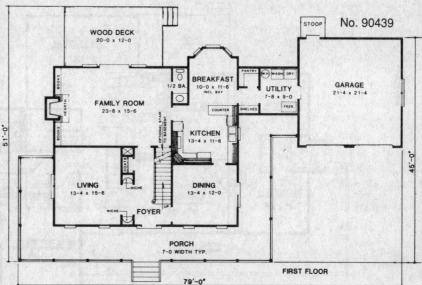

FIRST FLOOR

Design 99765

A LONG WRAP-AROUND PORCH

If sipping lemonade on a porch swing, or passing the time away on a hot summer's afternoon, chatting with friends are appealing fantasies, this home with its long wrap-around porch might be just the ticket. The railed porch stretches across most of the front of this one story, country-style ranch. Once inside, the ranch and country themes give way to a totally contemporary floor plan with all the modern amenities and plenty of extra storage space. The living room can be as formal or as relaxed as you like, with a fireplace mantel offering a natural display area. A dining room with double glass doors that lead to the deck is great for entertaining. In addition to two big double windows, the family room has skylights set high in the vaulted ceiling that positively shower the room with natural light. The master suite includes two closets, an oversized walk-in and a smaller one that is lined with cedar. The suite also has two vanities, one inside the water closet the other outside.

Main area — 1,998 sq. ft.
Basement — 1,998 sq. ft.
Garage — 635 sq. ft.
Width — 87'-0"
Depth — 48'-0"

Total living area:
1,998 sq. ft.

Refer to **Pricing Schedule C** on the order form for pricing information

FLOOR PLAN

No. 99765

ONE-STORY COUNTRY HOME

The entrance to the house is sheltered by the front porch that leads into the living room with its imposing high ceiling that slopes down to a normal height of eight feet focusing on the decorative heat-circulating fireplace at the rear wall. Widely open to the living room is the dining room. Its front wall is windowed from side to side. The adjoining fully equipped kitchen is also a feature of the house.

The convenient dinette can comfortably seat six people and leads to the rear terrace through six foot sliding glass doors. The master suite is arranged with a large dressing area that has a walk-in closet plus two linear closets and space for a vanity. The main part of the bedroom contains a media wall designed for TV viewing with shelving and cabinets for a VCR, radio, speakers, records and CD player.

Main area — 1,367 sq. ft.
Garage — 431 sq. ft.
Basement — 1,267 sq. ft.

Total living area:
1,367 sq. ft.

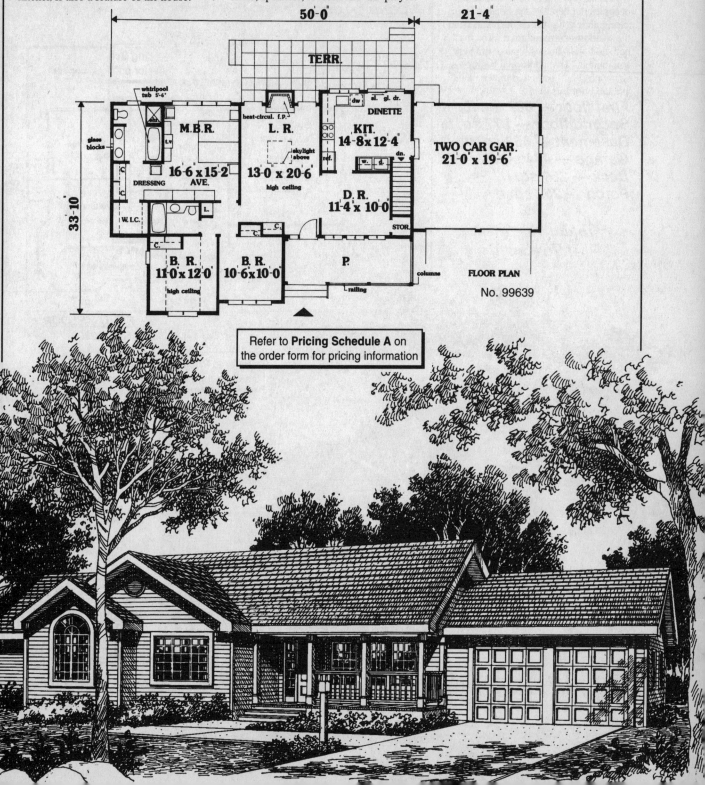

50'-0" 21'-4"

TERR.

whirlpool tub 5'-6"

heat-circul. f.p.

dw sl. gl. dr.

DINETTE

M.B.R. L. R. KIT.
14'-8 x 12'-4"

glass blocks t.v.

TWO CAR GAR.
21'-0" x 19'-6"

16'-6 x 15'-2 13'-0 x 20'-6
skylight above
high ceiling

DRESSING AVE.

ref.

w. d. dn.

33'-10" W.I.C.

D. R.
11'-4" x 10'-0"

STOR.

B. R.
11'-0 x 12'-0
high ceiling

B. R.
10'-6 x 10'-0

P.

columns FLOOR PLAN

railing No. 99639

Refer to **Pricing Schedule A** on the order form for pricing information

A TOUCH OF VICTORIAN STYLING

Design 93230

The covered porch and pointed roof on the sitting alcove of the master suite give this home a touch of victorian styling. Yet, the layout in the interior is certainly modern. The formal areas occupy the front of the home. The high traffic areas are in the rear of the home. The kitchen/breakfast area has a half-bath sandwiched between them and the family room, which enjoys a corner fireplace. On the second floor, the master suite occupies the depth of the house. The sitting alcove has the natural light from the windows surrounding it. The master bath and walk-in closet make life very convenient. Two additional bedrooms share a full hall bath. No materials list available for this plan.

First floor — 887 sq. ft.
Second floor — 877 sq. ft.
Basement — 859 sq. ft.
Garage — 484 sq. ft.
Deck — 261 sq. ft.
Porch — 252 sq. ft.

Total living area:
1,764 sq. ft.

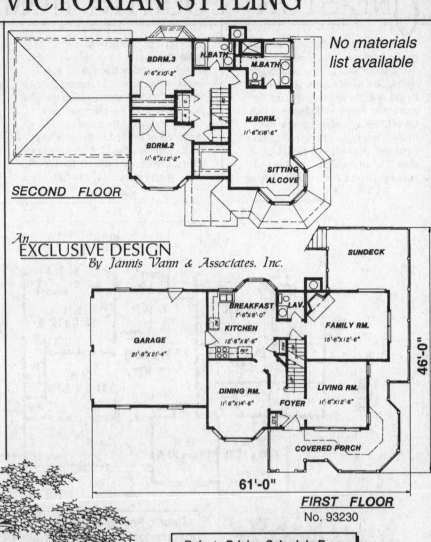

No materials list available

SECOND FLOOR

BDRM.3 11'-6"X10'-2"
H.BATH
M.BATH
BDRM.2 11'-6"X12'-2"
M.BDRM. 11'-6"X18'-6"
SITTING ALCOVE

An EXCLUSIVE DESIGN
By Jannis Vann & Associates, Inc.

SUNDECK
BREAKFAST 7'-6"X8'-0"
LAV.
KITCHEN 12'-6"X8'-6"
FAMILY RM. 15'-6"X12'-6"
GARAGE 21'-8"X21'-4"
DINING RM. 11'-6"X14'-6"
FOYER
LIVING RM. 11'-6"X12'-6"
COVERED PORCH
46'-0"
61'-0"

FIRST FLOOR
No. 93230

Refer to **Pricing Schedule B** on the order form for pricing information

GLORIOUS FRONT WINDOW

This home's many features accentuate your entertaining endeavors. The large front window enhances the curb appeal of this home, and illuminates the dining room. The expansive kitchen/breakfast room is close at hand. The cooktop island, double sinks and more than ample counter and cupboard space add to the room's efficiency. A private master suite, with a decorative ceiling, provides a personal getaway for the owner. The master bath and walk-in closet give convenience and privacy to the suite.

Two additional bedrooms on the second floor, with walk-in closets, share a full hall bath with a double vanity. No materials list available.

An
EXCLUSIVE DESIGN
By Greg Marquis

First floor — 1,901 sq. ft.
Second floor — 803 sq. ft.
Basement — 1,901 sq. ft.
Garage — 550 sq. ft.

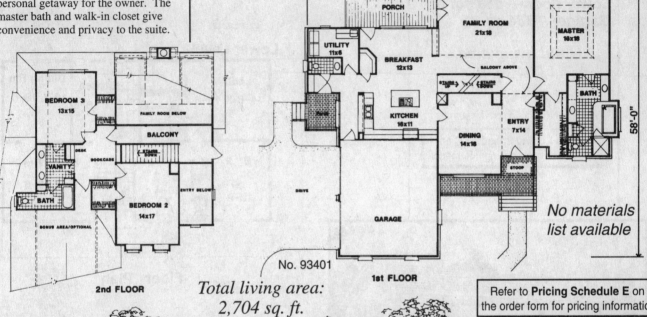

67'-0"

58'-0"

2nd FLOOR

No. 93401

1st FLOOR

Total living area: 2,704 sq. ft.

No materials list available

Refer to **Pricing Schedule E** on the order form for pricing information

ENTRY CROWNED BY CLERESTORY

The split foyer entry of this charmer has a half-flight of stairs that leads down to a family room, a utility room, a powder room, a study, and a two-car garage. Step up to a large living room, and an adjoining dining room and kitchen. A hall bath serves the two front bedrooms tucked down the hall while the rear master suite features a private bath.

Upper floor — 1,331 sq. ft.
Lower floor — 663 sq. ft.
Garage — 584 sq. ft.

Total living area:
1,994 sq. ft.

Refer to **Pricing Schedule C** on the order form for pricing information

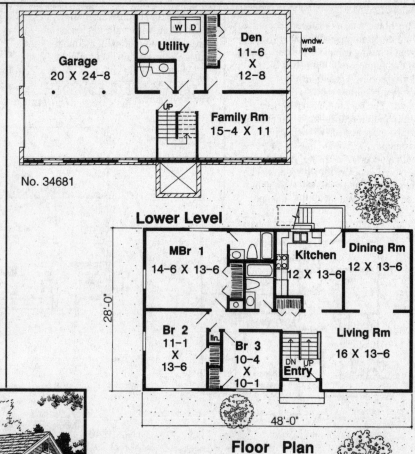

No. 34681

Lower Level

Floor Plan

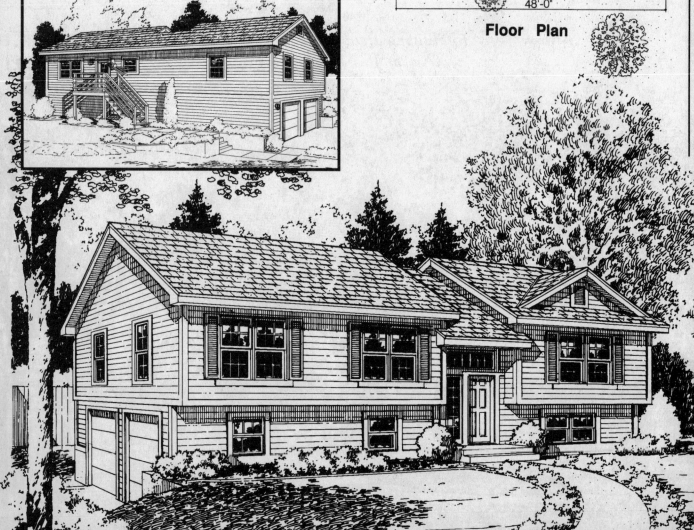

COMPACT, BUT ELEGANT

This Ranch home features a large sunken Great room, centralized with a cozy fireplace. The master bedroom has an unforgettable bathroom with a super skylight. The huge three-car plus garage can include a work area for the family carpenter. In the center of this home a kitchen includes an eating nook for family gatherings. The porch at the rear of the house has easy access from the dining room. One other bedroom and a den, which can easily be converted to a bedroom, are on the opposite side of the house from the master bedroom.

Main area — 1,738 sq. ft.
Basement — 1,083 sq. ft.
Garage — 796 sq. ft.

Total living area:
1,738 sq. ft.

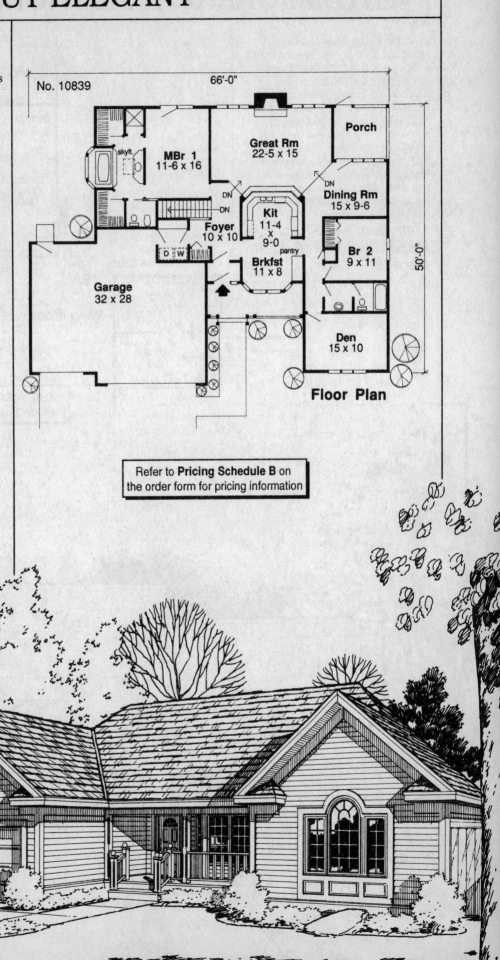

No. 10839 — 66'-0" — 50'-0"

MBr 1 11-6 x 16
skylt.
Great Rm 22-5 x 15
Porch
DN
Dining Rm 15 x 9-6
DN
DN
Kit 11-4 x 9-0
pantry
Foyer 10 x 10
Br 2 9 x 11
D W
Brkfst 11 x 8
Garage 32 x 28
Den 15 x 10

Floor Plan

Refer to **Pricing Schedule B** on the order form for pricing information

Design 99339

CONTEMPORARY TRADITIONS

Traditional elements such as half-round and divided sash, covered front porch, gable louver detail and wrap-around plant shelf under corner windows all create a nostalgic appeal. Dramatic views await guests from the front entry, with a vaulted ceiling above the living room and clerestory glass, fireplace corner windows with half-round transom, and a long view through the dining room slider to the rear deck. The main floor master suite has corner windows, walk-in wardrobe and private bath access.

Main floor — 857 sq. ft.
Upper floor — 446 sq. ft.
Garage — 2-car

No. 99339

Main Floor

38'-8"

Deck

Dining
9x9-6

Kit
12x9

Mas. Suite
14x12-8

Living Rm
12-4x17
vaulted

DN

P

UP

38'-8"

Garage
20x20

Upper Floor

Br 2
11-6x10

Br 3
13x9

open to below

DN

L

Refer to **Pricing Schedule A** on the order form for pricing information

Total living area:
1,303 sq. ft.

ANGLES AND WINDOWS ADD EYE APPEAL

The outdoor trellis leads to the front entrance into an energy-saving vestibule. The dramatic combined living room and dining "L" have a 16-foot ceiling and high windows flanking a natural stone, heat-circulating fireplace. A large outdoor terrace is reached through sliding glass doors of the dining room or from the fully windowed semi-circular dinette adjoining the kitchen. Two bedrooms are located on the first floor sharing a luxurious bath with a whirlpool tub and two sinks set in a long counter. Bedrooms three and four are located upstairs with bedroom five, which can also be used as a den, open to the living room below. Here too is another large bath with two sinks and an oval whirlpool tub. This second floor can be finished at a later date.

Refer to **Pricing Schedule C** on the order form for pricing information

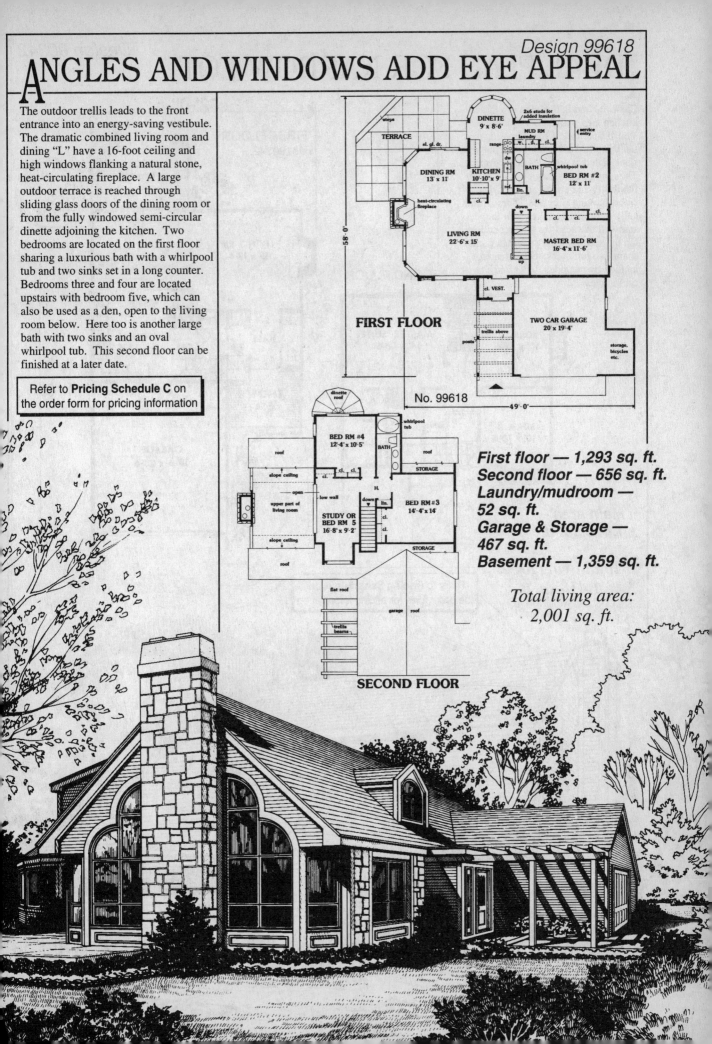

FIRST FLOOR

No. 99618

SECOND FLOOR

First floor — 1,293 sq. ft.
Second floor — 656 sq. ft.
Laundry/mudroom — 52 sq. ft.
Garage & Storage — 467 sq. ft.
Basement — 1,359 sq. ft.

Total living area: 2,001 sq. ft.

IDEAL PLAN FOR NARROW LOT

Design 90342

Close at hand in this plan is a large kitchen area with laundry facilities. You'll find it ideal for a growing family. The first level has an open floor plan that provides needed space. The living/dining room has both flexibility and charm and enjoys a wood-burning fireplace. Through the hallway, a half-bath lies near the stairwell that leads to the second level. On the second floor, three bedrooms share two full baths. Other features include two wooden decks and a two-car garage.

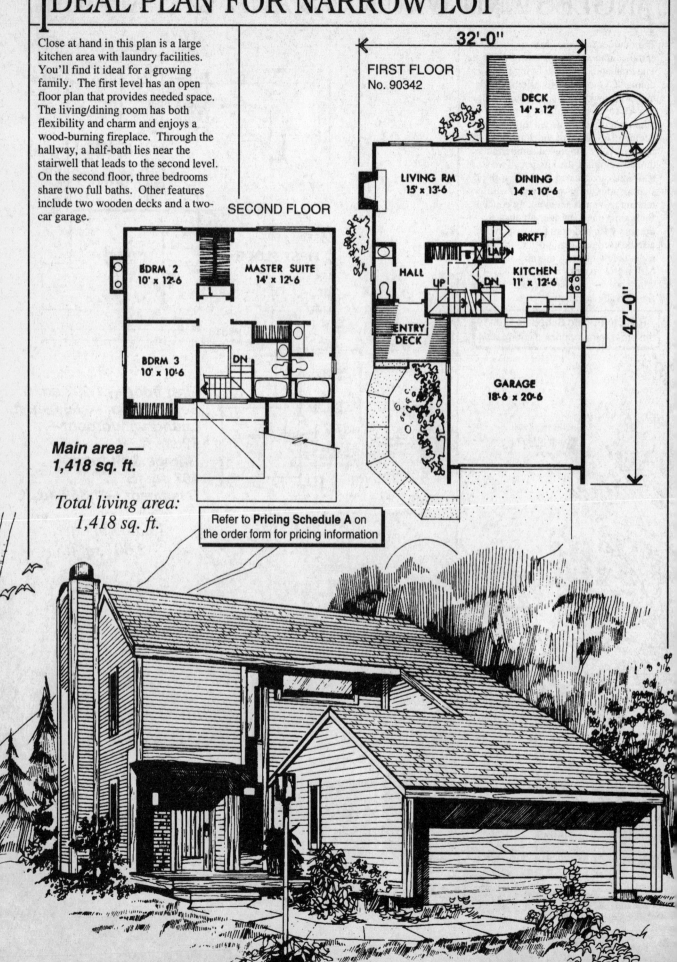

FIRST FLOOR
No. 90342

32'-0"

47'-0"

DECK
14' x 12'

LIVING RM
15' x 13'-6

DINING
14' x 10'-6

BRKFT

HALL

LAUN

KITCHEN
11' x 12'-6

UP

DN

ENTRY
DECK

GARAGE
18'-6 x 20'-6

SECOND FLOOR

BDRM 2
10' x 12'-6

MASTER SUITE
14' x 12'-6

BDRM 3
10' x 10'-6

DN

**Main area —
1,418 sq. ft.**

*Total living area:
1,418 sq. ft.*

Refer to **Pricing Schedule A** on
the order form for pricing information

HAPPY HILL HOUSE

Built into a hill, this vacation house takes advantage of your wonderful view. It features a Great room that opens out on a deck and brings earth and sky into the home through sweeping panels of glass. The open plan draws the kitchen into the celebration of the outdoors and shares the warmth of the sturdy wood stove. Two bedrooms on the main level share a bath. Two large, upstairs lofts, one overlooking the Great room, have a full bath all to themselves. This house feels as airy and delightful as a tree house. This plan is available with a basement foundation only.

Main level — 988 sq. ft.
Upper level — 366 sq. ft.
Basement — 988 sq. ft.

Total living area:
1,354 sq. ft.

Refer to **Pricing Schedule A** on the order form for pricing information

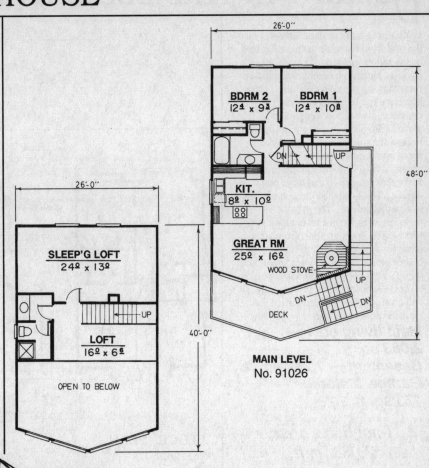

26'-0"

SLEEP'G LOFT
24² x 13²

LOFT
16² x 6²

UP

OPEN TO BELOW

40'-0"

UPPER LEVEL

26'-0"

BDRM 2
12⁴ x 9³

BDRM 1
12⁴ x 10⁸

DN   UP

KIT.
8² x 10²

GREAT RM
25² x 16²

WOOD STOVE

UP

DN   DN

DECK

48'-0"

MAIN LEVEL
No. 91026

Design 99627

DELIGHT IN THIS ELEGANT HOME

Walk through the landscaped courtyard into the front entrance of this elegant home and be greeted by a spacious foyer and a ceiling height of almost 10 feet. Among the many features of this home are the living room with conveniently located wetbar and glazed end in the shape of a hexagon. Follow the folding doors of the dining room into the family room that is accented by a heat-circulating fireplace and opens to a porch and huge rear terrace. The U-shaped kitchen is open to a bayed dinette. The private bedroom wing is on a level about two feet higher, setting it apart from all other living areas. The master bedroom has plentiful closet space while its bath is equipped with two basins, a whirlpool tub, private stall, and a vanity. The hall bath also includes double vanities.

**Main living area —
2,083 sq. ft.
Basement — 1,242 sq. ft.
Garage & storage —
473 sq. ft.**

*Total living area:
2,083 sq. ft.*

79'-4"

TERRACE

L R
13'-0" x 18'-6"

whirlpool tub

MBR
13' x 17'

MB

WET
BAR

D R
12'-0" x 13'-8"

FAM. R
16'-2" x 13'-8"

sl. gl. dr.

media wall

SCREENED
PORCH

C

WIC

B

C

C

ref.

STORAGE

C

up

K
13' x 10

LAUN

C

F

BR
13' x 13' AV.

BR
11' x 13' AV.

D N TE
8'-0" x 13'-5"

W
D

TWO CAR GAR
20' x 19'

stone or brick wall

COURT YARD

up

FLOOR PLAN
No. 99627

Refer to **Pricing Schedule C** on the order form for pricing information

ONE-STORY AFFORDABLE HOME

Design 99637

This energy-saving house was designed for comfortable living as well as a handsome exterior. In 1,460 total square feet it contains effective and efficient spaces for all family requirements. The entrance is through an inviting porch with a skylight. Once inside the house, the view through the foyer and then the living room is spectacular. The fireplace is flanked by two patio doors, one of which is operable to the rear terrace. The dining room can easily accommodate ten people around a table. The efficient U-shaped kitchen is conveniently accessible to the front door. These, with the family room/dinette, form the casual and informal portion of the house. On the other side of the house is the compact bedroom wing composed of three bedrooms and two full baths. The master bedroom is the largest. Contributing to the lower cost of this house is the simplicity in construction. None of the wood joists have a dimension greater than eight inches.

**Main living area —
1,460 sq. ft.
Garage — 427 sq. ft.**

*Total living area:
1,460 sq. ft.*

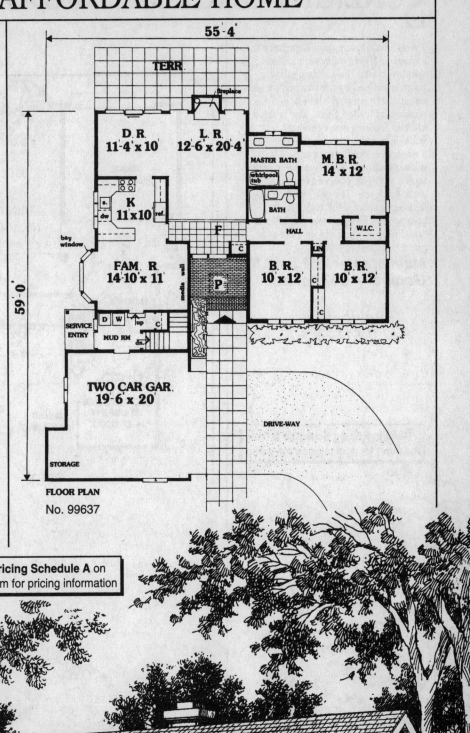

Refer to **Pricing Schedule A** on the order form for pricing information

SUNLIGHT STREAMS WINDOWS

Twelve-foot beamed ceilings grace the expansive living room with its facing window wall. The adjoining dining room is defined by a lower ceiling and enhanced by an over-sized bay window of leaded glass. The spacious kitchen features many cabinets, a walk-in pantry, center work-island, and a nook overlooking the patio. The master bedroom has a five-piece bath with a skylight, plus an extra large walk-in closet. The two smaller bedrooms share a full bath. A third bedroom located between the kitchen and dining room might find use as a guest bedroom or study.

Main area — 2,511 sq. ft.
Garage — 517 sq. ft.

Total living area:
2,511 sq. ft.

Refer to **Pricing Schedule D** on the order form for pricing information

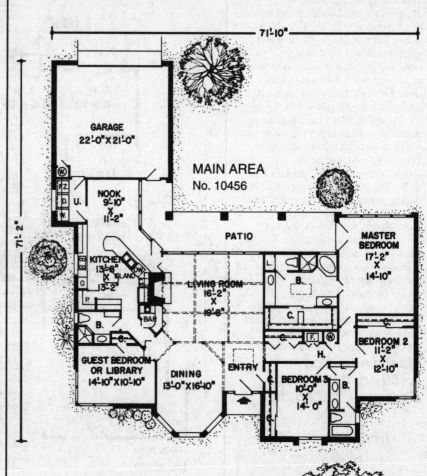

MAIN AREA
No. 10456

CABIN IN THE COUNTRY

Enjoy an up-to-date improvement on a vacation classic. You'll like the echoes of the past in this rustic looking, easy-to-maintain cabin, while you'll love the modern touches like 1-1/2 baths. The large screened porch invites you to relax or eat in style and take advantage of this country comfort. If the air gets nippy, you may want to sit by the fire in the cozy living room. Or, snuggle up in one of two bedrooms, each with its own bathroom. If you've overdone your outside exploring, a long, hot bath will restore you. This design, similar to classic cabins of the past, will always be a joy. Please specify a crawl space or slab foundation when ordering.

Main area — 928 sq. ft.
Screen porch —
230 sq. ft.
Storage area — 14 sq. ft.

Total living area:
928 sq. ft.

Refer to **Pricing Schedule A** on the order form for pricing information

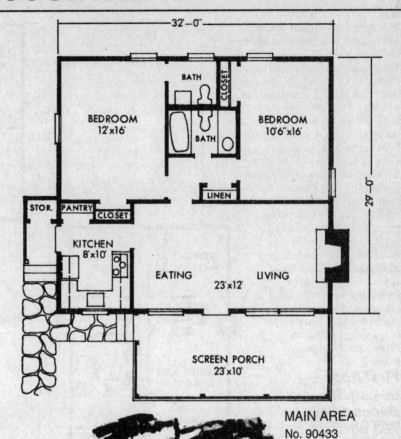

MAIN AREA
No. 90433

Design 90406

VICTORIAN IDEAL FOR NARROW LOT

This compact Victorian design incorporates four bedrooms and three full baths into a 30 foot wide home. The upstairs master suite features two closets, an oversized tub, and a sitting room with vaulted ceiling and bay window. Two additional bedrooms and a second full bath are included in the upper level. A fourth bedroom and third full bath on the main floor can serve as an in-law or guest suite. Between the dining and breakfast rooms is a galley kitchen. The dining room has a bay window and the breakfast room, a utility nook. A large parlor with a raised-hearth fireplace completes the main floor. The porches add to the overall exterior appearances and help to protect the front and side entrances. This plan is available with a basement or crawl space foundation. Please specify when ordering.

**First floor —
954 sq. ft.
Second floor —
783 sq. ft.**

No. 90406

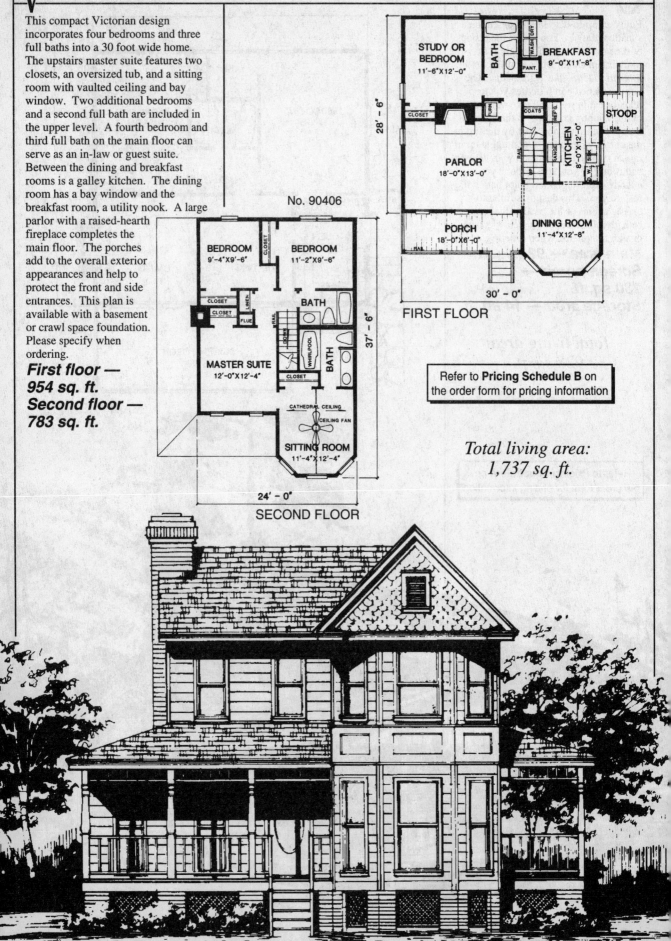

FIRST FLOOR

Refer to **Pricing Schedule B** on the order form for pricing information

*Total living area:
1,737 sq. ft.*

SECOND FLOOR

COUNTRY LIVING

Put out the rocking chairs and watch the world go by from the covered porch of this appealing family classic. Inside, a cozy atmosphere pervades living spaces, from the fireplace in the expansive family room to the bay windows in both dining and breakfast rooms. You'll appreciate the strategic location of the large, well-appointed kitchen, just steps away from eating areas. You'll also love the first floor placement of the master suite. And, look at the double-vanitied bath that wraps around his-and-her closets in this luxurious retreat. Both upstairs bedrooms feature dormer nooks, and private dressing rooms with an adjoining bath. Please specify a basement, slab or crawl space foundation when ordering.

First floor — 1,477 sq. ft.
Second floor —
704 sq. ft.
Basement — 1,374 sq. ft.
Garage — 2-car

Total living area:
2,181 sq. ft.

Refer to **Pricing Schedule C** on the order form for pricing information

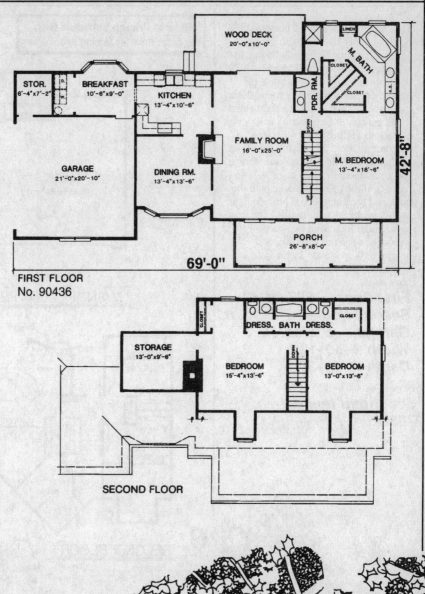

FIRST FLOOR
No. 90436

SECOND FLOOR

CONTEMPORARY IN STYLE

This contemporary styled home fits the needs of either families with young children, or empty-nesters who like to accommodate occasional visitors. Each of the three basic components of the main living area; the living room, dining room and kitchen, is set at a right angle to the garage. A large eating nook gives a spacious feeling to the otherwise compact kitchen. The eating bar offers additional food preparation and storage space and there is also a large walk-in pantry. Sliding glass doors in both the nook and the dining room provide light as well as access to the patio. The master bath is luxurious, with two garden windows, a spa tub, a shower and a nearby walk-in closet. In the third bedroom, the dormer window forms a cozy nook.

First floor — 887 sq. ft.
Second floor — 748 sq. ft.
Garage — 576 sq. ft.
Width — 50'-1"
Depth — 45'-3"

Total living area:
1,635 sq. ft.

Refer to **Pricing Schedule B** on the order form for pricing information

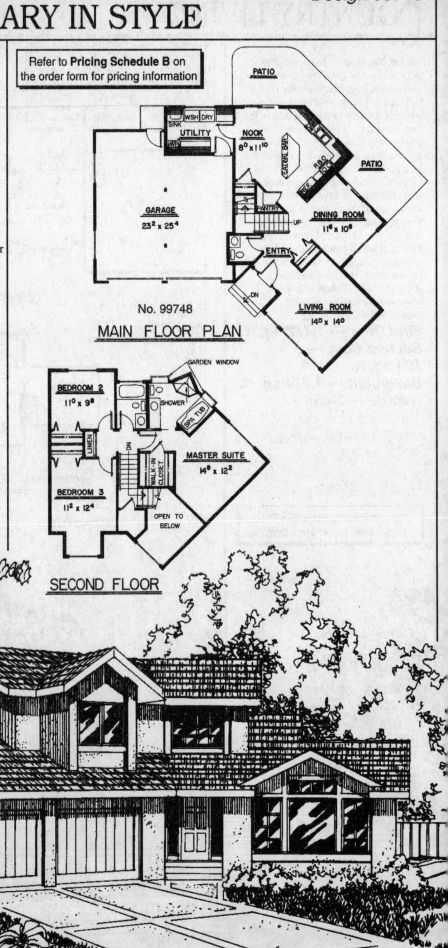

No. 99748
MAIN FLOOR PLAN

SECOND FLOOR

A UNIQUELY SHAPED HOME

Designed to take full advantage of a view facing out over a gentle slope or a corner lot, this uniquely shaped home will fill either requirement. The windows along the back offer striking vistas from the living room, dining room, master suite and bedroom, while high multi-panned windows on the front and side make the home equally attractive from either viewing angle. A tiled entry with skylights, opens into a living/dining room with a high ceiling. The odd angle created by the entry is used for a fireplace in the living room. Four steps up is an elevated kitchen with a walk-in pantry, double sink and spacious nook area. The master suite is equipped with a walk-in closet and private bath with a dressing area. The second bedroom is close to the master suite, convenient for small children, and has use of a hall bath with skylights. No materials list available for this plan.

Main area — 1,655 sq. ft.
Garage — 597 sq. ft.
Width — 72'-0"
Depth — 66'-0"

Total living area:
1,655 sq. ft.

Refer to **Pricing Schedule B** on the order form for pricing information

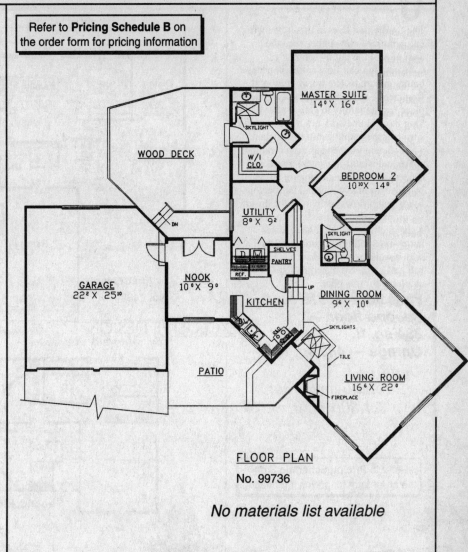

FLOOR PLAN

No. 99736

No materials list available

WITH A FOCUS ON THE FAMILY

The family that lives in this home will enjoy the open layout between the kitchen and the family room. Conversation can flow while dinner is being prepared. The warm glow of the fireplace in the family room is a good place for the family to gather after a long day. Homework is sure to be done sitting at the eating bar in the kitchen. The efficient kitchen has ample cabinet space and a built-in pantry. Formal dinners in the dining room are crowned by a pan-vaulted ceiling. The spacious living room flows easily into the dining room. Upstairs, the master suite has a walk-in closet and a private master bath. Two additional bedrooms, one with a walk-in closet, share the use of a full hall bath. No materials list available for this plan.

First floor — 916 sq. ft.
Second floor — 884 sq. ft.
Garage — 480 sq. ft.

Total living area: 1,800 sq. ft.

Refer to **Pricing Schedule B** on the order form for pricing information

40'-0"

48'-0"

Dining 9-6 x 11
pan vault clg.

Kit. 10-4 x 11
bar
pantry

Family 14 x 14-10

Living 14-1 x 15-9
railing
open to above
UP
DN
DN

Util.

Garage 19-5 x 23-8

First Floor
No. 24324

Alternate Crawl Option
crawl access
open to above
furn. w/h

An
EXCLUSIVE DESIGN
By Marshall Associates

No materials list available

whirlpool tub

Br 3 10-6 x 11

Mst. Br 14-1 x 15-9
9' clg.

DN
storage
open to below

Br 2 10-6 x 11-9

Second Floor

BALCONY OVERLOOKS GREAT ROOM

The Great room of this home is made more elegant by the fireplace and the fact that it is two stories high. A beautiful multi-paned, arched window naturally illuminates the room and provides a view of the front yard. An efficient kitchen is located at the rear of the home. The conveniences included in the layout of the kitchen are many. A central island, a built-in pantry, double sinks, not to mention the ample storage and counter space, give the advantages today's family demands. The second floor overlooks the Great room. The master bedroom has a private bath and a walk-in closet. The two additional bedrooms share a full hall bath. No materials list available for this plan.

First floor — 891 sq. ft.
Second floor — 894 sq. ft.
Basement — 891 sq. ft.
Garage — 534 sq. ft.

Total living area:
1,785 sq. ft.

Refer to **Pricing Schedule B** on the order form for pricing information

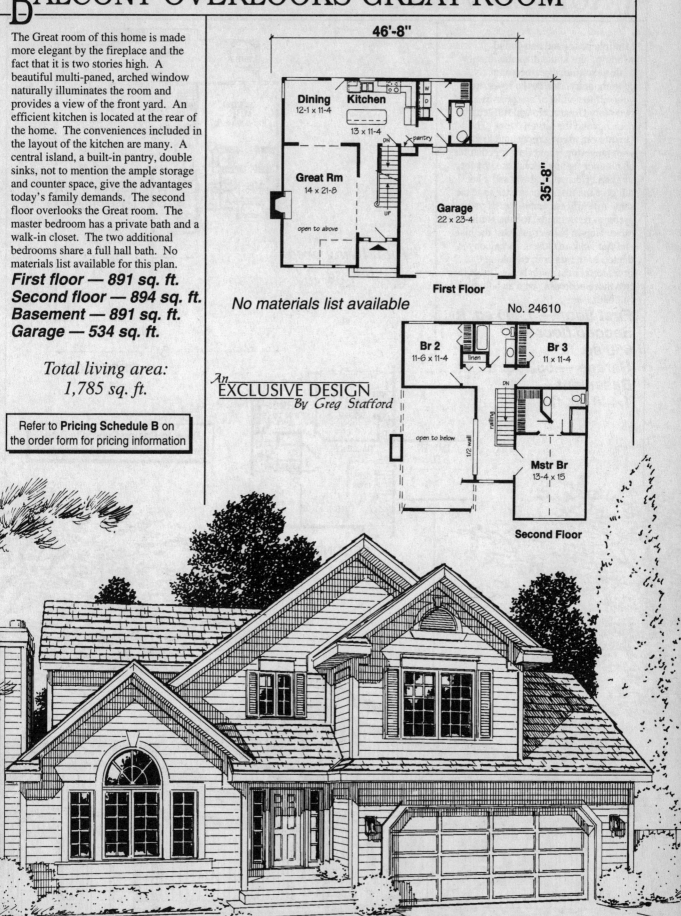

No materials list available

An
EXCLUSIVE DESIGN
By Greg Stafford

First Floor

No. 24610

Second Floor

VAULTED VIEWS

Multiple peaks and half-round windows hint at the dramatic interior of this exciting, three-bedroom contemporary. Inside the foyer, treat yourself to a view of an expansive, two-story Great room and full-length deck beyond the atrium doors. The Great room, dining room, and kitchen with range-top island flow together for an outdoor feeling accentuated by lots of glass. Corner windows and a hot tub give the first-floor master suite the same magnificent ambiance. If you prefer to relax inside, use the garden tub or step-in shower just past the his-and-her walk-in closets. A balcony at the top of the stairs overlooking the fireplaced Great room below, leads to two more bedrooms with an adjoining full bath.

First floor — 1,440 sq. ft.
Second floor — 650 sq. ft.
Garage — 552 sq. ft.
Basement — 1,440 sq. ft.

Total living area: 2,090 sq. ft.

FIRST FLOOR
No. 91416

HOT TUB

DECK

VAULTED MBR
17/6 X 13/6

VAULTED GREAT ROOM
19 X 15/6 AVG

DINE
12/6 X 12

W. CLO   W. CLO

MB

FOYER   UTIL   KIT

GARAGE
23/6 X 23/6

52'

50'

SECOND FLOOR

GREAT ROOM BELOW

BR
11/6 X 10/6

STR

LIMITED STOR

BALCONY

BATH

OPEN TO FOYER

DEN
10 X 11/6

BR
10/6 X 11/6

Refer to **Pricing Schedule C** on the order form for pricing information

BRICK STABILITY

This home offers one floor convenience. The large den has a stepped ceiling and a fabulous fireplace. Shelves and cabinets have been built-in to the side of the fireplace, resulting in even more convenience. The formal dining room and the informal breakfast bay sandwich the kitchen. The efficient kitchen includes a cooktop island, double ovens, built-in pantry and more than ample cabinet and counter space. The master bedroom includes a master bath and a large walk-in closet. Two additional bedrooms share a full hall bath. There is added storage behind the garage.

Main area — 1,869 sq. ft.
Garage and storage — 561 sq. ft.

Total living area: 1,869 sq. ft.

Refer to **Pricing Schedule C** on the order form for pricing information

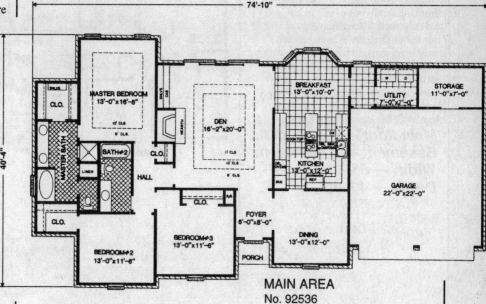

MAIN AREA
No. 92536

Design 93901

COZY RANCH-STYLED HOME

The large tiled foyer of this home leads to a front facing living room crowned by a volume ceiling. Decorative columns accent the entrance of the dining room which is topped by a camphered ceiling. The kitchen is open to the family room, separated only by a breakfast bar, allowing the cook a view of the central gas fireplace. Sliding glass doors lead from the family room to a large privacy deck, affording plenty of sunlight. The master bedroom has a walk-in closet and a private bath with a shower. Two additional bedrooms share the full hall bath. The laundry room is located by the two-car garage and serves as a mudroom. No materials list available for this plan.

Main floor — 1,538 sq. ft.
Basement — 1,488 sq. ft.
Width — 65'-0"
Depth — 40'-0"

Total living area:
1,538 sq. ft.

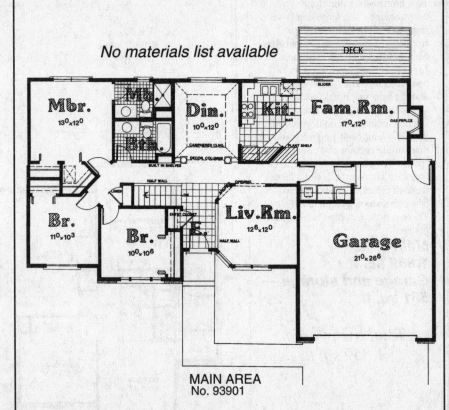

No materials list available

MAIN AREA
No. 93901

Refer to **Pricing Schedule B** on
the order form for pricing information

START WITH STYLE

Economical with style, describes this starter home. The generously sized Great room, leaves you with a light, open and airy feeling; due to taking advantage of the volume that is created with the vaulted ceilings. The Great room opens through a convenient serving bar into the cozy efficient kitchen, with eating area, that brings you to an outside deck. The master bedroom includes a full bath and walk-in closet. All of this is enhanced by a pleasant exterior that includes a charming porch. No materials list available for this plan.

Main floor — 1,200 sq. ft.
Width — 36'-0"
Depth — 54'-0"

Total living area:
1,200 sq. ft.

Refer to **Pricing Schedule A** on the order form for pricing information

No materials list available

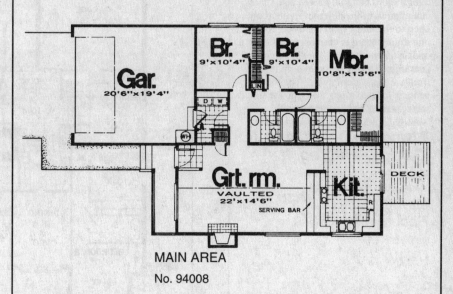

MAIN AREA

No. 94008

An
EXCLUSIVE DESIGN *By*
CRANE DESIGN inc.

BEAMED CEILING ACCENTS

Design 10465

The beamed ceiling, plus the fireplace and built-in bookcase of the comfortable family room, make this design an ideal plan for casual elegance. The family room also shares a wetbar with the adjacent living room. Across the entry from the living room, the dining room is easily reached from the efficient kitchen. Three bedrooms are aligned along one side with two full baths just steps away. The master suite is located along the opposite side with its own bath, complete with skylight, and spacious walk-in closet.

Living Area — 2,144 sq. ft.
Garage — 483 sq. ft.

Total living area:
2,144 sq. ft.

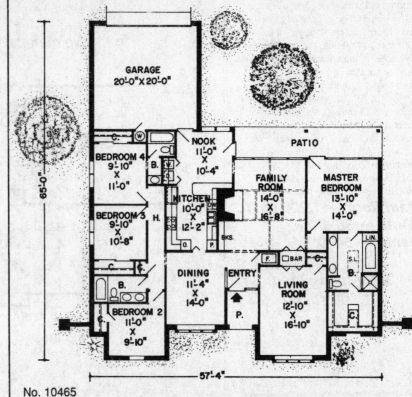

No. 10465

Refer to **Pricing Schedule C** on the order form for pricing information

CAREFREE COMFORT

Easy living awaits you in this one-level traditional designed with privacy in mind. A dramatic, vaulted foyer separates active areas from the three bedrooms. Down the skylit hall lies the master suite, where you'll discover the luxury of a private patio off the book-lined reading nook, decorative ceilings, and a well-appointed bath. The soaring roof line of the foyer continues into the Great room, which combines with the bayed dining room to create a celebration of open space enhanced by abundant windows. The cook in the house will love the rangetop island kitchen and nook arrangement, loaded with storage inside, and surrounded by a built-in planter outside that's perfect for an herb garden.

Main area — 1,665 sq. ft.
Garage — 2-car

Total living area:
1,665 sq. ft.

Refer to **Pricing Schedule B** on the order form for pricing information

ALTERNATE BASEMENT PLAN

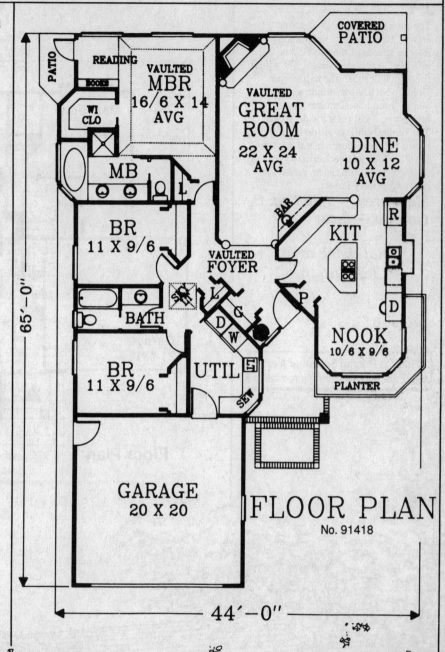

PATIO

READING
BOOKS

VAULTED
MBR
16/6 X 14
AVG

W1
CLO

MB

COVERED
PATIO

VAULTED
GREAT ROOM
22 X 24
AVG

DINE
10 X 12
AVG

BR
11 X 9/6

VAULTED
FOYER

BAR

KIT

R

BATH

NOOK
10/6 X 9/6

P

D

BR
11 X 9/6

UTIL

SEW

PLANTER

65'-0"

GARAGE
20 X 20

FLOOR PLAN
No. 91418

44'-0"

Design 99321

NOSTALGIA RETURNS

The return to a nostalgic exterior around contemporary volumetric interior spaces of the late 80's is reflected in this appealing 1,368 square foot ranch design. The half-round Great room transom window with quarter round detail makes for an interesting focal point inside and out. The vaulted ceilings inside make the rooms feel spacious, while the corner fireplace and side deck entered through the breakfast room sliders create an interesting entry impact.

Main area — 1,368 sq. ft.
Garage — 2-car

Total living area: 1,368 sq. ft.

Refer to **Pricing Schedule A** on the order form for pricing information

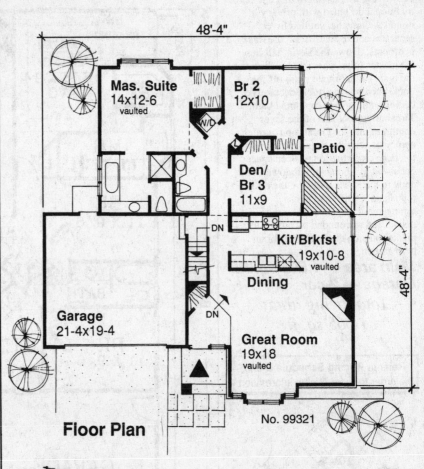

Floor Plan

No. 99321

SINGLE-LEVEL LIVING

For the move-up or empty-nest buyer who is looking for lots of features, but wants them all on one floor, consider this 1,642 square foot home. The interior offers many surprises like a vaulted ceiling in the living room and a built-in plant shelf. A fireplace forms the focus of this room. The angled kitchen has a sunny breakfast room. The formal dining room has stately divider details. Two bedrooms and two full baths in the sleeping wing of the home include the master suite.

Main area — 1,642 sq. ft.
Garage — 2-car

Total living area:
1,642 sq. ft.

Refer to **Pricing Schedule B** on the order form for pricing information

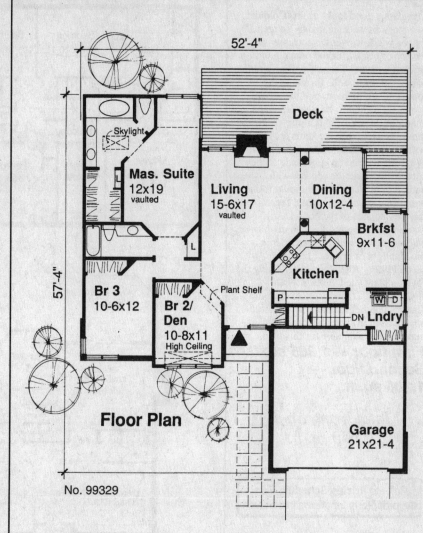

Floor Plan

No. 99329

LUXURY PERSONIFIED

The classic good looks of this Colonial two-story are accentuated by an arch topped window over the entrance and the use of brick trim and dental molding across the front. The tray ceiling and the corner columns in the formal living room and dining room pull these two rooms into a unit to create a large and charming area for entertaining. For family convenience the stairs are located with access directly into the kitchen. Windows located on either side of the corner sink flood the counter with natural light. The sunken family room with fireplace brings a warm feeling to this private area of the house. A luxurious bedroom suite with double walk-in closets and a sloped ceiling is the highlight of this four bedroom second floor. A balcony overlooking the foyer, a plant shelf, arched window, skylight, and a laundry chute are extra features that help to make this a home unsurpassed in style and value. No materials list available for this plan.

First floor — 1,365 sq. ft.
Second floor — 1,288 sq. ft.

Total living area:
2,653 sq. ft.

Refer to **Pricing Schedule E** on the order form for pricing information

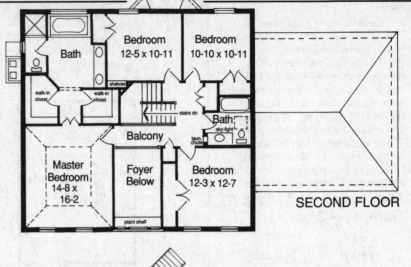

SECOND FLOOR

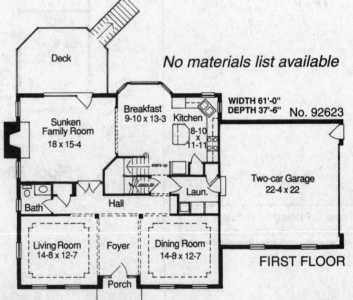

No materials list available

WIDTH 61'-0"
DEPTH 37'-6"   No. 92623

FIRST FLOOR

Stucco Opulence

An open foyer leads to a two-story living room with a great fireplace. The well-appointed kitchen has a cooktop island/snack bar, built-in pantry and desk, and an abundance of cabinet and counter space. The kitchen expands to the breakfast nook and the keeping room creating a feeling of spaciousness. His and her walk-in closets, a luxuriant bath and private sitting room create a master suite sure to be a personal retreat for the owner of this home. The library is in close proximity to the master suite for those late nights working at home. The additional bedrooms are on the second floor. The children's den give the children needed space and the two full baths are situated close to the bedrooms. No materials list available for this plan.

First floor — 2,329 sq. ft.
Second floor —
1,259 sq. ft.
Basement — 1,806 sq. ft.
Garage — 528 sq. ft.

Total living area:
3,656 sq. ft.

Refer to **Pricing Schedule F** on the order form for pricing information

No materials list available

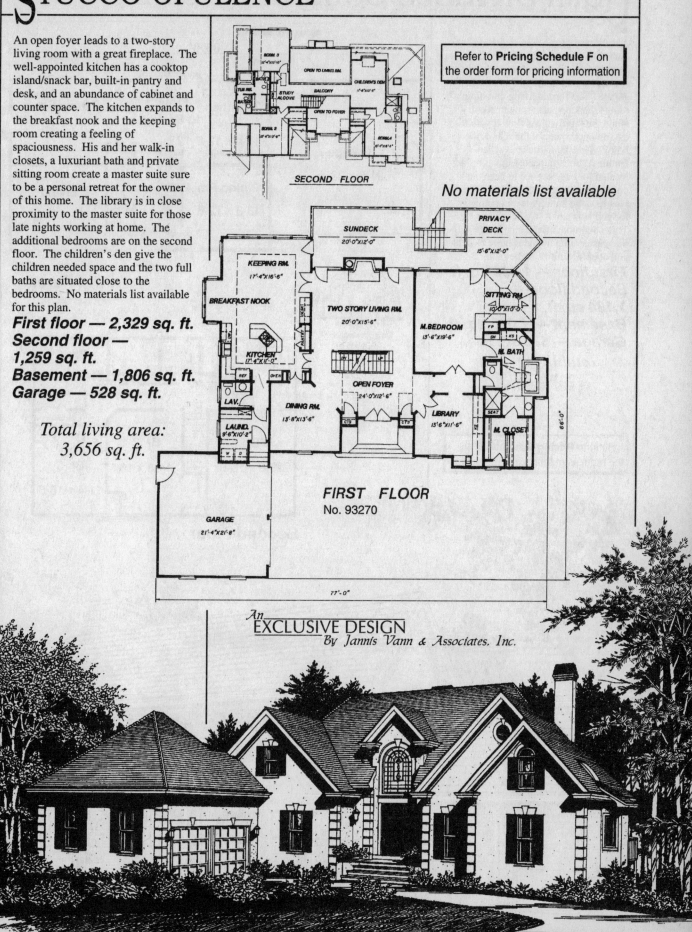

SECOND FLOOR

FIRST FLOOR
No. 93270

An
EXCLUSIVE DESIGN
By Jannis Vann & Associates, Inc.

Design 34705

COMFORTABLE COLONIAL HOME

A two-story plan keeps active and quite areas separate in this classic design which features four bedrooms, two-and-a-half baths and an attached garage. The formal living and dining rooms flank a spacious central entry while the family areas flow together into an open space at the rear of the house. An island kitchen, which features a built-in pantry, is centrally located for easy service to both the dining room and the breakfast nook. Upstairs, the laundry is conveniently located adjacent to the bedrooms. Three bedrooms share a hall bath and the master suite includes large closets and double vanities in the bath.

First floor — 1,090 sq. ft.
Second floor —
1,134 sq. ft.
Basement — 1,090 sq. ft.
Garage — 576 sq. ft.
Total living area:
2,224 sq. ft.

Refer to **Pricing Schedule D** on the order form for pricing information

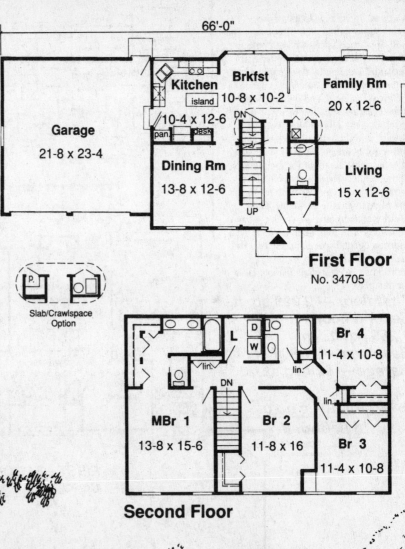

First Floor

No. 34705

Slab/Crawlspace Option

Second Floor

WINDOWS ADD WARMTH

Plenty of windows brighten this beautiful home with natural lighting and fresh air. More than enough closet space keeps clutter under control. A laundry room is located conveniently near all three bedrooms. The master suite features huge his-and-her walk-in closets and a private bath. Between the second and third bedroom is the second bathroom and linen closet. The family room is open to the dining area and kitchen. The kitchen is equipped with island counter and has access to an optional garage. Please indicate slab, crawl space or basement when ordering.

Main living area — 1,672 sq. ft.
Optional Garage — 566 sq. ft.

Total living area: 1,672 sq. ft.

Refer to **Pricing Schedule B** on the order form for pricing information

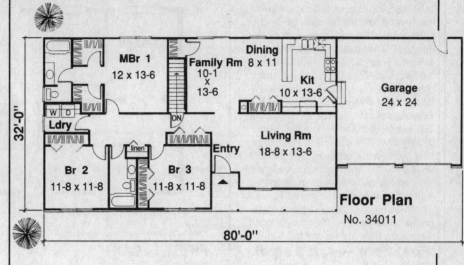

Floor Plan
No. 34011

32'-0"

80'-0"

MBr 1
12 x 13-6

Family Rm
10-1 x 13-6

Dining
8 x 11

Kit
10 x 13-6

Garage
24 x 24

Ldry

W D

Living Rm
18-8 x 13-6

Br 2
11-8 x 11-8

linen

Br 3
11-8 x 11-8

Entry

DN

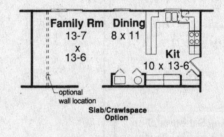

Family Rm
13-7 x 13-6

Dining
8 x 11

Kit
10 x 13-6

optional wall location

Slab/Crawlspace Option

Design 91053

UPDATED VICTORIAN

Although the exterior has the antique charm of Victorian features, the interior of this three bedroom home is truly modern. The charming features include a covered veranda, turreted sitting room, and a private deck for the master suite. Spaciousness is apparent in the family living areas with no separation of the nook and the family room. An efficient, modern kitchen serves both the casual living areas as well as the formal dining and living room enhanced by a patio door leading to the front veranda. A touch of elegance is added upstairs in the master suite with its turreted sitting room, walk-in closet, and a separate dressing room with double vanities. Two ample sized bedrooms share the second full bathroom.

First floor — 1,150 sq. ft.
Second floor — 949 sq. ft.
Garage — 484 sq. ft.

Total living area: 2,099 sq. ft.

Refer to **Pricing Schedule C** on the order form for pricing information

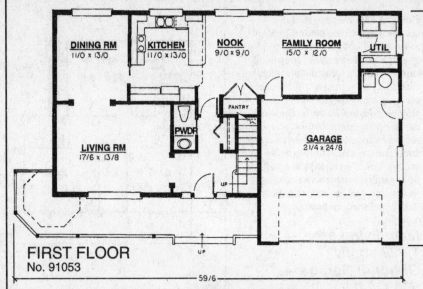

FIRST FLOOR
No. 91053

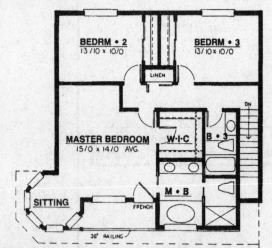

SECOND FLOOR

Design 91070

RUSTIC OPEN-CONCEPT FLOOR PLAN

Log columns and a stone chimney create a rustic appearance for this two-story home. Vaulted ceilings and an open-concept floor plan lend a feeling of spaciousness. The double door entry is flanked by a spiral stairway and a den/guest bedroom. A cozy fireplace heats both the living room and the dining area. An efficiently designed kitchen features a pantry. A secondary master bedroom includes a walk-in closet, private bath and French doors leading to the deck. The upper level master suite overlooks the living and dining rooms below. It is complete with a walk-in closet and private bath. No materials list available for this plan.

**First floor — 1,428 sq. ft.
Second floor —
376 sq. ft.
Garage — 450 sq. ft.**

*Total living area:
1,804 sq. ft.*

No materials list available

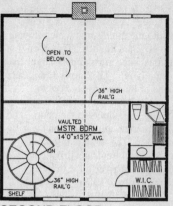

SECOND FLOOR

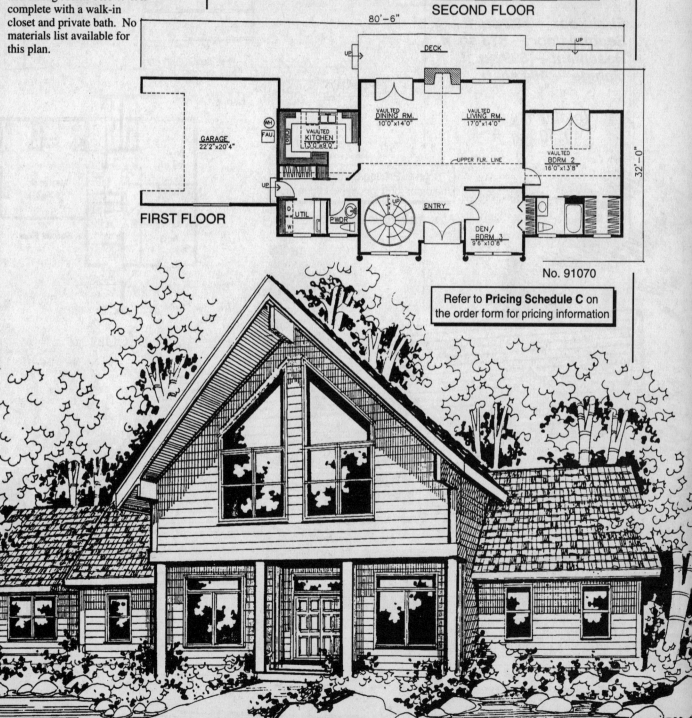

FIRST FLOOR

No. 91070

Refer to **Pricing Schedule C** on the order form for pricing information

FIREPLACE-EQUIPPED FAMILY ROOM

Design 24326

A lovely front porch shades the entrance of this home. A spacious living room opens into the dining area which flows into the efficient kitchen. This open layout makes the areas appear larger than they actually are. The family room, sure to be one of the busiest areas of the home, is equipped with a cozy fireplace and sliding glass doors to the patio. The sleeping quarters are located on the second floor. The master suite has a large walk-in closet and a private bath with a step-in shower. The three additional bedrooms share a full hall bath. No materials list available for this plan.

First floor — 692 sq. ft.
Second floor — 813 sq. ft.
Basement — 699 sq. ft.
Garage — 484 sq. ft.

Total living area:
1,505 sq. ft.

An
EXCLUSIVE DESIGN
By Marshall Associates

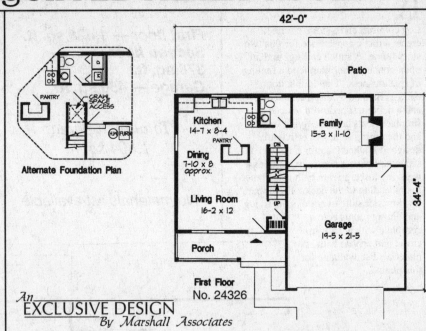

Refer to **Pricing Schedule B** on the order form for pricing information

No materials list available

BRIDGE IS A UNIQUE FEATURE

A dynamic foyer opens into a cathedral-ceiling great room, complete with a cozy fireplace framed on both sides with bookshelves. The unique octagonal breakfast nook is tucked into a spacious kitchen with a view of the backyard. The master bedroom boasts a quaint, but roomy, sitting room. Three full baths and two half baths are conveniently located for family and guests.

First floor — 2,335 sq. ft.
Second floor — 1,157 sq. ft.
Basement — 2,281 sq. ft.
Garage — 862 sq. ft.

Total living area: 3,492 sq. ft.

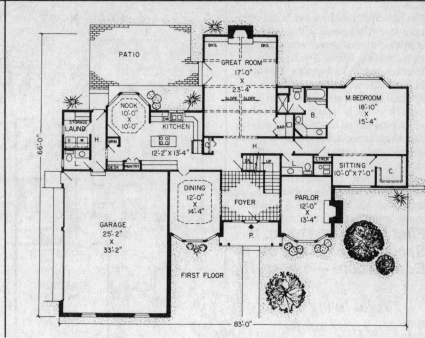

No. 10535

Refer to **Pricing Schedule F** on the order form for pricing information

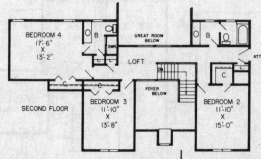

An **EXCLUSIVE DESIGN** *By Karl Kreeger*

Design 91514

STREAMING WITH NATURAL LIGHT

This beautiful three bedroom home offers a two-story Great room with an attractive front window that almost wraps around the front of the home. An exquisite fireplace provides a warm focal point for the room. There is formal as well as informal eating space. The formal dining room flows easily from the large kitchen which provides an eating nook. A vaulted ceiling adds interest to the master suite which includes a spa tub, double vanity, separate shower and large wardrobe space. The two bedrooms upstairs have ample closet space and share a full hall bath. There is even a bonus option for a fourth bedroom.

First floor — 1,230 sq. ft.
Second floor — 477 sq. ft.
Bonus room — 195 sq. ft.

Total living area:
1,707 sq. ft.

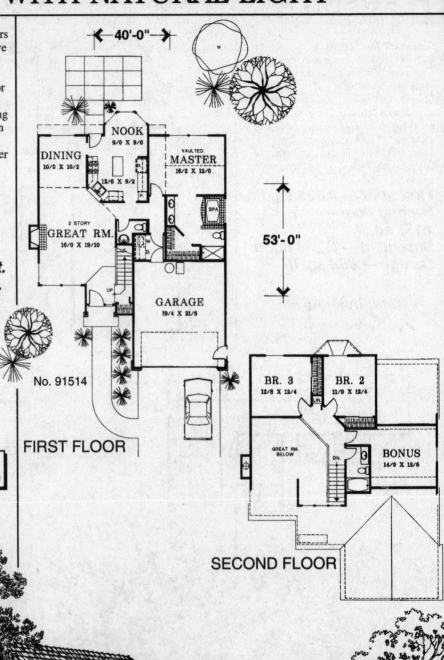

No. 91514

FIRST FLOOR

SECOND FLOOR

Refer to **Pricing Schedule C** on the order form for pricing information

AN OPEN CONCEPT HOME

An angled entry creates the illusion of space and makes this split bedroom home feel larger. Two square columns flank the bar separating the kitchen from the living room and add detail to this open concept home. A dining room located off the kitchen services both formal and informal occasions. The master bedroom has a large walk-in closet and functional master bath with double vanities, linen closet and whirlpool tub/shower combination. Two additional bedrooms and a full bath area located on the opposite side of the home and complete the layout. No materials list available for this plan.

**Main living area —
1,282 sq. ft.
Garage — 501 sq. ft.**

*Total living area:
1,282 sq. ft.*

Refer to **Pricing Schedule A** on the order form for pricing information

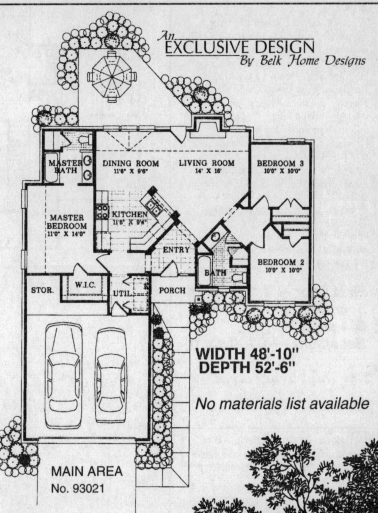

An EXCLUSIVE DESIGN
By Belk Home Designs

MASTER BATH

DINING ROOM
11'6" X 9'6"

LIVING ROOM
14' X 16'

BEDROOM 3
10'0" X 10'0"

MASTER BEDROOM
11'0" X 14'0"

KITCHEN
11'6" X 9'4"

ENTRY

BEDROOM 2
10'0" X 10'0"

BATH

STOR.

W.I.C.

UTIL.

PORCH

**WIDTH 48'-10"
DEPTH 52'-6"**

No materials list available

MAIN AREA
No. 93021

RUSTIC WARMTH

While the covered porch and huge, fieldstone fireplace lend a rustic air to this three-bedroom classic, the interior is loaded with the amenities you've been seeking. Doesn't a book-lined, fireplaced living room sound nice? Haven't you been longing for a fully-equipped island kitchen? This one adjoins a sunny dining room with sliders to a wood deck. Does the idea of a first-floor master suite just steps away from your morning coffee sound good? Tucked upstairs with another full bath, two bedrooms feature walk-in closets and cozy, sloping ceilings. There's even plenty of extra storage space in the attic. This plan can be built with a basement or crawl space foundation. Please specify when ordering.

First floor — 1,100 sq. ft.
Second floor —
664 sq. ft.
Basement — 1,100 sq. ft.

Total living area:
1,764 sq. ft.

Refer to **Pricing Schedule B** on the order form for pricing information

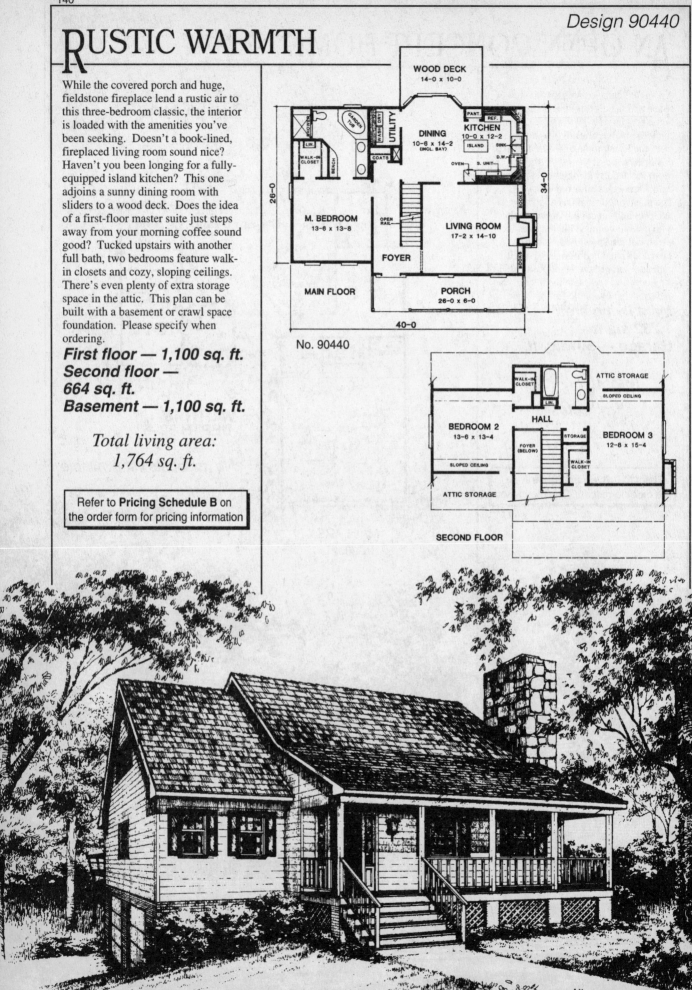

No. 90440

ELEGANT BRICK TWO-STORY

The bay windows and brick quoins enhance the front of this two story Traditional home. The large two-story Great room gives an open feeling to this home. The balcony on the second floor looks over into the Great room as well as the two-story foyer. The secluded master suite has two walk-in closets and a super bath. The downstairs study can also serve as a nursery, office, etc. The large kitchen is open to a bright breakfast room. The dining room with bay window is for more formal occasions. The second floor has three more bedrooms and another full bath. Another bath and closet can be finished at a later time. The bonus room over the garage has a private entrance from below, making it a perfect office. This plan is available with either a basement or crawl space foundation. Please specify when ordering.

Main floor — 1,637 sq. ft.
Second floor — 761 sq. ft.
Opt. bath & closet — 106 sq ft.
Opt. bonus — 347 sq. ft.
Volume space — 344 sq. ft.

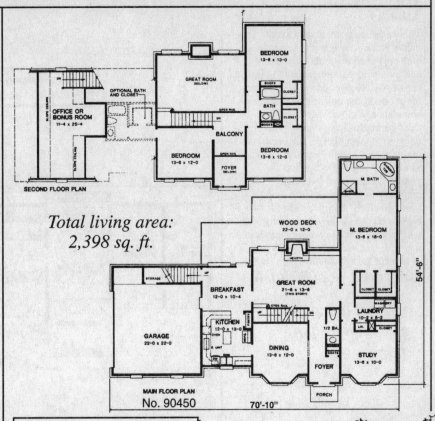

Total living area: 2,398 sq. ft.

SECOND FLOOR PLAN

No. 90450   MAIN FLOOR PLAN   70'-10"   54'-6"

Refer to **Pricing Schedule D** on the order form for pricing information

UNDERGROUND DELIGHT

This three bedroom, underground masterpiece is designed to fight the high cost of living through its many energy-saving features, including the use of passive solar energy. The large master bedroom on one end shows an abundance of closet space. Each of the three bedrooms have sliding glass doors to the front lawn. Also featured in this area is a multi-purpose room, easily converted to individual use, graciously separated from the entryway by ornately carved wood room dividers. The plan calls for two baths, one delightfully designed with a whirlpool. The family room opens to a greenhouse via sliding glass doors. A two-car garage completes this home.

Main area — 2,086 sq. ft.

Total living area:
2,086 sq. ft.

Refer to **Pricing Schedule C** on the order form for pricing information

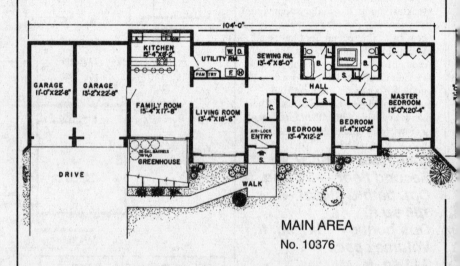

MAIN AREA

No. 10376

LIVING ROOM FOCUSED

Equipped with fireplace and sliding glass doors to the bordering deck, the two-story living room creates a sizeable and airy center for family activity. A well planned traffic pattern connects the dining area, kitchen, laundry niche and bath. Closets are plentiful, and a total of three 15-foot bedrooms are shown. A balcony overlooking the open living room is featured on the second floor.

First floor — 1,024 sq. ft.
Second floor — 576 sq. ft.
Basement — 1,024 sq. ft.

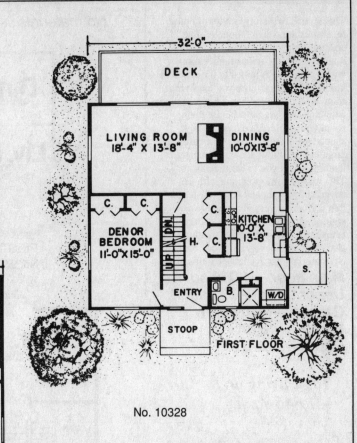

FIRST FLOOR

32'-0"

DECK

LIVING ROOM 18'-4" X 13'-8"

DINING 10'-0"X13'-8"

C. C.

DEN OR BEDROOM 11'-0"X 15'-0"

UP DN

H.

C.

C.

KITCHEN 10'-0" X 13'-8"

ENTRY

B.

W/D

S.

STOOP

No. 10328

32'-0"

OPEN TO LIVING ROOM

32'-0"

C.

BALCONY

C. C.

DN

H.

S.

L.

BEDROOM 11'-0"X15'-0"

BEDROOM 10'-0"X15'-0"

BATH

DECK

SECOND FLOOR

Total living area: 1,600 sq. ft.

Refer to **Pricing Schedule B** on the order form for pricing information

WINDOWS ARE FOCAL POINTS

This stylish two-story is a lot of house in a minimum square footage. The spacious entry welcomes you to the main floor. A spacious family room with a fireplace is joined to the efficient kitchen by a nook. The vaulted living room with a squared bay window and a fireplace, adjoins the separate dining room with coffered ceilings. The U-shaped staircase, a focal point with the large half round window at the middle landing, leads you to the second story. The master suite is unique with the bayed sitting area and large master bath that includes a very generously sized walk-in closet. The two secondary bedrooms, one with corner windows, also share another second floor bath. No materials list available for this plan.

Main floor —1,069 sq. ft.
Upper floor — 777 sq. ft.
Garage — 420 sq. ft.
Width — 48'-0"
Depth — 42'-0"

Total living area:
1,846 sq. ft.

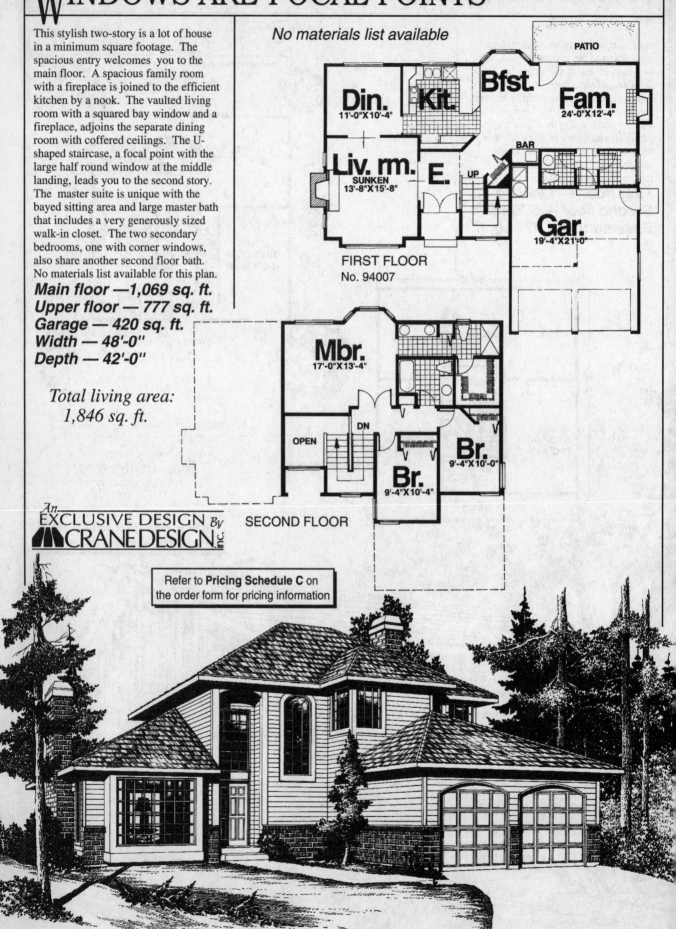

No materials list available

FIRST FLOOR
No. 94007

Din. 11'-0"X10'-4"
Kit.
Bfst.
Fam. 24'-0"X12'-4"
Liv. rm. SUNKEN 13'-8"X15'-8"
E.
UP
BAR
Gar. 19'-4"X21'-0"

SECOND FLOOR

Mbr. 17'-0"X13'-4"
OPEN
DN
Br. 9'-4"X10'-4"
Br. 9'-4"X10'-0"

An EXCLUSIVE DESIGN *By* CRANE DESIGN inc.

Refer to **Pricing Schedule C** on the order form for pricing information

PATIO

PACKED WITH EFFICIENCY

A modest-sized two-story home with consideration for cost-efficient construction and the value-oriented consumer. This home features an open plan with minimum circulation. The kitchen is large enough for an informal eating area. The entry views the spacious living room. The master suite has a large walk-in closet and private bath. The secondary bedrooms are conveniently equipped with an upper level laundry area. No materials list available for this plan.

First floor — 684 sq. ft.
Second floor — 727 sq. ft.
Garage — 400 sq. ft.
Basement — 684 sq. ft.

Total living area: 1,411 sq. ft.

No materials list available

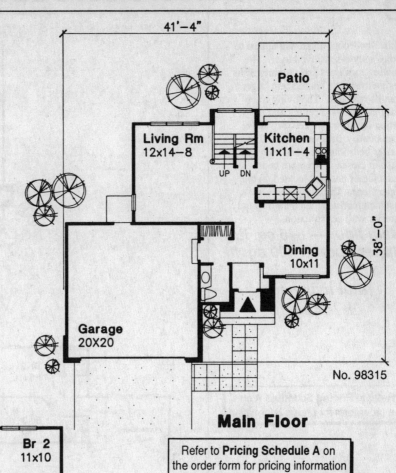

Main Floor

Refer to **Pricing Schedule A** on the order form for pricing information

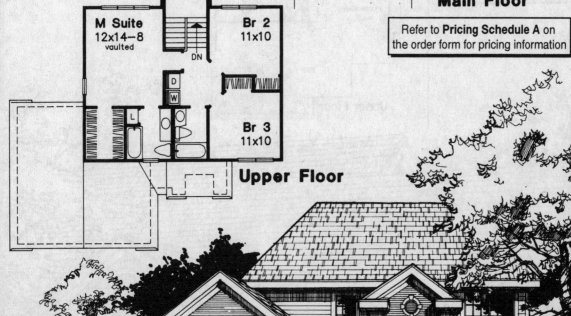

Upper Floor

STYLISH DESIGN FOR TODAY

This 3-bedroom home will appeal to today's style-sensitive buyer. The flowing roof lines and volumes of its design make the house seem larger than its real size. The living room features a vaulted ceiling and the dining room, with clerestory above, opens onto a backyard patio. The master bedroom has a full bath and walk-in closet. Two more bedrooms and another bath are located on the upper floor. The design features basement construction detailing and exterior wall construction.

Main floor — 846 sq. ft.
Upper floor — 400 sq. ft.

Total living area:
1,246 sq. ft.

Refer to **Pricing Schedule A** on the order form for pricing information

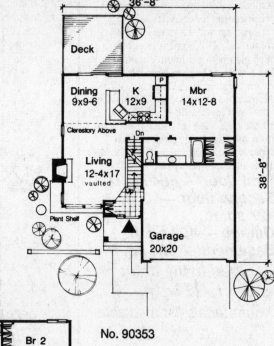

No. 90353

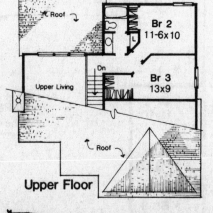

Upper Floor

LOTS O' SPACE IN A SMALLER PLAN

Here's a compact gem that won't break your budget. Well-placed windows, an open plan, and vaulted ceilings lend a spacious feeling to this contemporary home. The dynamic, soaring angles of the living room are accentuated by the fireplace that dominates the room. Eat in the dining room adjoining the kitchen, or step through the sliders for dinner on the deck. And, when it's time to make coffee in the morning, you'll love the first-floor location of the master suite, just steps away from the kitchen. Upstairs, a full bath serves two bedrooms, each with a walk-in closet.

Refer to **Pricing Schedule A** on the order form for pricing information

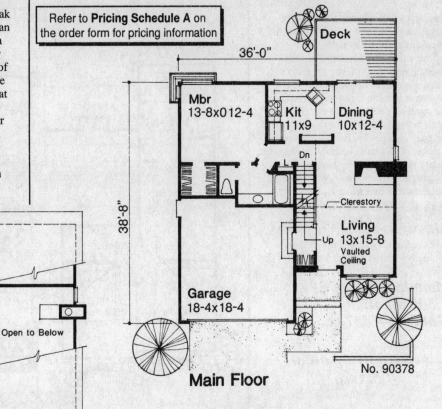

Deck

36'-0"

Mbr
13-8x0 12-4

Kit
11x9

Dining
10x12-4

38'-8"

Dn

Clerestory

Living 13x15-8
Vaulted Ceiling

Up

Garage
18-4x18-4

No. 90378

Main Floor

Loft/Br3
12x12-4

Br2
9-8x12-8

Dn

Open to Below

Upper Floor

First floor — 878 sq. ft.
Second floor —
405 sq. ft.
Garage — 2-car

Total living area:
1,283 sq. ft.

Design 93027

FOR TODAY'S SOPHISTICATED OWNER

This best seller features a traditional elevation and a floor plan full of all the amenities required by today's sophisticated homeowner. A formal dining room opens off the foyer and features a classic bay window. The kitchen is notable for an angled eating bar opening the kitchen to the living room beyond, and providing a view of the cozy living room fireplace from the kitchen. The master bedroom includes a luxury master bath with his-and-her vanities and knee space. A whirlpool tub/shower combination and walk-in closet area standard. Ten foot ceilings in the major living areas including the master bedroom and one of the bedrooms give the impression of a much larger home. No materials list available for this plan.

**Main living area —
1,500 sq. ft.
Garage — 437 sq. ft.**

*Total living area:
1,500 sq. ft.*

Refer to **Pricing Schedule A** on the order form for pricing information

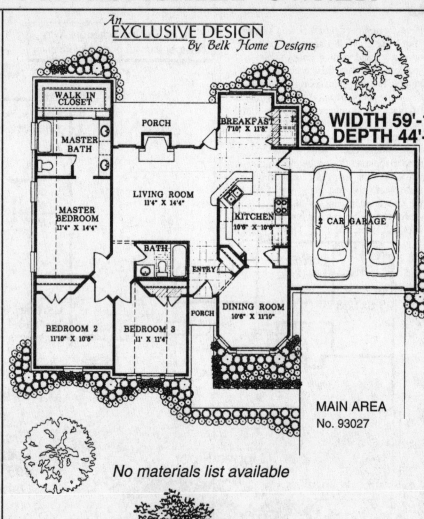

An
EXCLUSIVE DESIGN
By Belk Home Designs

WIDTH 59'-10
DEPTH 44'-4

WALK IN CLOSET

PORCH

BREAKFAST
7'10" X 11'8"

MASTER BATH

LIVING ROOM
11'4" X 14'4"

2 CAR GARAGE

KITCHEN
10'6" X 10'6"

MASTER BEDROOM
11'4" X 14'4"

BATH

ENTRY

DINING ROOM
10'6" X 11'10"

PORCH

BEDROOM 2
11'10" X 10'8"

BEDROOM 3
11' X 11'4"

MAIN AREA
No. 93027

No materials list available

SPACIOUS FAMILY AREAS

The attractive exterior of this home is just the icing on the cake. The layout of this plan is just perfect for the young family. The kitchen, breakfast room and family room are in an open layout, giving a feeling of spaciousness and making family interaction simple. The efficient kitchen includes a cooktop peninsula and a corner sink. The sunny breakfast area will start the day on a bright note. A cozy family room with focal point fireplace will add to a relaxing evening. The formal living and dining rooms are located at the front of the house. The second floor includes three bedrooms, two full baths and a bonus room to be decided on in the future. One of the bedrooms, the master bedroom, has a private master bath with a walk-in closet and a decorative ceiling. The two additional bedrooms are spacious with ample closet space.

First floor — 902 sq. ft.
Second floor — 819 sq. ft.
Finished staircase — 28 sq. ft.
Bonus room — 210 sq. ft.
Basement — 874 sq. ft.
Garage — 400 sq. ft.

Total living area: 1,749 sq. ft.

An EXCLUSIVE DESIGN
By Jannis Vann & Associates, Inc.

Refer to **Pricing Schedule C** on the order form for pricing information

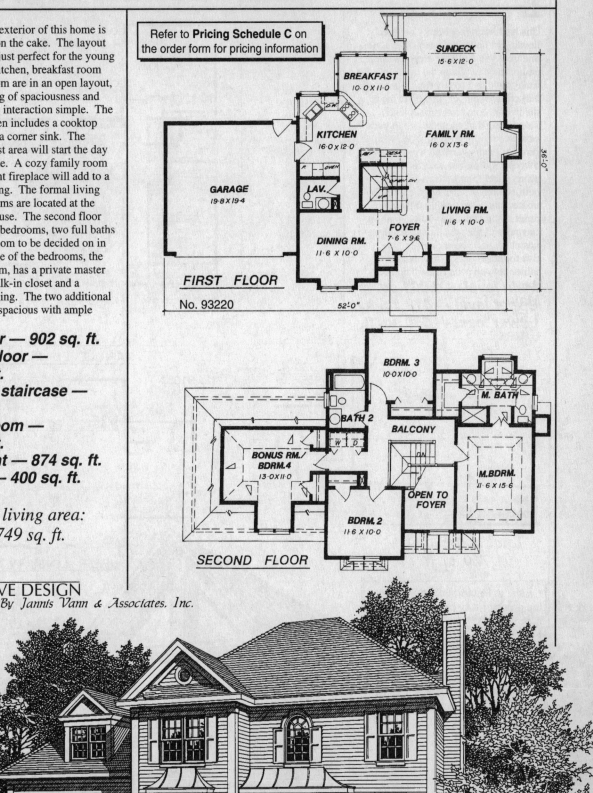

FIRST FLOOR
No. 93220

SECOND FLOOR

ENJOY A LOFTY RETREAT

This contemporary beauty on three levels will house your family in style and give you a private escape at the end of the day. From the main entry, walk down to a roomy fourth bedroom and utility room, or, step up to the to the living room on the main level. There, you'll be treated to a full view of active family areas, flooded with sunlight from oversized windows. Two bedrooms, one with its own private deck, flank a convenient full bath. Climb the stairs to the lofty master suite overlooking the living room. With a double vanity, walk-in shower and spa tub all to yourself, you'll be glad you chose this comfortable home. This plan is available with a slab foundation only.

Main level — 1,021 sq. ft.
Upper level — 418 sq. ft.
Lower level — 330 sq. ft.

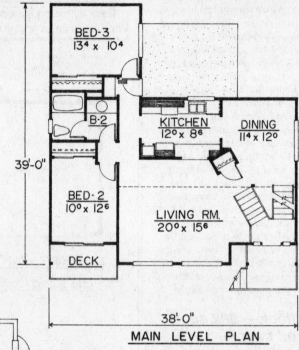

MAIN LEVEL PLAN

No. 91039

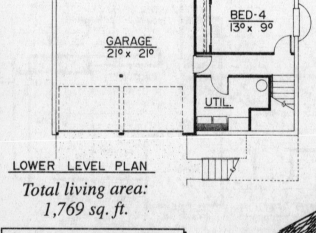

LOWER LEVEL PLAN

Total living area:
1,769 sq. ft.

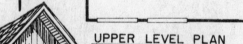

UPPER LEVEL PLAN

Refer to **Pricing Schedule B** on the order form for pricing information

FARMHOUSE FLAVOR

This exciting home combines elements borrowed from the New England barns of long ago with the desirable features of contemporary design. The octagonal stair tower is sure to be a conversation piece, and offers a quiet spot away from it all when you're in the mood. The foyer opens to a living and dining room combination enhanced by a striking glass wall. A heat-circulating fireplace adds welcome warmth when the sun goes down. The galley kitchen includes a large pantry, snackbar, and laundry area. The first-floor master suite has a private deck overlooking the backyard, as well as a luxurious bath with whirlpool tub. Two bedrooms and a full bath share the second floor with a balcony overlooking the living room.

First floor — 1,073 sq. ft.
Second floor — 604 sq. ft.
Retreat tower — 93 sq. ft.
Garage — 428 sq. ft.
Total living area: 1,770 sq. ft.

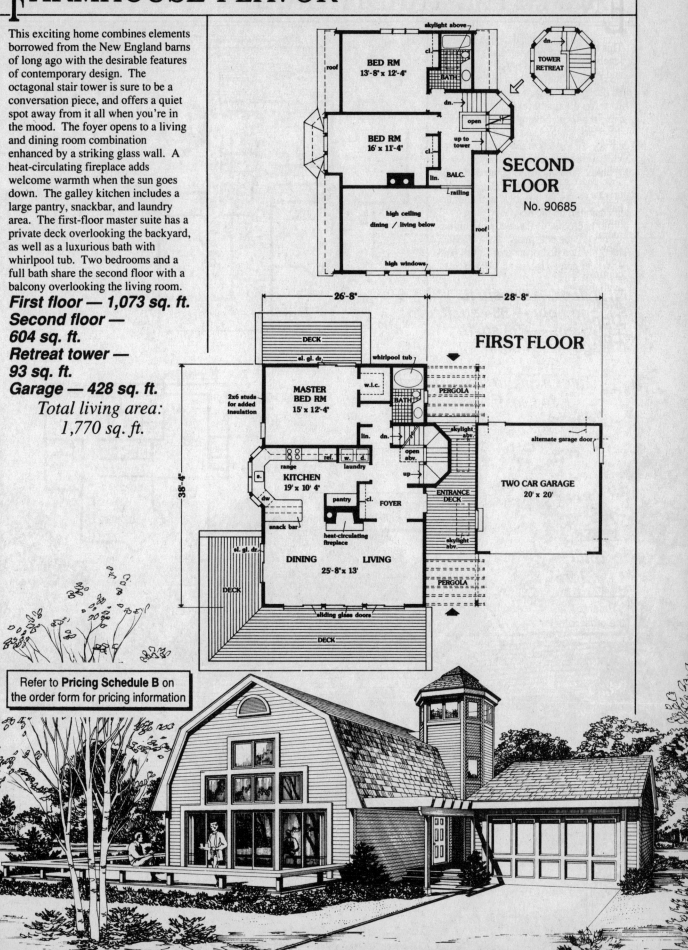

SECOND FLOOR
No. 90685

BED RM
13'-8" x 12'-4"

BED RM
16' x 11'-4"

TOWER RETREAT

high ceiling
dining / living below

high windows

FIRST FLOOR

MASTER BED RM
15' x 12'-4"

2x6 studs for added insulation

KITCHEN
19' x 10' 4"

DINING   LIVING
25'-8" x 13'

whirlpool tub

PERGOLA

TWO CAR GARAGE
20' x 20'

alternate garage door

FOYER

pantry

ENTRANCE DECK

26'-8"   28'-8"

38'-4"

Refer to **Pricing Schedule B** on the order form for pricing information

FARM-TYPE TRADITIONAL

This pleasant Traditional design has a farmhouse flavor exterior that incorporates a covered porch and features a circle wood louver on its garage, giving this design a feeling of sturdiness. Inside, on the first level to the right of the foyer, is a formal dining room complete with a bay window and an elevated ceiling. To the left of the foyer is the living room with a wood-burning fireplace. The kitchen is connected to the breakfast room and there is also a room for the laundry facilities. A half-bath is also featured on the first floor. The master bedroom, on the second floor, has its own private bath and walk-in closet. The other two bedrooms share a full bath. A two-car garage is also added into this design.

First floor — 909 sq. ft.
Second floor — 854 sq. ft.
Basement — 899 sq. ft.
Garage — 491 sq. ft.

Total living area:
1,763 sq. ft.

An
EXCLUSIVE DESIGN
By Karl Kreeger

Refer to **Pricing Schedule B** on the order form for pricing information

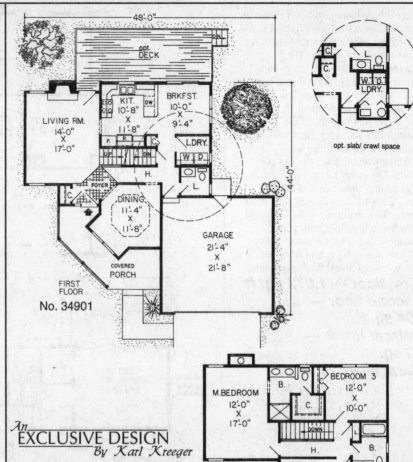

NATURAL LIGHT GIVES BRIGHT SPACES

The generous use of windows throughout this home creates bright living spaces. The welcoming covered front porch and lovely bay window give this home great curb appeal. Notice the separate entrance close to the den making a third bedroom a practical possibility. The kitchen has a great center island and large pantry. There is a bright sunny breakfast nook to start your day. The formal dining area is close by to make entertaining easy. The living room has a fireplace to add atmosphere to the room as well as warmth. There is access to the optional patio from the dining room to add living space. The master bedroom has a private bath and double closets. The second bedroom has ample closet space and shares a full, compartmented hall bath with the possible third bedroom.

Main area — 1,620 sq. ft.

Total living area: 1,620 sq. ft.

Refer to **Pricing Schedule B** on the order form for pricing information

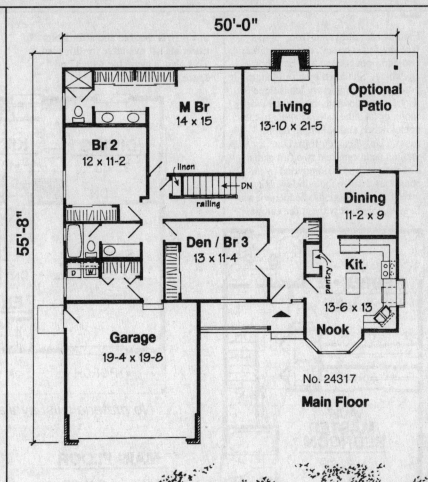

50'-0"

55'-8"

M Br
14 x 15

Living
13-10 x 21-5

Optional Patio

Br 2
12 x 11-2

linen

DN

railing

Dining
11-2 x 9

Den / Br 3
13 x 11-4

pantry

Kit.

D W

13-6 x 13

Garage
19-4 x 19-8

Nook

No. 24317

Main Floor

An
EXCLUSIVE DESIGN
By Marshall Associates

EASY-TO-BUILD

From the smallest lake-front lot to a faraway forest retreat, this affordable, two-bedroom cottage will be at home anywhere. Sheltered by a full-length porch, the inviting entry leads three ways. Step down to the sunken living room, or take the hallway route to the open kitchen and adjoining dining room. Upstairs, you'll find the vaulted bedrooms and two full baths. The master suite is dominated by an enormous, half-round window that takes full advantage of vacation views. Easy to construct without the garage, this plan is flexible and affordable. No materials list available for this plan. This plan is available with a crawl space foundation only.

Refer to **Pricing Schedule A** on the order form for pricing information

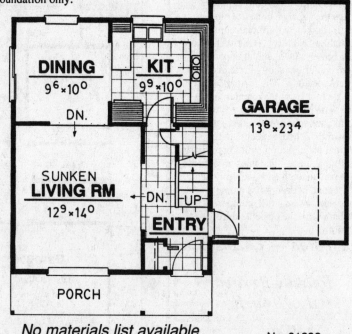

No materials list available

No. 91038

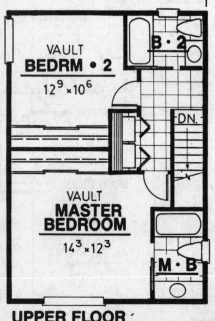

UPPER FLOOR

MAIN FLOOR

Width — 34'-0"
Depth — 31'-0"

First floor — 500 sq. ft.
Second floor — 550 sq. ft.
Total living area: 1,050 sq. ft.

CONTEMPORARY FLAIR

Come right off the beach and into this contemporary style home. Open to the dining room, the great room is lined with windows overlooking the large deck — great for entertaining. The upper level of this home houses three good sized bedrooms. The master suite, complete with a deck of it's own, also includes a large walk-in closet that leads you to the bathroom with a double vanity and a stylish window over the tub. Having the laundry area on the upper level is an added bonus for those who don't want to travel the stairs with the laundry basket. This home is designed with an unfinished basement that can be finished at a later time.

Main floor — 852 sq. ft.
Upper floor — 822 sq. ft.
Lower floor — 336 sq. ft.
Garage— 513 sq. ft.
Width — 30'-0"
Depth — 44'-0"

Total living area:
2,010 sq. ft.

No materials list available

Kit.

Din.
11'-0"X9'-0"

UP

E.

Liv. rm.
24'-0"X15'-0"

DN

Deck

MAIN FLOOR

No. 94000

An **EXCLUSIVE DESIGN** *By*
CRANE DESIGN inc.

Refer to **Pricing Schedule C** on the order form for pricing information

UPPER FLOOR

Br.
10'-0"X11'-0"

Br.
10'-0"X11'-0"

LIN.

DN

W D

Mbr.
VAULTED
14'-0"X15'-0"

Deck

STOR.

Bsmt.
22'-0"X14'-0"

UP

F WH

Gar.
24'-0"X21'-0"

LOWER FLOOR

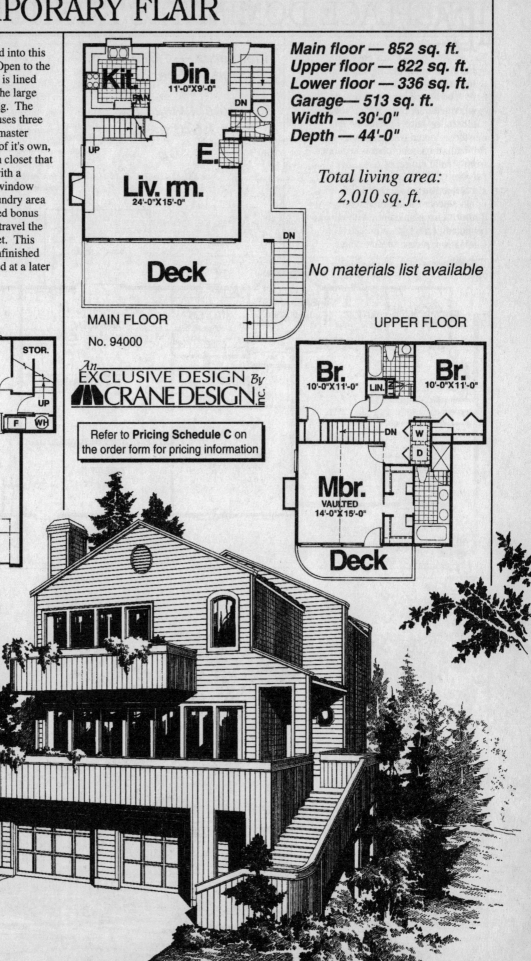

Design 90409

FIREPLACE DOMINATES RUSTIC DESIGN

The ample porch of this charming home deserves a rocking chair, and there's room for two or three if you'd like. The front entry opens to an expansive Great room with a soaring cathedral ceiling. Flanked by the master suite and two bedrooms with a full bath, the Great room is separated from formal dining by a massive fireplace. The convenient galley kitchen adjoins a sunny breakfast nook, perfect for informal family dining. This plan comes with either a basement, crawl space or slab foundation, please specify when ordering.

Main area — 1,670 sq. ft.
Garage — 2-car

Total living area:
1,670 sq. ft.

Refer to **Pricing Schedule B** on the order form for pricing information

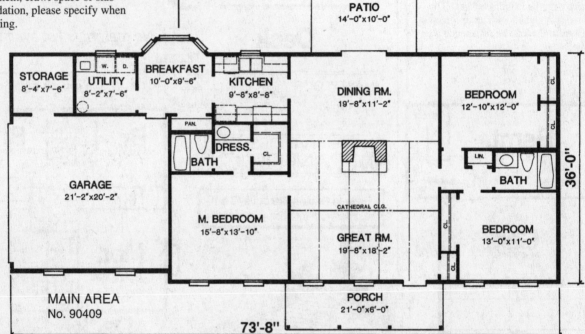

STORAGE 8'-4"x7'-6"

UTILITY 8'-2"x7'-6"

BREAKFAST 10'-0"x9'-6"

KITCHEN 9'-8"x8'-8"

PATIO 14'-0"x10'-0"

DINING RM. 19'-8"x11'-2"

BEDROOM 12'-10"x12'-0"

GARAGE 21'-2"x20'-2"

PAN.

DRESS.

BATH

M. BEDROOM 15'-8"x13'-10"

CATHEDRAL CLG.

GREAT RM. 19'-8"x18'-2"

LIN.

BATH

BEDROOM 13'-0"x11'-0"

MAIN AREA No. 90409

PORCH 21'-0"x6'-0"

36'-0"

73'-8"

FEATURES OF A MUCH LARGER PLAN

This rustic Ranch design has only 1,811 square feet, yet it offers many amenities found in much larger homes. The large Great room has a vaulted ceiling and a stone fireplace with book shelves on either side. The kitchen is spacious with a lot of cabinet space, and is located between the large dining room with a bay on one side, and the screened porch on the other. The master suite has a large bath with a garden tub and double vanities. The large walk-in closet offers plenty of space. Two other large bedrooms, each with a walk-in closet, share another full bath. The utility room is located conveniently off of the main hall. The large wood deck in the rear of the house offers a space for outdoor living. This plan is available with a basement, slab or crawl space foundation. Please specify when ordering.

Main area — 1,811 sq. ft.

*Total living area:
1,811 sq. ft.*

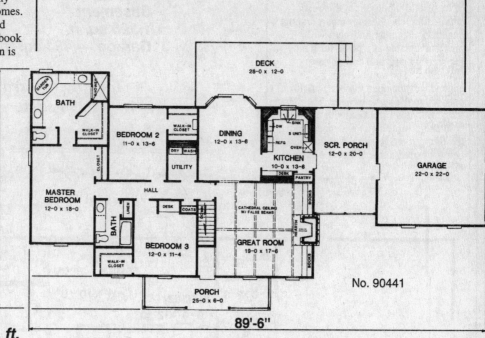

No. 90441

Refer to **Pricing Schedule C** on the order form for pricing information

Design 9812

Mudroom Conveniently Located

Gardening and woodworking tools will find a home in the storage closet of the useful mudroom in this rustic detailed Ranch. Besides incorporating a laundry area, the mudroom will prove invaluable as a place for removing snowy boots and draining wet umbrellas. The family room appendages the open kitchen and flows outward to the stone terrace. The master bedroom is furnished with a private bath and protruding closet space, and the living room retains a formality by being situated to the left of the entryway.

First floor — 1,396 sq. ft.
Basement —
1,396 sq. ft.
Garage — 484 sq. ft.

Total living area:
1,396 sq. ft.

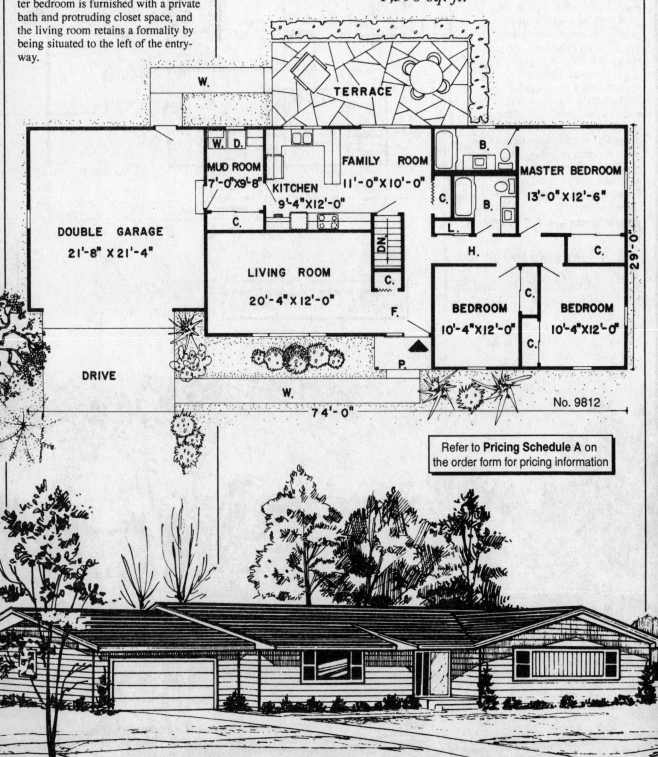

TERRACE

W.

W. D.

MUD ROOM
7'-0"X9'-8"

KITCHEN
9'-4"X12'-0"

C.

DOUBLE GARAGE
21'-8" X 21'-4"

LIVING ROOM
20'-4" X 12'-0"

FAMILY ROOM
11'-0"X10'-0"

DN.

C.

F.

B.

C.

B.

L.

MASTER BEDROOM
13'-0" X 12'-6"

C.

H.

C.

BEDROOM
10'-4"X12'-0"

C.

C.

BEDROOM
10'-4"X12'-0"

P.

DRIVE

W.

74'-0"

29'-0"

No. 9812

Refer to **Pricing Schedule A** on the order form for pricing information

LOTS OF SPACE AND DRAMA

Here's a one-level home with an airy feeling accentuated by oversized windows and well-placed skylights. You'll love the attractive garden court that adds privacy to the front facing bedroom, the sheltered porch that opens to a central foyer, and the wide-open active areas. Two bedrooms, tucked down a hall off the foyer, include the sunny master suite with its sloping ceilings, private terrace entry, and luxurious garden bath with adjoining dressing room. The gathering room, study, and formal dining room flow together along the rear of the house, sharing the warmth of the gathering room fireplace, and a magnificent view of the terrace. Convenient pass-throughs add to the efficiency of the galley kitchen and adjoining breakfast room.

**Main living area —
1,387 sq. ft.
Garage — 2-car**

*Total living area:
1,387 sq. ft.*

Refer to **Pricing Schedule A** on the order form for pricing information

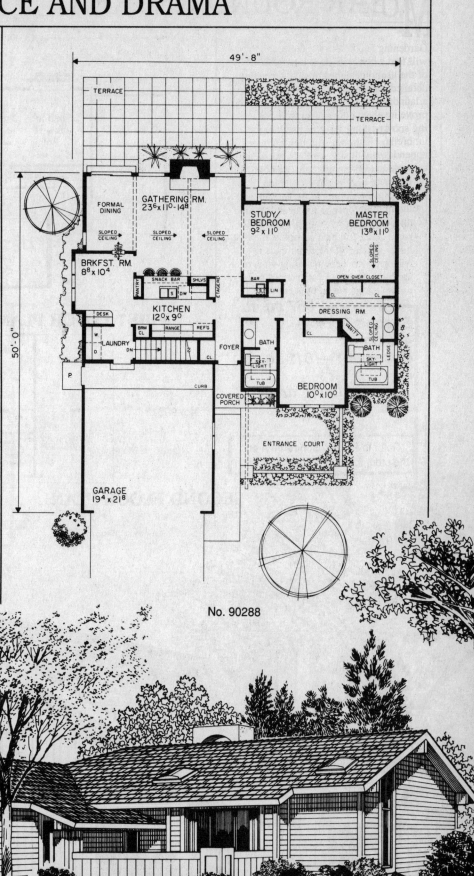

No. 90288

YEAR ROUND RETREAT

This compact home is a bargain to build and designed to save on energy bills. Large glass areas face south, and the dramatic sloping ceiling of the living room allows heat from the wood-burning stove to rise into the upstairs bedrooms through high louvers on the inside wall. In hot weather, just open the windows on both floors for cooling air circulation. Sliding glass doors in the kitchen and living room open to the deck for outdoor dining or relaxation. One bedroom and a full bath complete the first floor. A stair off the foyer ends in a balcony with a commanding view of the living room. Two spacious bedrooms are separated by a full bath.

First floor — 967 sq. ft.
**Second floor —
465 sq. ft.**
Basement — 811 sq. ft.

*Total living area:
1,432 sq. ft.*

Refer to **Pricing Schedule A** on the order form for pricing information

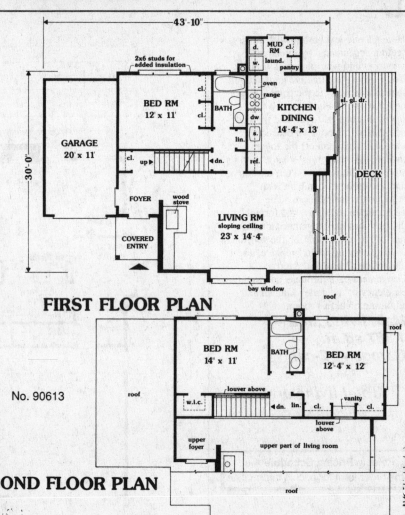

FIRST FLOOR PLAN

No. 90613

SECOND FLOOR PLAN

LEAVE YOUR CARES BEHIND

All you'll have to do in this snug retreat is relax and enjoy the view. Outside on your deck or inside looking though the three large windows or the double glass living room door, you'll appreciate the wonders of nature. But you won't be roughing it. You'll enjoy the cozy bedroom, comforts like a hot shower, and the joys of cooking in a kitchen open to the two-story living space. If you do invite guests to this cottage to share your privacy, they can bed down upstairs in the loft bedroom. This plan is available with a crawl space foundation only.

Main area — 572 sq. ft.
Loft — 308 sq. ft.

Total living area:
880 sq. ft.

Refer to **Pricing Schedule A** on the order form for pricing information

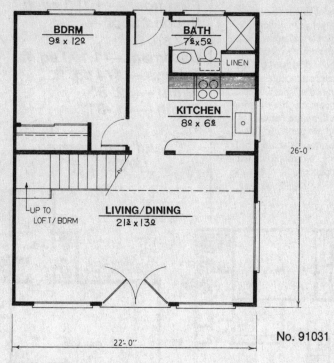

MAIN LEVEL

No. 91031

BDRM
9⁰ x 12⁰

BATH
7⁰ x 5⁰

LINEN

KITCHEN
8⁰ x 6⁰

UP TO
LOFT / BDRM

LIVING / DINING
21³ x 13⁰

26'-0"

22'-0"

LOFT / BDRM
308 SQ. FT.

DOWN

COZY FOUR BEDROOM DESIGN

Design 94103

The covered entry of this home leads to the two story foyer. On either side of the foyer are the formal areas, the living room and the dining room. An open layout has been designed for the family room, dinette and kitchen, giving the appearance of spaciousness. The second floor contains the sleeping quarters. The master suite features a walk-in closet and private bath. The three additional bedrooms share a full bath in the hallway. No materials list available for this plan.

First floor — 1,100 sq. ft.
Second floor — 892 sq. ft.
Basement — 1,100 sq. ft.
Garage — 474 sq. ft.
Width — 52'-8"
Depth — 41'-8"

Refer to **Pricing Schedule C** on the order form for pricing information

No materials list available

Total living area: 1,992 sq. ft.

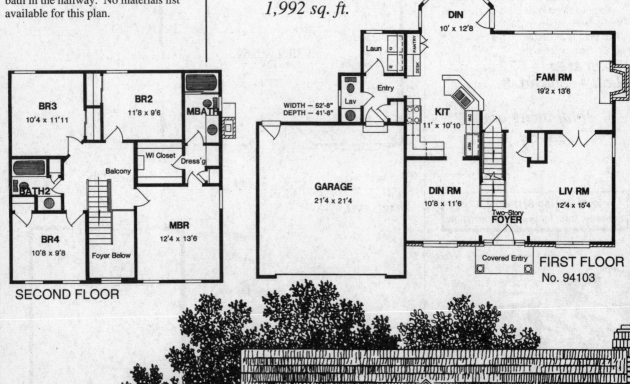

SECOND FLOOR

FIRST FLOOR
No. 94103

LATTICE TRIM ADDS NOSTALGIC CHARM

Thanks to vaulted ceilings and an ingenious plan, this wood and fieldstone classic feels much larger than its compact size. The entry, dominated by a skylit staircase to the bedroom floor, opens to the vaulted living room with a balcony view and floor-to-ceiling corner window treatment. Eat in the spacious, formal dining room, in the sunny breakfast nook off the kitchen, or, when the weathers nice, out on the adjoining deck. Pass-through convenience makes meal service easy wherever you choose to dine. A full bath at the top of the stairs serves the kids' bedrooms off the balcony hall. The master suite boasts its own, private bath, along with a private dressing area.

First floor — 668 sq. ft.
Second floor — 691 sq. ft.
Garage — 2-car

Total living area:
1,359 sq. ft.

Refer to **Pricing Schedule A** on the order form for pricing information

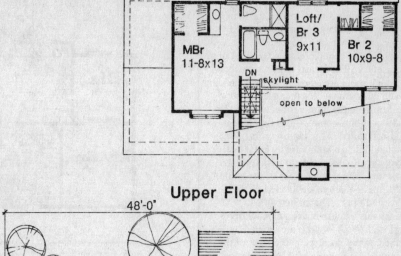

Upper Floor

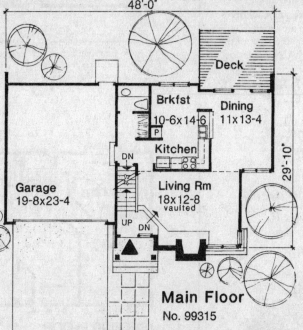

Main Floor
No. 99315

COUNTRY PORCH SHELTERS ENTRY

Design 93904

A country porch offers a warm welcome to visitors. Inside, the two-story foyer attains natural light from the arched window above. A convenient coat closet is to the right of the entry. The formal living room and dining room are adjoined through an arched opening. Another arched opening to the family room adds to the decor of this home. A gas fireplace is also featured in the family room. An island kitchen with a sunny breakfast bay, serves efficiently to both the formal and informal areas of the home. Sleeping quarters are located on the second floor. The master suite includes a lavish bath and a walk-in closet. Window seats are created by the country dormers on the front of the house. No materials list available for this plan.

**First floor — 1,121 sq. ft.
Second floor — 748 sq. ft.
Width — 61'-0"
Depth — 32'-0"**

Total living area: 1,869 sq. ft.

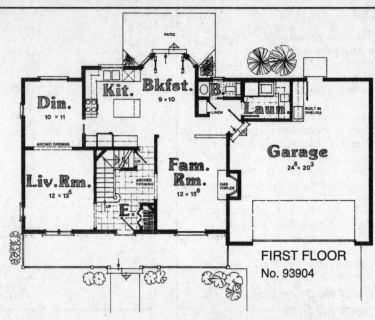

FIRST FLOOR
No. 93904

Refer to **Pricing Schedule C** on the order form for pricing information

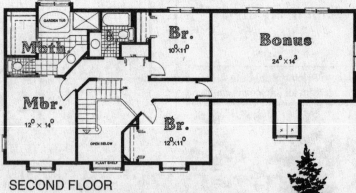

SECOND FLOOR

No materials list available

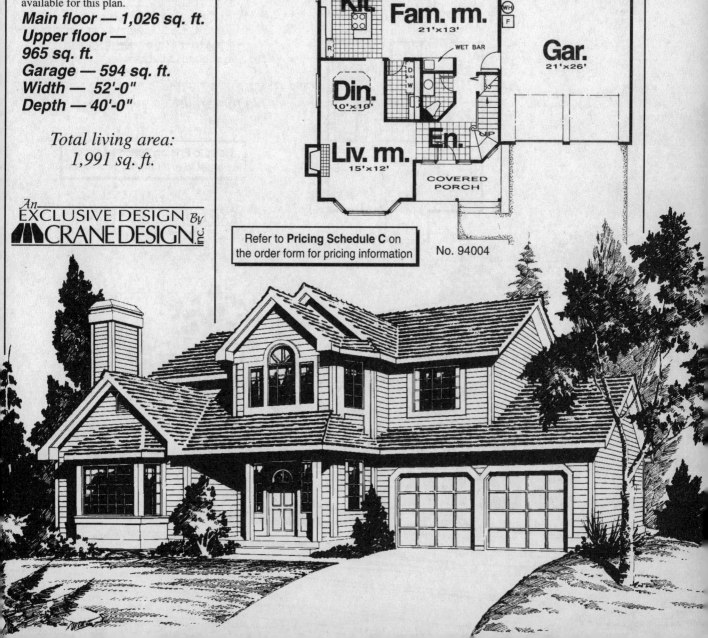

Design 94004

WELL DESIGNED PLAN

Enter this well-designed Traditional style home from a cozy covered porch to an open, inviting two-story entrance with lavish window details. The vaulted, bayed living room and dining room are together on one side and the open living areas to the rear of the house, make this an excellent family home. The open kitchen, with cooktop island and corner windows, makes this an enjoyable feature for the family. The winding staircase leads you to an "open to below" landing, welcoming you to the second floor bedrooms. Three good-sized bedrooms join the master suite to make this home suitable for any family. The generously sized master suite has a lovely master bath with a whirlpool tub, a double cornered vanity, and a large walk-in closet. All of this is enhanced with a great exterior. No materials list available for this plan.

Main floor — 1,026 sq. ft.
Upper floor — 965 sq. ft.
Garage — 594 sq. ft.
Width — 52'-0"
Depth — 40'-0"

Total living area: 1,991 sq. ft.

An EXCLUSIVE DESIGN By CRANE DESIGN inc.

SECOND FLOOR
No materials list available

FIRST FLOOR

Refer to **Pricing Schedule C** on the order form for pricing information

No. 94004

MORE HOUSE FOR YOUR DOLLAR

This plan works for growing families, empty-nesters, and single folk. With every turn there is drama and function. Notice the upper floor economically tucked under the roof line. The great hall leads into the island kitchen with eating nook. The family and living rooms feature a fireplace. The master bedroom features a walk-in closet and master bath with spa tub. The two additional bedrooms upstairs feature walk-in closets and, they share a full bath. No materials list available for this plan.

Main floor — 1,928 sq. ft.
Upper floor — 504 sq. ft.
Bonus room — 335 sq. ft.
Garage — 440 sq. ft.

Total living area:
2,432 sq. ft.

MAIN FLOOR   No. 91672

55' 0"

54' 0"

NOOK 8/6X9/6
MASTER 12/6X14/6
SPA
KIT
FAMILY 16/0X14/6
WIC
DESK
DINING 11/0X11/0
UP
STORAGE
BED 2 11/0X10/0
GREAT HALL
UTIL
LIVING 13/0X16/0
DEN 10/0X10/0
GARAGE 22/0X20/0

No materials list available

Refer to **Pricing Schedule D** on the order form for pricing information

An
EXCLUSIVE DESIGN
By Mark Stewart

BED 3 11/6X10/3
BED 4 11/6X10/3
WIC
WIC
DN
BONUS 28/8X12/0

UPPER FLOOR

TRIPLE TANDEM GARAGE

The large foyer of this gracious ranch leads you back to the bright and spacious living room. The large open kitchen features a central work island with lots of extra storage space and there is also a handy laundry room with pantry and garage access. The master suite features a private master bath with oversized tub, corner shower, room-sized walk-in closet, as well as a bay shared sitting area and French doors. The two front bedrooms share a full bath. The lower level has plenty of open space for future expansion. The triple tandem garage provides space for a third car, boat, or just plenty of storage and work space. No materials list available for this plan.

Main area — 1,761 sq. ft.
Basement — 1,761 sq. ft.
Garage — 658 sq. ft.

Total living area:
1,761 sq. ft.

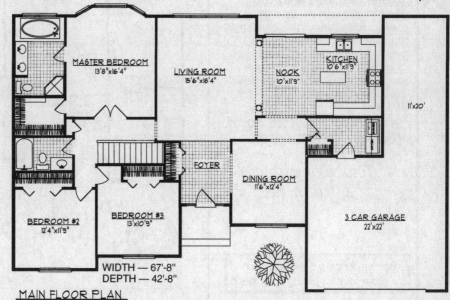

An
EXCLUSIVE DESIGN
By Ahmann Design Inc.

MASTER BEDROOM
13'8"x16'4"

LIVING ROOM
15'6"x18'4"

NOOK
10'x11'9"

KITCHEN
10'6"x11'9"

11'x20'

FOYER

DINING ROOM
11'6"x12'4"

BEDROOM #2
12'4"x11'9"

BEDROOM #3
13'x10'9"

3 CAR GARAGE
22'x22'

WIDTH — 67'-8"
DEPTH — 42'-8"

MAIN FLOOR PLAN
No. 93133

No materials list available

Refer to **Pricing Schedule B** on the order form for pricing information

UNIQUE OPEN QUALITY IN EVERY ROOM

Design 84040

The angular windows and recessed ceilings separate the island kitchen from the formal dining and breakfast rooms. Twelve foot ceilings in the soaring, skylit living room add to its sophistication, along with a cozy fireplace and access to the outdoor deck. Separated from the active areas, the master suite boasts bump-out windows, a personal bath and a huge, walk-in closet. The two bedrooms off the foyer share a full, double-vanitied bath. No materials list available for this plan.

Main area — 2,026 sq. ft.
Garage — 545 sq. ft.

Total living area:
2,026 sq. ft.

Refer to **Pricing Schedule C** on the order form for pricing information

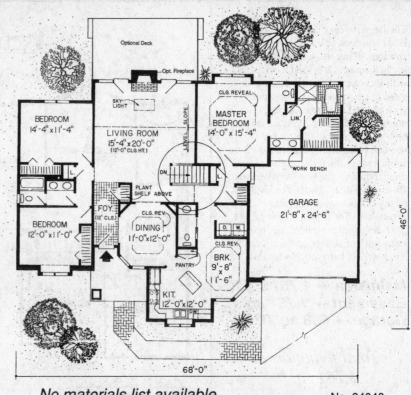

No materials list available

No. 84040

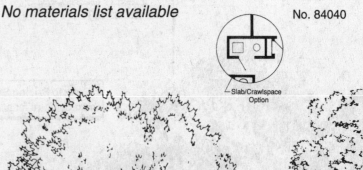

Slab/Crawlspace Option

ROOM FOR FAMILY GATHERINGS

This classic Ranch features a large open Great room for family gatherings. The sunny kitchen sports a separate dining area. On the other side of the house three good-size bedrooms share two full bathrooms. A great hide-away laundry closet is located outside the large linen closet. A two-car optional garage attaches to this all inclusive home. This plan is available with a basement, slab or crawl space foundation. Please specify when ordering. No materials list available for this plan.

**Main living area —
1,644 sq. ft.
Garage — 576 sq. ft.**

*Total living area:
1,644 sq. ft.*

Refer to **Pricing Schedule B** on the order form for pricing information

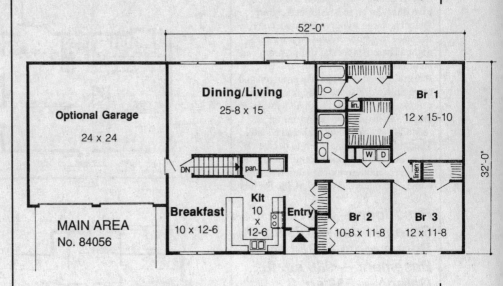

MAIN AREA
No. 84056

No materials list available

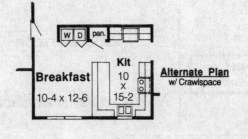

Design 93212

OLD-FASHIONED MODERN TOUCHES

No one can resist a cool drink served on an old-fashioned country porch on a hot day. A country-style porch and dormers give this plan an old-fashioned country feel. The large living room has a cozy fireplace to gather around on a winter's night. There is a formal dining room and an informal breakfast room. The U-shaped kitchen is efficiently arranged and has ample work space. The master suite offers a private master bath and a walk-in closet. There are two bedrooms on the second floor, a full hall bath and a study. There is even a bonus room to decide on later. An old-fashioned country feel with some very modern touches describes this home. No materials list available for this plan.

First floor — 1,362 sq. ft.
Second floor — 729 sq. ft.
Bonus room — 384 sq. ft.
Basement — 988 sq. ft.
Garage — 559 sq. ft.
Porch — 396 sq. ft.

Total living area:
2,091 sq. ft.

Refer to **Pricing Schedule C** on the order form for pricing information

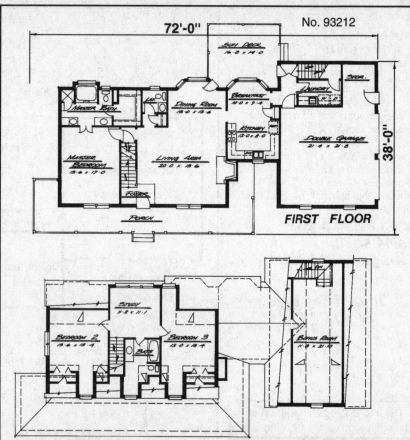

No. 93212

FIRST FLOOR

SECOND FLOOR

No materials list available

An
EXCLUSIVE DESIGN
By Jannis Vann & Associates, Inc.

FAMILY ROOM WITH A FIREPLACE

This beautiful family home includes all the amenities you have been looking for. The island kitchen includes a built-in pantry, double sink and dinette area. The dinette area flows into the family room. A cozy fireplace enhances the family room and can be seen from the formal living room. The formal dining room is easily accessible from the kitchen. All the bedrooms are located on the second floor. The master suite includes a walk-in closet, double vanity, separate shower and tub and compartmented toilet. The three additional bedrooms share a full hall bath.

First floor — 1,228 sq. ft.
Second floor — 1,191 sq. ft.
Basement — 1,228 sq. ft.
Garage — 528 sq. ft.

Total living area: 2,419 sq. ft.

Refer to **Pricing Schedule D** on the order form for pricing information

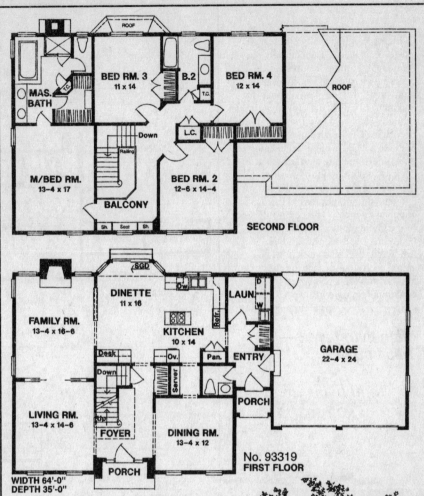

NO WASTED SPACE

The open floor plan of this modified A-frame design virtually eliminates wasted hall space. The centrally located Great room features a cathedral ceiling with exposed wood beams and large areas of fixed glass on both front and rear. Living and dining areas are virtually separated by a massive stone fireplace. The isolated master suite features a walk-in closet and sliding glass doors opening onto the front deck. A walk-thru utility room provides easy access from the carport and outside storage areas to the compact kitchen. On the opposite side of the Great room are two additional bedrooms and a second full bath. A full length deck and vertical wood siding with stone accents on the corners provide a rustic, yet contemporary exterior. Specify crawl space, basement or slab foundation when ordering.

Main living area — 1,454 sq. ft.

Total living area: 1,454 sq. ft.

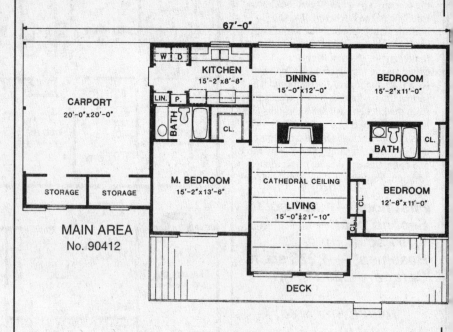

MAIN AREA
No. 90412

Refer to **Pricing Schedule A** on the order form for pricing information

TWO-SINK BATHS EASE RUSH

Save energy and construction costs by building this friendly farmhouse colonial. The inviting covered porch opens to a center hall, enhanced by the stairway leading to the four-bedroom second floor. Flanked by formal living and dining rooms, the foyer leads right into the open-beamed family room, island kitchen and bay window dinette. The rear porch adjoins both family and living rooms.

First floor — 983 sq. ft.
**Second floor —
1,013 sq. ft.**
Mudroom — 99 sq. ft.
Garage — 481 sq. ft.

*Total living area:
2,095 sq. ft.*

Refer to **Pricing Schedule C** on the order form for pricing information

SECOND FLOOR PLAN

2x6 studs for added insulation

BED RM 2
12' x 11'-6"

BATH   BATH   W.I.C.

cl   cab

cl

lin.

BALCONY

cl   cl   H   dn   railing

MASTER
BED RM
18'-8" x 12'-6"

BED RM 3
13'-4" x 10'

BED RM 4
12' x 9'-8"

cl

FIRST FLOOR PLAN

No. 90622

DINETTE

KITCHEN
14'-10" x 8'-8"

dw

laundry

MUD RM

w. d.   ref

range top   ov

wood beam ceiling

FAMILY RM
15' x 11'-6"

PORCH

sliding glass doors

SERVICE
PORCH

cl

STORAGE

heater rm. for slab version

LAV.   pantry

dn

cl

LIVING RM
19' x 12'-6"

heat-circulating fireplace

TWO CAR GARAGE
20'-2" x 20'

DINING RM
12' x 11'-8"

cl

FOYER

up

cl

PORCH

42'-0"

58'-0"

TRADITIONAL MULTI-LEVEL HOME

Design 93902

The Traditional exterior and brick accents of this home compliment the cozy four levels within. The living room is dramatic with decorative columns defining its entry and a boxed-out bay window bringing in streaming natural light. The efficient kitchen includes a corner sink, a built-in pantry and a breakfast bar. The dining room includes a sliding glass door to a private deck. One level up, the bedrooms have easy access to a full bath, while the master bedroom has a private bath. One level down an unfinished bedroom and a bath are located close to the family room, which includes a gas fireplace.

Main level — 531 sq. ft.
Second level — 717 sq. ft.
Lower level — 744 sq. ft.

Total living area: 1,992 sq. ft.

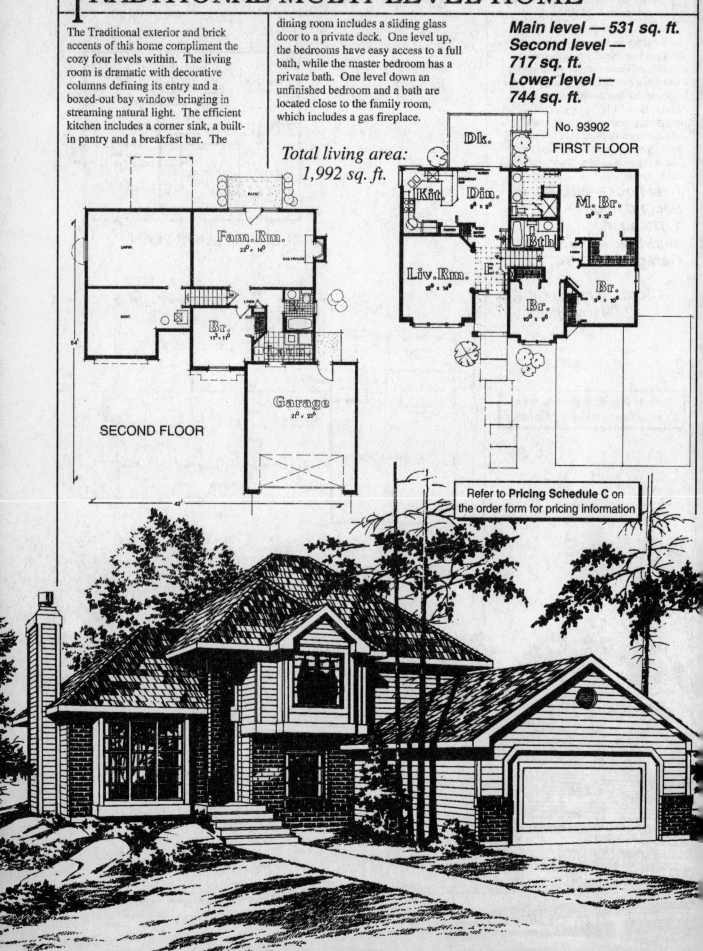

No. 93902
FIRST FLOOR

SECOND FLOOR

Refer to **Pricing Schedule C** on the order form for pricing information

A GRAND ENTRANCE

Enter this lovely, Traditional styled home, through the massive two story entrance, and feel the warmth and elegance it offers. With the vaulted living room nestled off to one side, and open to the formal dining room, any occasion could be considered formal. The family room, with a wetbar, is open to the breakfast nook and kitchen. The cooking island is a delight. A den is also conveniently located on the main floor, along with the ample laundry area, which separates the garage from the living area. The second story landing opens to the main floor foyer area, creating an excellent use of space. All of the bedrooms feature unique details with bay and corner windows, and window seats. The splendid master suite, with romantic fireplace, and whirlpool tub offers the homeowner a place to retreat. No materials list available for this plan.

Main floor —
1,425 sq. ft.
Upper floor —
1,099 sq. ft.
Garage —
763 sq. ft.
Width — 62'-0"
Depth — 51'-0"

DECK

Bfst.

Fam. rm.
25'x14'6"

Kit.
BAR

Din.
12'6"x14'4"

WET BAR

PANT

UP

Den
10'x10'8"

F
HW

W
D

LAUN

LINEN

En.

DN 7"

Liv. rm
VAULTED
13'x15'8"

DN 7"

Gar.

COV. PORCH

FIRST FLOOR
No. 94006

Br.
10'x12'

Br.
10'6"x12'

Mbr.
14'x17'

LINEN

JACUZZI

DN

OPEN TO FOYER

PLANT SHELF

Br.
10'x12

SECOND FLOOR

An EXCLUSIVE DESIGN *By* CRANE DESIGN inc.

Refer to **Pricing Schedule D** on the order form for pricing information

Total living area:
2,524 sq. ft.

No materials list available

PERFECT FOR A CORNER LOT

Design 90444

This Ranch plan is ideal for a corner lot, with a rear garage that enters from the side. The focal point of this plan is the Great room with a vaulted ceiling, and loft above. The French doors on either side of the fireplace open onto a screened porch. The large double-L kitchen is open to the breakfast room, which has a bay window. The master bedroom has a large walk-in closet, and the master bath features a corner tub, as well as double vanities. Two other bedrooms on the opposite end of the house make this split-bedroom design popular. Each of these bedrooms has a walk-in closet, and a desk for school-age children. The loft has a vaulted ceiling and overlooks the Great room with an open rail balcony. This plan is available with either a basement or crawl space foundation. Please specify when ordering.

Main floor — 1,996 sq. ft.
Loft — 305 sq. ft.

Total living area: 2,301 sq. ft.

Refer to **Pricing Schedule D** on the order form for pricing information

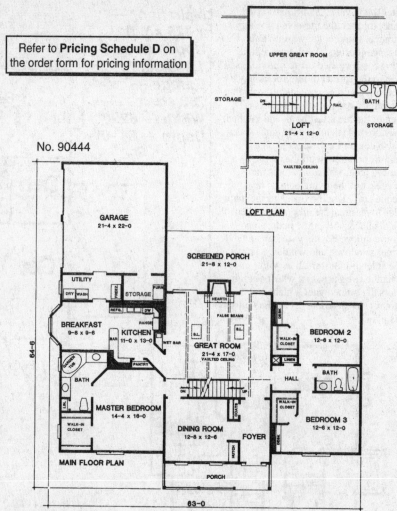

No. 90444

INVITING PORCH ADORNS HOME

You don't have to give up storage space to build an affordable home. With large closets just inside the front door and in every bedroom, a walk-in pantry by the kitchen, and an extra-large storage area tucked behind the garage, you can build this house on an optional slab foundation and still keep the clutter to a minimum. The L-shaped living and dining room arrangement, brightened by triple windows and sliding glass doors, adds a spacious feeling to active areas. Eat in formal elegance overlooking the patio, or have a family meal in the country kitchen. Tucked in a private wing for a quiet bedtime atmosphere, three bedrooms and two full baths complete this affordable home loaded with amenities.

Main area — 1,160 sq. ft.
Mud/laundry room — 83 sq. ft.
Garage — 2-car

Total living area:
1,243 sq. ft.

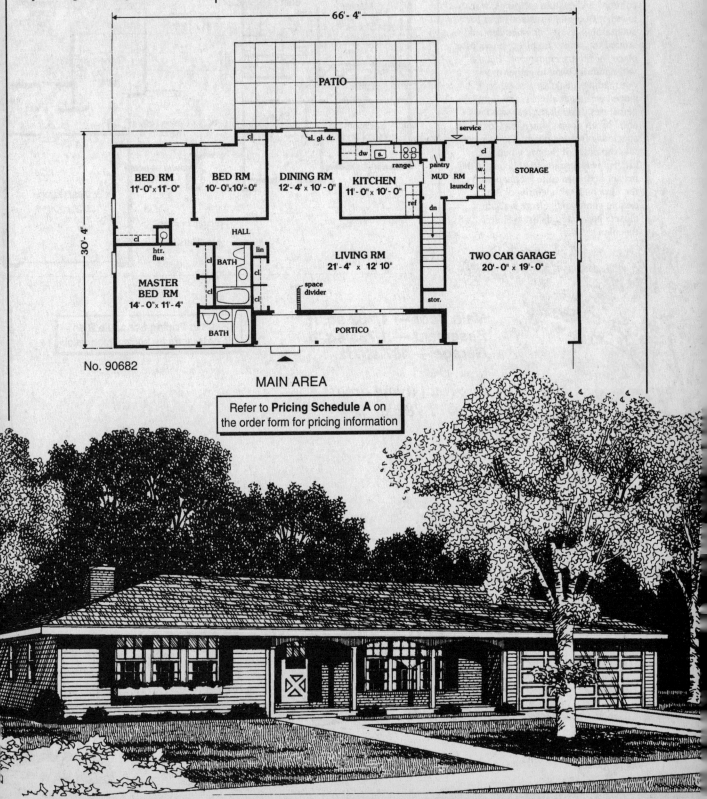

No. 90682

MAIN AREA

Refer to **Pricing Schedule A** on the order form for pricing information

CHARMING RANCH STYLE

The appeal of this ranch style home is not only in its charm and exterior style, but extends to the classic interior as well. Designed to provide an efficient floor plan, the real excitement lies in the amenities. Whether you enjoy formal entertaining, or a more casual lifestyle, this home can adapt to your needs. The Great room and dining room, accented by a sloped ceiling, columns and custom moldings, work together to create a spacious area for entertaining guests, or when centered around the corner fireplace, provides a place for family enjoyment. People will naturally want to gather in this outstanding breakfast area where the sloped ceiling continues, and light permeates through the rear windows and French doors, which lead to the spacious screened porch. Convenience was the order of the day when this kitchen was designed. Relaxing in the master bedroom suite is enhanced by the ultra bath with whirlpool tub, double vanity and a large walk-in closet. No materials list available for this plan.

No materials list available

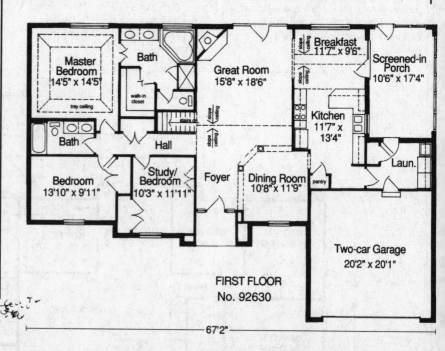

FIRST FLOOR
No. 92630

— 67'2" —

Main floor — 1,782 sq. ft.
Basement — 1,735 sq. ft.
Garage — 407 sq. ft.

Refer to **Pricing Schedule B** on the order form for pricing information

Total living area:
1,782 sq. ft.

CONVENIENT AND EFFICIENT RANCH

The one floor convenience of a ranch cannot be matched. The floor plan of this home keeps the private areas—the bedrooms—to one side and the high traffic areas to the other. The foyer features a barrel vault ceiling. Turning left from the foyer into the dinette, one can't help but notice another decorative ceiling, a stepped ceiling. There is also a stepped ceiling in the formal dining room. The kitchen features a work island and built-in pantry. An expansive gathering room has a tray ceiling and a large fireplace. The master suite affords the owner the luxury of privacy. A private master bath features separate shower and tub as well as a double vanity. The walk-in closet provides more than adequate storage space. Two additional bedrooms share the full hall bath. No materials list available for this plan.

**Main living area —
1,810 sq. ft.
Garage — 528 sq. ft.**

*Total living area:
1,810 sq. ft.*

An
EXCLUSIVE DESIGN
By Patrick Morabito, A.I.A. Architect

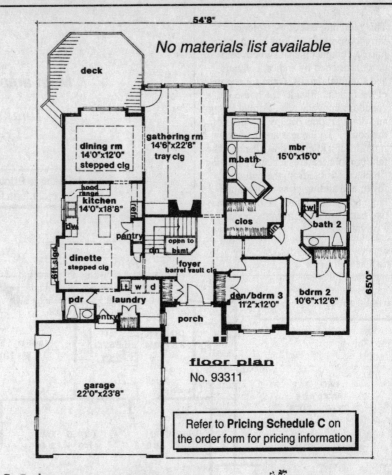

54'8"

No materials list available

deck

dining rm
14'0"x12'0"
stepped clg

gathering rm
14'6"x22'8"
tray clg

m.bath

mbr
15'0"x15'0"

hood range
kitchen
14'0"x18'8"

ref

clos

twl

bath 2

pantry

open to bsmt

dn

dinette
stepped clg

foyer
barrel vault clg

65'0"

t   w   d

den/bdrm 3
11'2"x12'0"

bdrm 2
10'6"x12'6"

pdr

laundry

entry

porch

floor plan
No. 93311

garage
22'0"x23'8"

Refer to **Pricing Schedule C** on the order form for pricing information

VARIED ROOF HEIGHTS

This rambling one-story Colonial farmhouse packs a lot of living space into its compact plan. The covered porch, enriched by arches, columns and Colonial details, is the focal point of the facade. Inside, the house is zoned for convenience. Formal living and dining rooms occupy the front of the house. To the rear are the family room, island kitchen, and dinette. The family room features a heat-circulating fireplace, visible from the entrance foyer, and sliding glass doors to the large rear patio. Three bedrooms and two baths are away from the action in a private wing.

Main area — 1,613 sq. ft.

Total living area:
1,613 sq. ft.

Refer to **Pricing Schedule B** on
the order form for pricing information

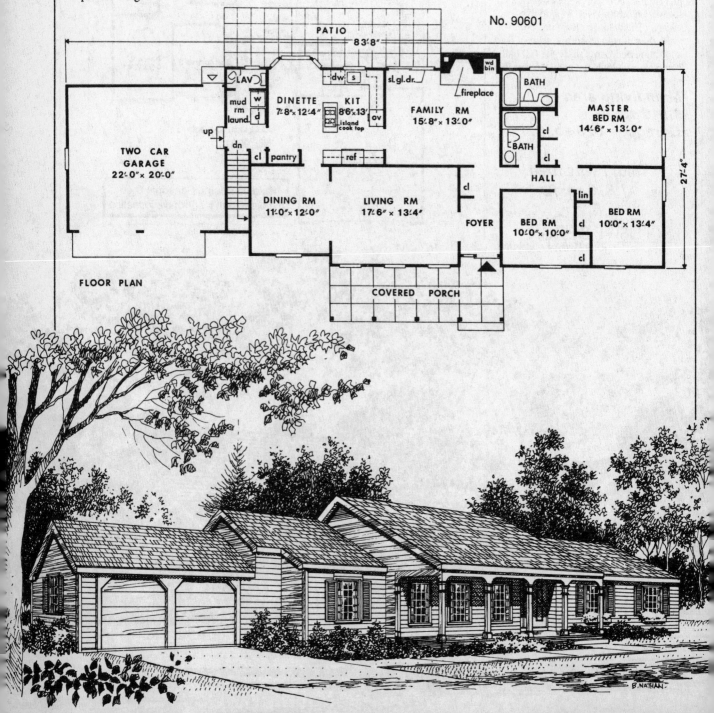

FLOOR PLAN

No. 90601

B. NATHAN

COLONIAL RANCH

Endowed with the trimmings of a traditional colonial, this three-bedroom ranch is doubly attractive. The master bedroom is complete with a full bath, walk-in closet and spacious dressing area. Warmed by a wood-burning fireplace, the living room spills onto a large redwood deck via a sliding glass door. A functional kitchen is separated from the family room by a cooking peninsula. A utility room and hobby shop edge the double garage.

First floor — 1,612 sq. ft.
Basement — 1,612 sq. ft.
Garage, utility room and storage — 660 sq. ft.

Refer to **Pricing Schedule B** on the order form for pricing information

Total living area:
1,612 sq. ft.

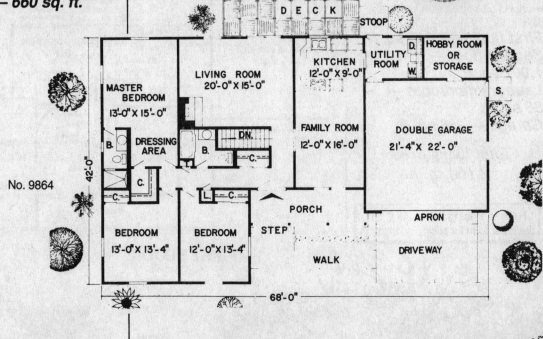

No. 9864

REDWOOD DECK

STOOP

MASTER BEDROOM
13'-0" X 15'-0"

LIVING ROOM
20'-0" X 15'-0"

KITCHEN
12'-0" X 9'-0"

UTILITY ROOM

HOBBY ROOM OR STORAGE

DRESSING AREA

DN.

FAMILY ROOM
12'-0" X 16'-0"

DOUBLE GARAGE
21'-4" X 22'-0"

BEDROOM
13'-0" X 13'-4"

BEDROOM
12'-0" X 13'-4"

PORCH

STEP

WALK

APRON

DRIVEWAY

42'-0"

68'-0"

COUNTRY COMFORTS

The farmhouse flavor of a covered porch, window boxes, and two chimneys give this house a welcoming feeling that couldn't be friendlier. And, the interior's just as nice, with the cozy living and dining rooms beckoning guests as they step into the foyer. Cabinets and a greenhouse bay separate the kitchen, dinette, and family room overlooking the backyard without compromising the spacious atmosphere throughout. And, a covered porch just off the fireplaced family room is a great place for a barbecue, rain or shine. Four bedrooms and two full baths are tucked up the circular staircase for privacy. You'll love the luxury of your own whirlpool tub at the end of your busy days.

First floor — 1,065 sq. ft.
Second floor — 1,007 sq. ft.
Laundry/mudroom — 88 sq. ft.
Garage — 428 sq. ft.

Total living area: 2,160 sq. ft.

Refer to **Pricing Schedule C** on the order form for pricing information

SECOND FLOOR

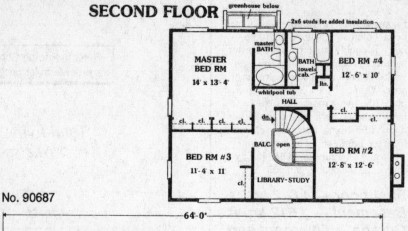

FIRST FLOOR

No. 90687

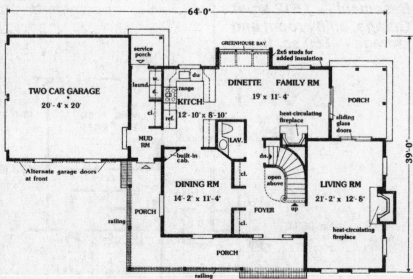

COLONIAL CHARMER

Design 93523

This charming Colonial gives you four bedrooms in only 1,920 sq. ft. The oversized family room opens onto the kitchen/nook area to create a feeling of openness. The family room features a large fireplace and access to the patio. A peninsula counter in the kitchen doubles as an eating bar. There is a formal living room and dining room for entertaining. The master suite has two closets and a private master bath with a jacuzzi and double vanity. The three additional bedrooms, one with a walk-in closet, share a full hall bath.

First floor — 970 sq. ft.
Second floor — 950 sq. ft.
Basement — 970 sq. ft.

Total living area: 1,920 sq. ft.

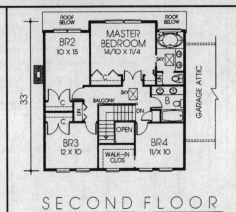

SECOND FLOOR

Refer to **Pricing Schedule C** on the order form for pricing information

OPTIONAL BASEMENT

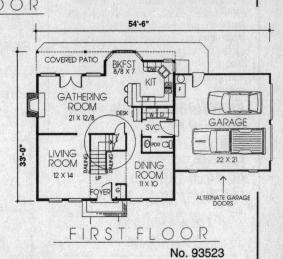

FIRST FLOOR

No. 93523

ENERGY-SAVING CAPE

Shutters, twin porches with wooden railings, and a brightening bay window are traditional elements that bring a warm feeling to the classic facade of this updated Cape. Inside, wood beams and a heat-circulating fireplace continue the cozy atmosphere into the large living room. Step back to reach the sunny dining and family room, enlarged by a bay with sliding glass doors to the rear deck. The adjoining country kitchen, with its generous cabinet space and efficient plan, is large enough for a table. Down a short hall, you'll find the handy first-floor master suite, double-vanitied bath, and a second bedroom. Upstairs, there's another full bath and two more bedrooms, each with cozy sitting nook and skylight.

First floor — 1,382 sq. ft.
Second floor — 688 sq. ft.
Garage — 1-car (w/2-car option)
Total living area: 2,070 sq. ft.

Refer to **Pricing Schedule C** on the order form for pricing information

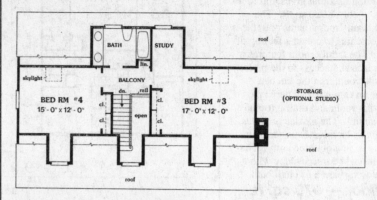

SECOND FLOOR PLAN

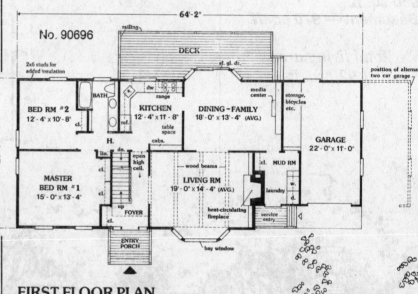

FIRST FLOOR PLAN

WINDOWS ADD DISTINCTION

The windows of this home give it character and distinction. The formal areas are located at the front of the home. The living room and the dining room enjoy the natural light from the bayed windows. The expansive family room is enhanced by a fireplace and view of the rear yard. A U-shaped kitchen efficiently serves the dining room and the breakfast bay. Both the breakfast bay the the family room have access to the patio. The master suite is elegantly crowned by a decorative ceiling. The private master bath offers a garden tub and a step-in shower. Two large additional bedrooms share a full hall bath. There is a convenient second floor laundry center. No materials list available for this plan.

First floor — 1,126 sq. ft.
Second floor — 959 sq. ft.
Basement — 458 sq. ft.
Garage — 627 sq. ft.

Total living area:
2,085 sq. ft.

An
EXCLUSIVE DESIGN
By Jannis Vann & Associates, Inc.

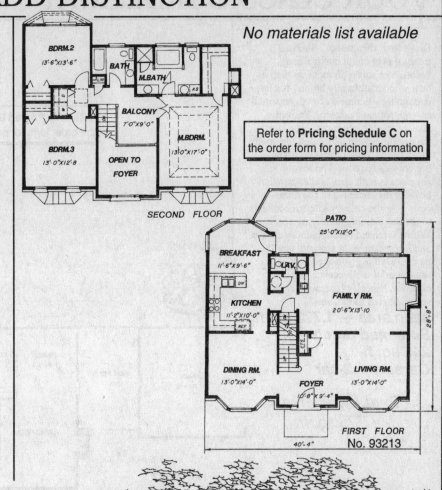

No materials list available

Refer to **Pricing Schedule C** on the order form for pricing information

SECOND FLOOR

BDRM.2 13'-6"X13'-6"
BATH
M.BATH
BALCONY 7'-0"X9'-0"
BDRM.3 13'-0"X12'-8"
OPEN TO FOYER
M.BDRM. 13'-0"X17'-0"

PATIO 25'-0"X12'-0"
BREAKFAST 11'-6"X9'-6"
LDY.
KITCHEN 11'-2"X10'-0"
FAMILY RM. 20'-6"X13'-10
DINING RM. 13'-0"X14'-0"
FOYER 10'-8"X9'-4"
LIVING RM. 13'-0"X14'-0"
FIRST FLOOR No. 93213
40'-4"
28'-8"

YOUR CLASSIC HIDEAWAY

Don't limit this design. Such a tranquil plan could maximize a vacation or suit retirement, as well as be a wonderful family home. It's large enough to welcome a crowd, but small enough for easy upkeep. The only stairs go to the basement. The lavish master suite, with its sunken tub, melts away cares. Either guest bedroom is big enough for two. The lovely fireplace is both cozy and a source of heat for the core area of the home. Note how the country kitchen connects to the large dining and living space. With a screened porch, laundry alcove, and large garage for storage, you'll have everything you need with a minimum of maintenance and cleaning. Specify basement, crawl space, or slab foundation.

Main area — 1,773 sq. ft.
Screened porch —
240 sq. ft.
Garage — 2-car

Total living area:
1,773 sq. ft.

Refer to **Pricing Schedule B** on the order form for pricing information

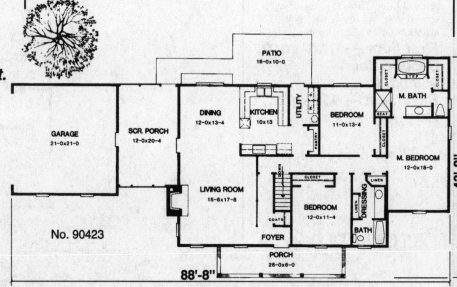

FARMHOUSE WITH A MODERN FLAIR

Enjoy this updated treatment of the classic salt box design. Don't worry about the kids tracking mud all over the house. The old-fashioned porch that surrounds this inviting home shelters two convenient entrances: one for guests and one for the kids with muddy shoes! The central foyer is flanked by the family room and a lovely sunken living room with an efficient heat-circulating fireplace. At the rear of the house, the kitchen serves formal and family dining rooms with ease. Walking up the circular stairs, you'll find three roomy bedrooms, including the master suite with skylit bath and dressing area.

First floor — 1,238 sq. ft.
Second floor — 797 sq. ft.
Basement — 1,159 sq. ft.
Garage — 439 sq. ft.

Total living area:
2,035 sq. ft.

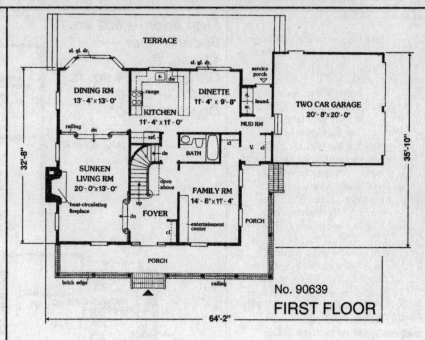

No. 90639
FIRST FLOOR

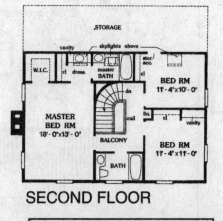

SECOND FLOOR

Refer to **Pricing Schedule C** on the order form for pricing information

LET THE SUN SHINE IN

It won't take long to notice how bright this home's interior is. Stepping into the solarium/living room from the main entry deck, you'll be bathed in sunlight and warmth from the skylights in the cathedral ceiling. Skylights distribute light more efficiently than windows and the open plan in this home makes full use of that capability. The centrally-located wood stove adds to the warmth. An open floor plan allows this Contemporary cottage to seem larger than it actually is. The kitchen is efficiently designed with convenience as a top priority. The pantry is located near the food preparation centers, and a garden window overlooks the backyard. The second floor exhibits careful planning. The bedrooms are well separated from each other for maximum privacy. This cottage, oriented with its solarium/living room to the South, should receive significant solar heat gains in the winter. Large but discrete window areas draw the sun inside, while six well-placed skylights spread the sun's energy towards the center of the house.

Refer to **Pricing Schedule A** on the order form for pricing information

First floor — 852 sq. ft.
Second floor — 414 sq. ft.
Garage — 624 sq. ft.
Width — 66'-0"
Depth — 26'-0"

Total living area: 1,266 sq. ft.

MORE THAN AMPLE MASTER SUITE

The master suite of this home covers about the same area as the combined family room/kitchen area. With about twice as much space as the average walk-in closet, the suite's oversize stroll-through closet is almost big enough to park a car. Another closet is located just outside the door of the large closet. Inadequate storage space won't be a problem here. Wedge in one corner of the suite, an oversized bathtub invites long leisurely baths to soak away the stresses of the day.

The toilet and shower are tucked into a separate cubicle, and twin basins are nestled behind a unique freestanding wall. The big country kitchen offers plenty of elbow room, counter space and cupboards. Triple sliding glass doors in the family room and master suite brighten both rooms and provide access to a long deck. The additional bedrooms have ample closet space and share a bathroom with a combined tub and shower.

Main area — 2,241 sq. ft.
Garage — 640 sq. ft.
Width — 90'-0"
Depth — 50'-0"

Total living area:
2,241 sq. ft.

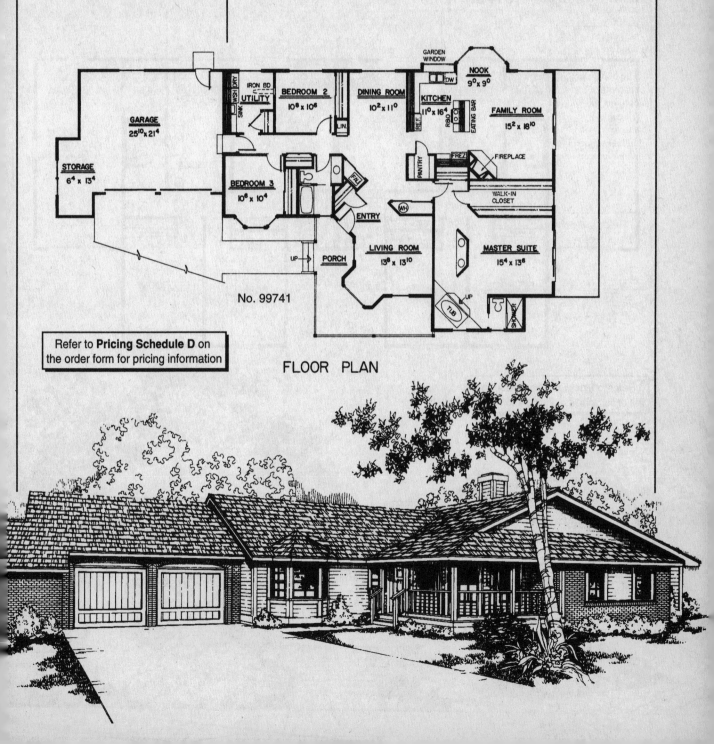

No. 99741

FLOOR PLAN

Refer to **Pricing Schedule D** on the order form for pricing information

CHOOSE YOUR OWN STYLE

Design 91333

This appealing duplex is available with either a Colonial or Contemporary style elevation. The central entry leads you directly into the living room or down the hall to the kitchen, bath and bedrooms without the need to pass through one room to reach another. The utility room is large enough to set up an ironing board and contains ample room for linen and additional storage. The compartmented bath with two lavatories can be used by three at the same time, thus making the early morning rush easier.

Width — 78'-0"
Depth — 36'-0"

Total living area:
914 sq. ft.

No materials list available

Main unit area — 914 sq. ft.

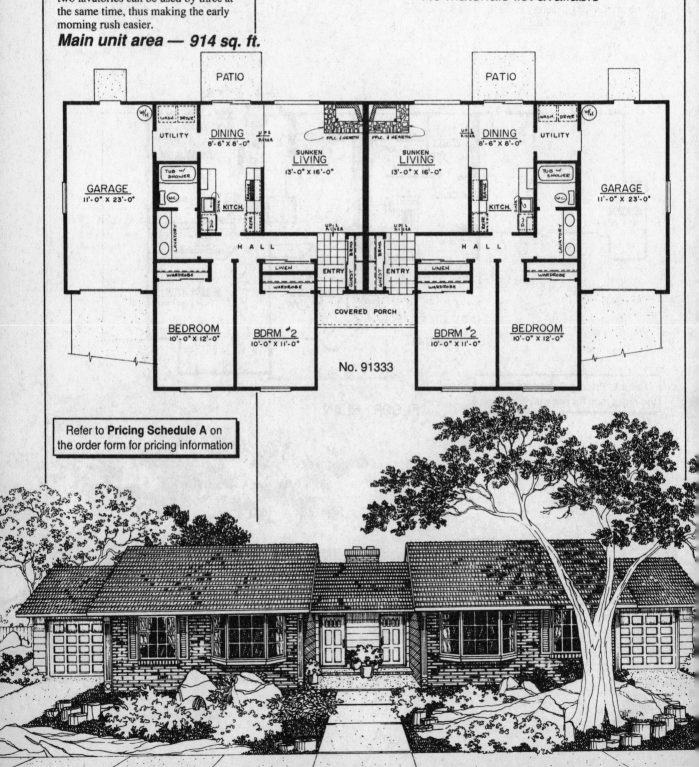

No. 91333

Refer to **Pricing Schedule A** on the order form for pricing information

REAR AS ATTRACTIVE AS FRONT

Design 90413

The rear of this contemporary home features a massive stone fireplace and a full length deck which make it ideal for a mountain, golf course, lake, or other location where both the front and rear are visible. Sliding glass doors in the family room and breakfast nook open onto the deck. The modified A-frame design combines a cathedral ceiling over the sunken family room with a large studio over the two front bedrooms. An isolated master suite features a walk-in closet and compartmentalized bath with double vanity and linen closet. The front bedrooms include ample closet space and share a unique bath-and-a-half arrangement. On one side of the U-shaped kitchen and breakfast nook is the formal dining room which opens onto the foyer. On the other side is a utility room which can be entered from either the kitchen or garage. The exterior features a massive stone fireplace, large glass areas, and a combination of vertical wood siding and stone. Please specify a basement, crawl space or slab foundation when ordering.

First floor — 2,192 sq. ft.
Second floor — 248 sq. ft.
Basement — 2,192 sq. ft.

Total living area: 2,440 sq. ft.

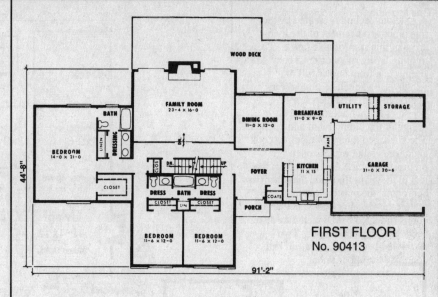

FIRST FLOOR
No. 90413

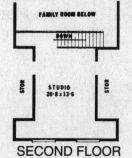

SECOND FLOOR

Refer to **Pricing Schedule D** on the order form for pricing information

Design 90327

CONTEMPORARY EXTERIOR

A spacious feeling is created by the ingenious arrangement of the living areas of this comfortable home. The inviting living room offers a cozy fireplace, a front corner full of windows, a vaulted ceiling and an open staircase. The clerestory windows further accent the open design of the dining room and kitchen. The U-shaped kitchen welcomes cook and tasters alike with its open preparation areas. Secluded from the rest of the main floor and the other two bedrooms, the master bedroom features a walk-in closet and a large, compartmented bath which may also serve as a guest bathroom. Two additional bedrooms and a full bath comprise the upper floor.

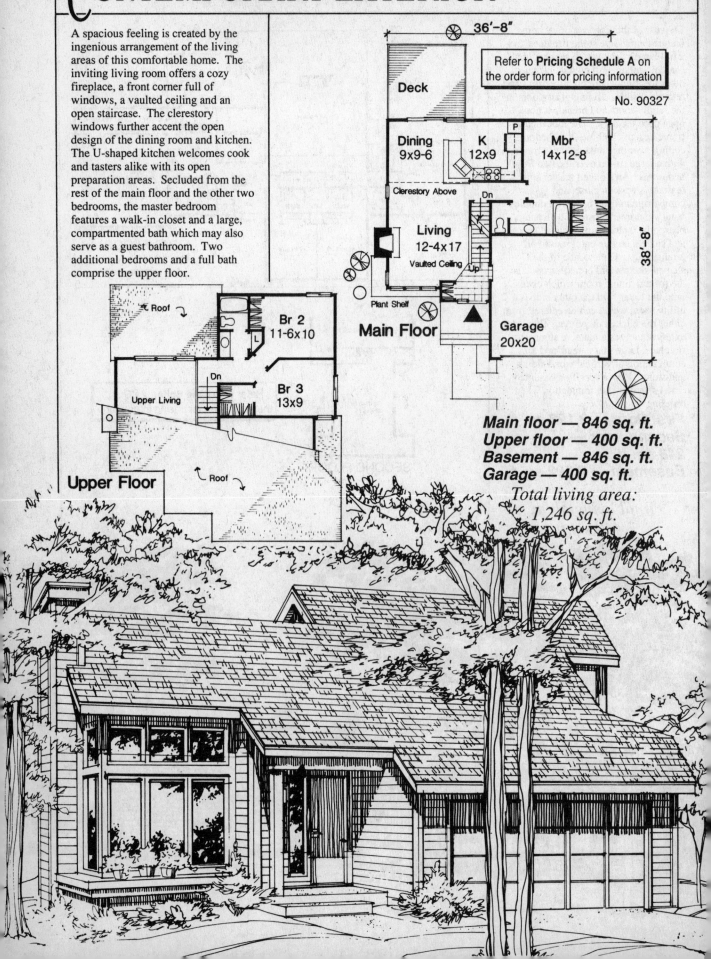

Refer to **Pricing Schedule A** on the order form for pricing information

No. 90327

36'-8"

Deck

Dining 9x9-6

K 12x9

P

Mbr 14x12-8

Clerestory Above

Dn

Living 12-4x17

Vaulted Ceiling

Up

38'-8"

Plant Shelf

Garage 20x20

Main Floor

Br 2 11-6x10

Roof

Dn

Br 3 13x9

Upper Living

Roof

Upper Floor

Main floor — 846 sq. ft.
Upper floor — 400 sq. ft.
Basement — 846 sq. ft.
Garage — 400 sq. ft.
Total living area:
1,246 sq. ft.

OPEN-SPACED RAISED RANCH

The space-saving, lower-level garage offers the option of finishing the adjacent area at any future date, with plenty of storage available immediately. The first floor of this home is complete with three bedrooms, two full baths and a master bedroom with walk-in closets. The activity area of the home combines living and dining areas into an open living space. The compact kitchen is packed with storage and has a conveniently located laundry nook.

First floor — 1,152 sq. ft.
Garage — 572 sq. ft.
Basement — 550 sq. ft.

Total living area:
1,152 sq. ft.

Refer to **Pricing Schedule A** on the order form for pricing information

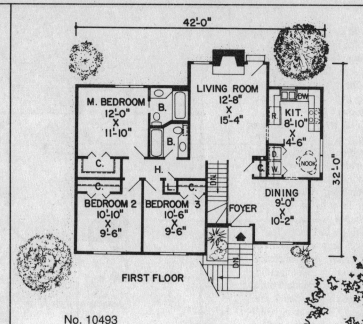

FIRST FLOOR

No. 10493

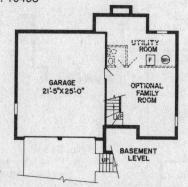

BASEMENT LEVEL

An
EXCLUSIVE DESIGN
By Karl Kreeger

FOUR BEDROOM CHARMER

Abounding with amenities, this single-level ranch home has an attractive street appearance with brick accents on cedar siding. A vaulted naturally lighted entry opens to a vaulted living room featuring a masonry fireplace and large windowed bay. The connecting dining room has a coffered ceiling and built-in china storage. To the rear of the house is a large vaulted family room with wood stove alcove, rear deck cooking island, large pantry and a telephone desk. A unique skylighted hall leads to the bedroom wing, consisting of two secondary bedrooms sharing a full bath. The luxurious master bedroom suite has a whirlpool garden tub, walk-in closet and double sink vanity. Completing this wing, is a storage abundant utility room. Hall access is provided to the three-car garage. Off the entry hall, is a study with window seat and built-in book shelves. This room can be used as a fourth bedroom.

Main area — 2,185 sq. ft.
Garage — 3-car
Width — 58-0"
Depth — 60'-0"

Refer to **Pricing Schedule C** on the order form for pricing information

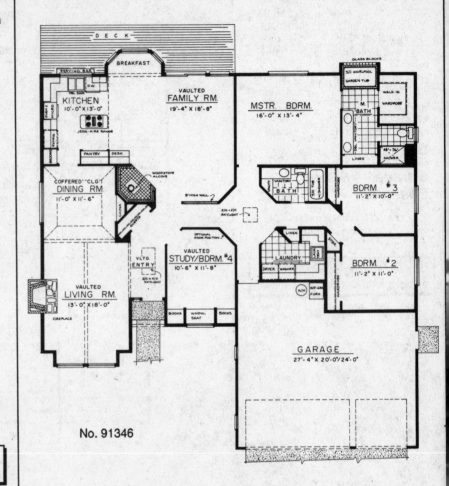

No. 91346

Total living area:
2,185 sq. ft.

EASY LIVING

Here's a pretty, one-level home designed for carefree living. The central foyer divides active and quiet areas. Step back to a fireplaced living room with dramatic, towering ceilings and a panoramic view of the backyard. The adjoining dining room features a sloping ceiling crowned by a plant shelf, and sliders to an outdoor deck. Just across the counter, a handy, U-shaped kitchen features abundant cabinets, a window over the sink overlooking the deck, and a walk-in pantry. You'll find three bedrooms tucked off the foyer. Front bedrooms share a handy full bath, but the master suite boasts its own private bath with both shower and tub, a room-sized walk-in closet, and a bump-out window that adds light and space.

**Main living area —
1,456 sq. ft.
Basement — 1,448 sq. ft.
Garage — 452 sq. ft.**

*Total living area:
1,456 sq. ft.*

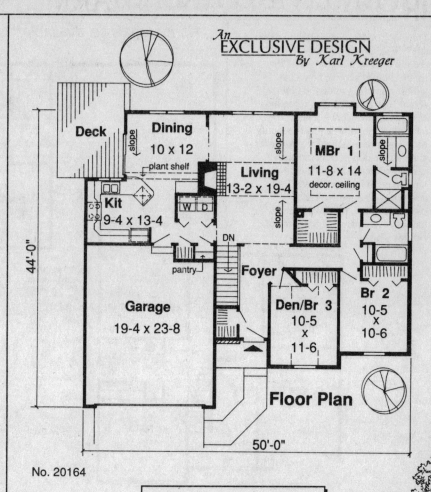

An **EXCLUSIVE DESIGN**
By Karl Kreeger

Deck

Dining
10 x 12

plant shelf

Living
13-2 x 19-4

MBr 1
11-8 x 14
decor. ceiling

slope

Kit
9-4 x 13-4

W D

DN

pantry

Foyer

Garage
19-4 x 23-8

Den/Br 3
10-5
x
11-6

Br 2
10-5
x
10-6

Floor Plan

44'-0"

50'-0"

No. 20164

Refer to **Pricing Schedule A** on the order form for pricing information

OPEN LIVING AREAS

The entry of this home leads to a two story foyer that is illuminated by a second floor window above. The living room is accented by a bay window and flows into the family room. The formal dining room has easy access from the kitchen. The island kitchen, dinette and the family room open into each other. A master suite with a double door entrance, walk-in closet and private bath is located on the second floor. Two additional bedrooms share the compartmented, full bath in the hallway. No materials list available for this plan.

No materials list available

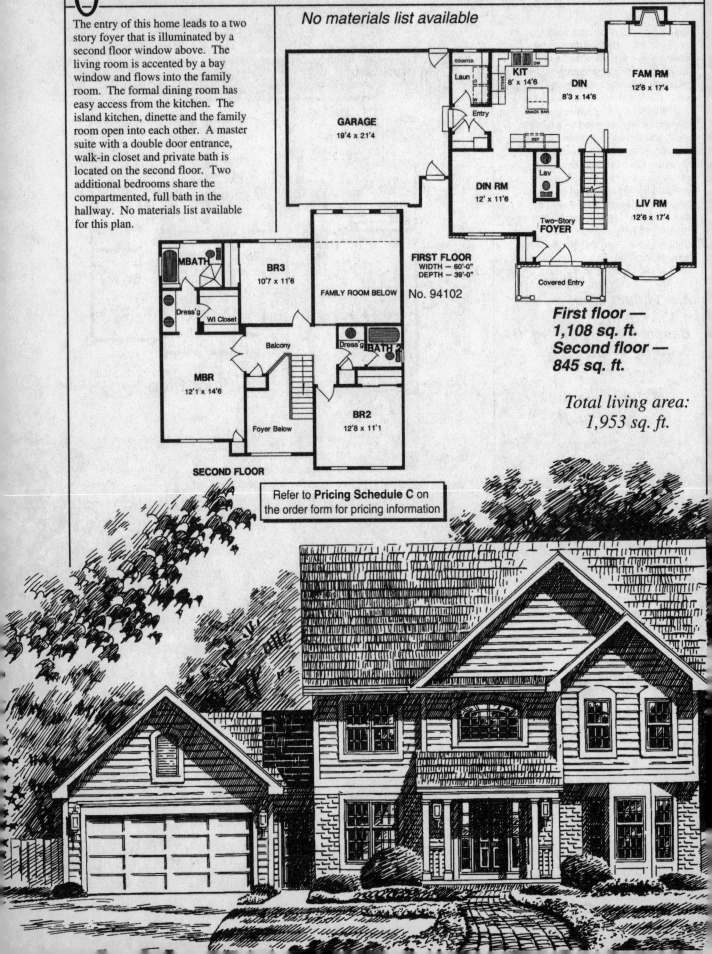

GARAGE 19'4 x 21'4

Laun

KIT 8' x 14'6

DIN 8'3 x 14'6

FAM RM 12'6 x 17'4

Entry

SNACK BAR

REF

DIN RM 12' x 11'6

Lav

LIV RM 12'6 x 17'4

Two-Story **FOYER**

FIRST FLOOR WIDTH — 60'-0" DEPTH — 39'-0"

No. 94102

Covered Entry

MBATH

BR3 10'7 x 11'6

FAMILY ROOM BELOW

Dress'g

WI Closet

Balcony

Dress'g **BATH 2**

MBR 12'1 x 14'6

Foyer Below

BR2 12'8 x 11'1

SECOND FLOOR

Refer to **Pricing Schedule C** on the order form for pricing information

First floor — 1,108 sq. ft. Second floor — 845 sq. ft.

Total living area: 1,953 sq. ft.

FOR MODERN FAMILY LIVING

A two-story foyer greets you as you enter this home. The spacious living room flows easily into the formal dining room adding to the comfort and convenience in entertaining. A large island kitchen includes a pantry, double sink and ample storage and counter space, while the expansive family room has a cozy fireplace and a stepped ceiling. The sleeping quarters are located on the second floor; the master suite is equipped with a private bath and walk-in closet, and the two family bedrooms share a full hall bath. A bonus room with a sloped ceiling will add to your family's living space. Today's lifestyle requires this modern, convenient house. No materials list available for this plan.

First floor — 1,166 sq. ft.
Second floor — 863 sq. ft.
Bonus room — 208 sq. ft.
Basement — 1,166 sq. ft.
Garage — 462 sq. ft.

Total living area:
2,029 sq. ft.

An
EXCLUSIVE DESIGN
By Patrick Morabito, A.I.A. Architect

Refer to **Pricing Schedule C** on the order form for pricing information

No materials list available

FIRST FLOOR
No. 93310

49'0"
42'8"

WOOD DECK 12X18'6"
DINETTE 8'6"X11'6"
KITCHEN 16'6"X11'6"
FAMILY RM 17X14 STEPPED CLG
DINING RM 11X14
REFR PANTRY
P.R.
FLR ABOVE
LAUND shelf
D. W.
ENTRY
FOYER HIGH CLG
LIVING RM 13X16
PORCH
STEP
UP
GARAGE 22X21
16FT. DOOR
PORCH
BRICK VENEER

SECOND FLOOR

B.R.#2 11X11
M.BATH
BATH
CLOSET
B.R.#3 12'6"X11
BALCONY
FOYER, BELOW
M.B.R. 13X15
PORCH, BELOW
BONUS RM 15'6"X17'6" SLOPED CLG
BRICK VENEER

Design 98316

FOR THE EMPTY-NESTER

This stylish Ranch markets to the empty-nester or the second home buyer. The second bedroom doubles as a guest suite and the den offers a comfortable secondary living space. The entry looks through the Great room out to the lanai. The Great room, breakfast area, master bedroom and the bathroom all access the lanai, for covered outdoor living. The high 10' flat ceilings are throughout the house. The den may function as a third bedroom. No materials list available for this plan.

Main area — 1,859 sq. ft.
Garage — 393 sq. ft.

Total living area: 1,859 sq. ft.

Refer to **Pricing Schedule C** on the order form for pricing information

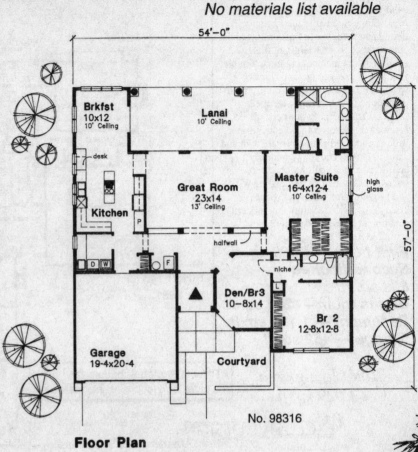

No materials list available

Floor Plan

No. 98316

YOU'VE GOT THE CHOICE

This design offers you a choice of three distinctively different exteriors. Blueprints show details for all three optional elevations. A study of the floor plan reveals a fine measure of livability. In less than 1,400 square feet, there are features galore. An excellent return on your construction dollar. In addition to the two eating areas and the open planning of the gathering room, the indoor-outdoor relationships are of great interest. The basement may be developed for recreational activities. Be sure to note the storage potential, particularly the linen closet, the pantry, the china cabinet and the broom closet.

Main living area — 1,366 sq . ft.
Garage — 484 sq.ft.
Basement — 1,281 sq. ft.

Total living area: 1,366 sq. ft.

Refer to **Pricing Schedule A** on the order form for pricing information

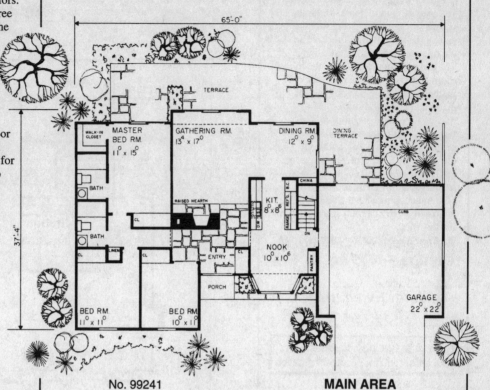

No. 99241

MAIN AREA

CATHEDRAL CEILINGS ADD VOLUME

This plan features the convenience of one floor living, with elegant touches you usually find in houses of larger square footage. The living room enjoys the warmth of a fireplace and the openness of a cathedral ceiling. The dining room flows from the living room and kitchen. The efficient kitchen provides and eating bar for informal eating and snacks. The master suite has a spacious feel because of its cathedral ceiling. A private master bath and a walk-in closet add to its appeal. Two additional bedrooms flank a hallway laundry center. There is a full hall bath to accommodate the additional bedrooms. No materials list available for this plan.

Main area — 1,346 sq. ft.
Garage — 449 sq. ft.

Total living area:
1,346 sq. ft.

Refer to **Pricing Schedule A** on the order form for pricing information

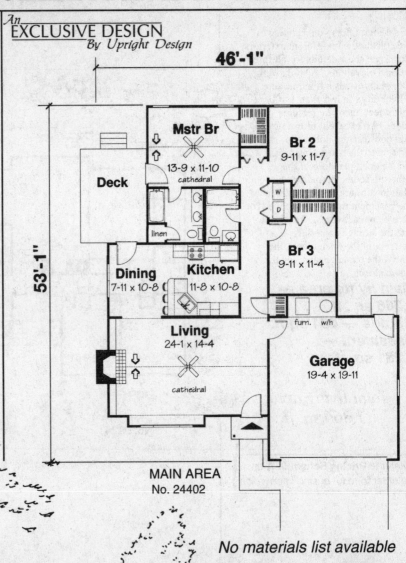

An **EXCLUSIVE DESIGN** *By Upright Design*

MAIN AREA
No. 24402

No materials list available

REFINED AND TASTEFUL

Through a covered entrance and into the foyer, the guest of this home is impressed by the refined taste it presents. A half wall, with columns, adorns the entrance of the formal dining room. French doors separate the formal living room from the family room. A U-shaped kitchen and breakfast room combination has access to the rear yard. A convenient mudroom entrance from the garage and side porch helps to keep the home clean. A vaulted ceiling adds architectural interest to the master suite, enhanced further by a fireplace and lavish bath. Three additional bedrooms share a full, double vanitied bath in the hall. No materials list available for this plan.

First floor — 1,206 sq. ft.
Second floor — 1,136 sq. ft.

Total living area: 2,342 sq. ft.

Refer to **Pricing Schedule D** on the order form for pricing information

First Floor

64'-0"

36'-6"

Garage
19-4 x 23-4

Kit./Brkfst
17-6 x 15-8
desk

Family
16-0 x 15-8

1/2 wall
w/ columns

DN railing

french doors

Dining
12-4 x 13-0

Living
12-6 x 13-0

Porch

UP

Foyer

First Floor

No. 24587

Second Floor

Master Br
19-0 x 13-2

whirlpool tub

linen

niche

linen

DN railing

Br 2
10-4 x 12-6

Br 3
9-0 x 13-0

Br 4
10-4x 10-4

Second Floor

An
EXCLUSIVE DESIGN
By Britt J. Willis

No materials list available

Welcoming Style

The two-story entrance welcomes you to this traditional home. With the angled staircase and the sunken bayed living room that invites you to the formal bayed dining room, any guest would feel welcomed. Along with the formal style comes warmth and efficiency for a living style you can't miss. This well designed four bedroom home gives you the maximum house in the minimum square footage. The generously sized master suite, enhanced with a window seat and a large walk-in closet, leaves you separated yet close enough to the three additional bedrooms. The exterior of the home lends itself the diversity and street appeal to fit well into any neighborhood. No materials list available for this plan.

No materials list available

**First floor —
947 sq. ft.
Second floor —
752 sq. ft.
Garage — 440 sq. ft.
Width — 40'-0"
Depth — 40'-0"**

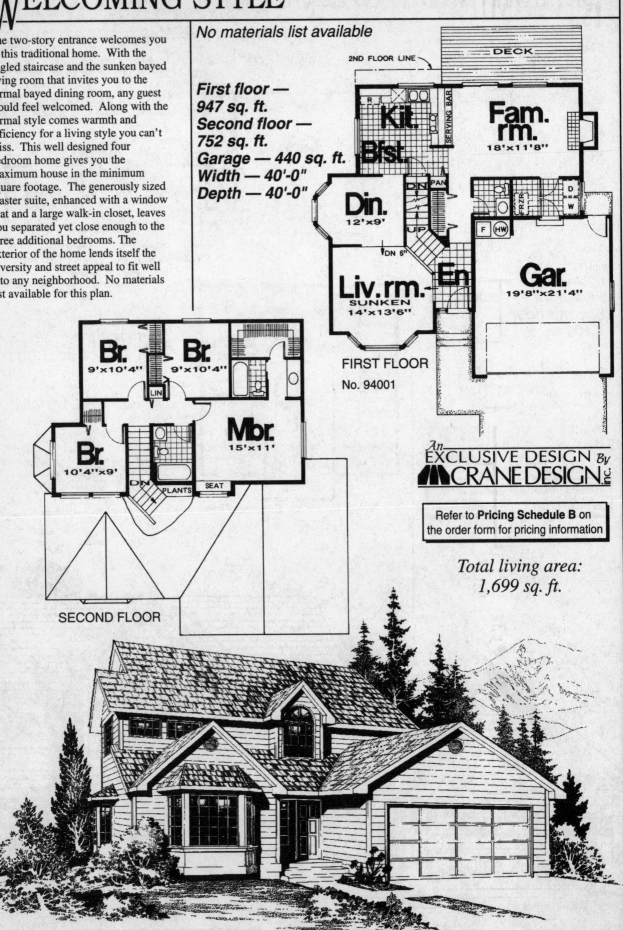

FIRST FLOOR

No. 94001

SECOND FLOOR

An
EXCLUSIVE DESIGN *By*
CRANE DESIGN inc.

Refer to **Pricing Schedule B** on the order form for pricing information

*Total living area:
1,699 sq. ft.*

CHARMING TOUCHES OF COUNTRY

The living room of this country charmer is accented by a large front window. Adjoining the living room is the dining room, allowing for a smooth transition for entertaining. The U-shaped kitchen directly accesses the dining room. A breakfast bar/peninsula counter separates the kitchen from the spacious family room. A gas fireplace in the family room enhances this entire open living space. The master suite with all the amenities is on the second floor. There are two additional second floor bedrooms sharing the full bath in the hallway. A bonus area allows for future expansion. No materials list available for this plan.

No materials list available

**First floor — 913 sq. ft.
Second floor — 771 sq. ft.**

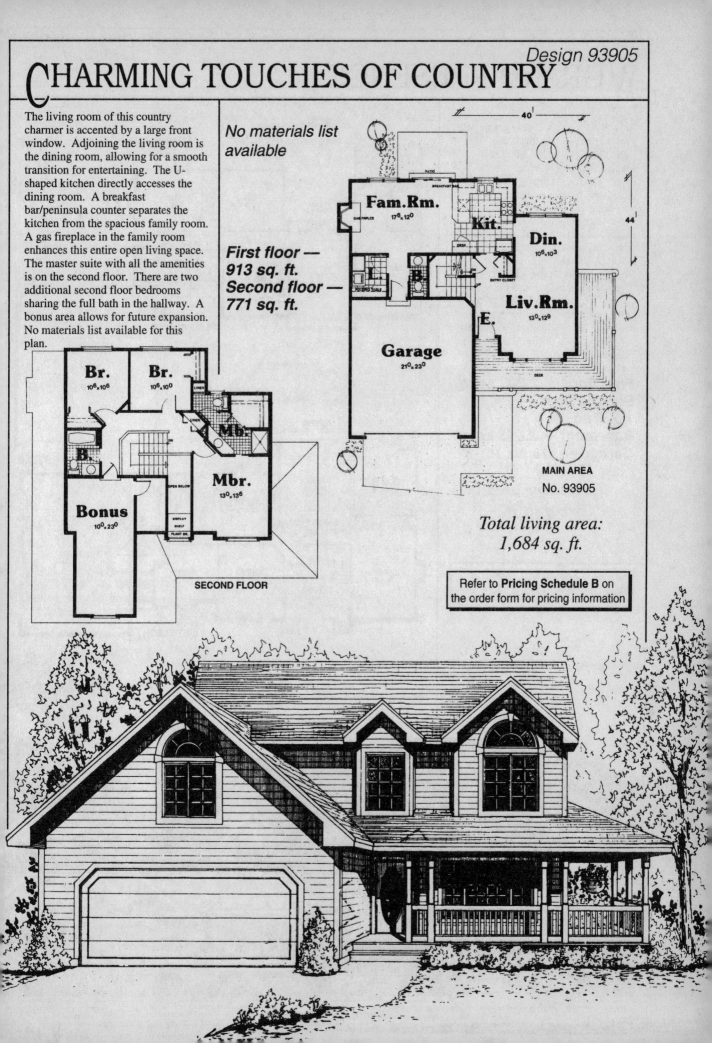

SECOND FLOOR

Br.
10⁶x10⁶

Br.
10⁶x10⁰

Mb.

Mbr.
13⁰x13⁶

B.

Bonus
10⁰x23⁰

OPEN BELOW

DISPLAY SHELF

PLANT BR.

LINEN

Fam.Rm.
17⁶x12⁰

Kit.

Din.
10⁶x10³

Liv.Rm.
13⁰x12⁹

Garage
21⁰x23⁰

GAS FIRPLCE

BREAKFAST BAR

PATIO

ENTRY CLOSET

DECK

E.

L.

B.

40'

44'

MAIN AREA

No. 93905

*Total living area:
1,684 sq. ft.*

Refer to **Pricing Schedule B** on the order form for pricing information

A GRAND PRESENCE

A foyer with a high ceiling greets your guests upon entering this home. The formal living room has a fantastic fireplace that can be seen from the foyer. The formal dining room includes intriguing pocket doors between it and the dinette area. The island kitchen includes a built-in pantry and planning desk, as well as more than ample counter and cabinet space. A tray ceiling crowns the family room, equipped with a cozy fireplace and a built-in entertainment center. A luxury bath highlights the master suite that also includes a walk-in closet. Three additional bedrooms, two having walk-in closets, share a full hall bath. No materials list available for this plan.

First floor — 2,093 sq. ft.
Second floor — 1,527 sq.. ft.
Basement — 2,093 sq. ft.
Garage — 816 sq. ft.

Total living area: 3,620 sq. ft.

Refer to **Pricing Schedule F** on the order form for pricing information

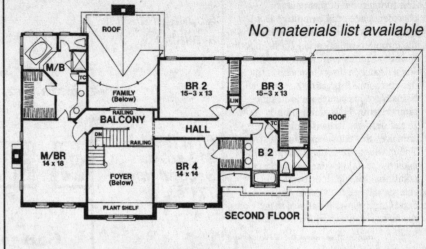

No materials list available

SECOND FLOOR

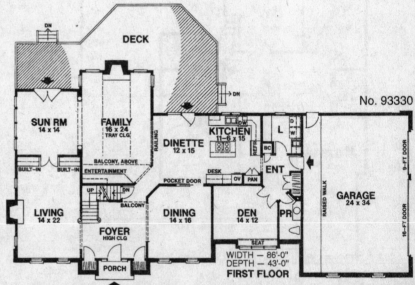

No. 93330

WIDTH — 86'-0"
DEPTH — 43'-0"
FIRST FLOOR

An EXCLUSIVE DESIGN
By Patrick Morabito, A.I.A. Architect

STREETSIDE APPEAL

Comfortable family living in this 1-1/2 story, three bedroom plus loft design is easy and stylish. The entry has a vaulted ceiling giving a feeling of open space as you enter the home. Walk right into the living room. It also has a vaulted ceiling and with its high glass windows there is a lot of natural light. To add elegance to your dinner parties, columns define the formal dining area. For less formal dining, the eat-in kitchen has access to the patio. The master suite features a walk-in closet and its own bath. The two other bedrooms are upstairs. Extra storage space is also located upstairs. No materials list available for this plan.

**First floor —
1,112 sq. ft.
Second floor —
490 sq. ft.**

Total living area:
1,602 sq. ft.

No materials list available

Refer to **Pricing Schedule B** on the order form for pricing information

Upper Floor

Br 2
10-6x13-8

Br 3
10x10

DN

open to below

unfinished storage

Plant Shelf

43'-4"

Patio

Kit/Brk
10-8x14

Master
12x13-8

Dining
11x10-6
vaulted

DN

Living
17x15
vaulted

W
D

UP

50'-0"

Garage
19-4x19-4

Main Floor
No. 99372

COUNTRY-STYLED DETAILING

This cozy front porch shelters the entrance with a country style welcome. The circle window and the double front window add illumination and detail to the front of the home. Directly from the foyer, to the right, are the formal living room and adjoining dining room. The informal areas are laid out in an open format, giving the rear of the home a spacious, airy feeling. The sleeping quarters are on the second floor. A roomy master suite equipped with a walk-in closet, double vanity, spa tub, separate shower and a compartmented toilet; will be a welcomed retreat at the end of the day. Two additional bedrooms share use of the full bath in the hallway. No materials list available for this plan.

FIRST FLOOR
No. 94100

No materials list available

FAM RM 16'2 x 17' cath cl'g · DIN 9' x 12'2 · KIT 10' x 14'2 · DIN RM 11'2 x 15' · GARAGE 21'8 x 21'8 · Entry · Lav. · Lsun · LIV RM 12'4 x 15'3 · FOYER · Covered Entry · 40' · 48'

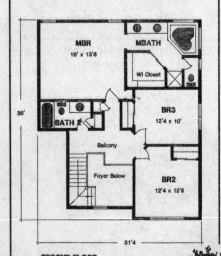

MBR 16' x 13'8 · MBATH · WI Closet · BATH 2 · BR3 12'4 x 10' · Balcony · Foyer Below · BR2 12'4 x 12'6 · 36' · 31'4

SECOND FLOOR

First floor — 1,228 sq. ft.
Second floor — 952 sq. ft.
Garage — 479 sq. ft.
Basement — 1,228 sq. ft.

Total living area: 2,180 sq. ft.

Refer to **Pricing Schedule C** on the order form for pricing information

CAPE FOR MODERN LIVING

For those interested in both traditional charm and modern convenience, this Cape Cod fits the bill. Enter the foyer and find a quiet study to the left and a living room with a fireplace to the right. Straight ahead from the foyer is the kitchen and breakfast room. The island counter top affords lots of room for meal preparation. The service entry introduces a laundry and powder room. Look for three bedrooms upstairs and a pampering master bath.

First floor — 964 sq. ft.
Second floor — 783 sq. ft.

Total living area: 1,747 sq. ft.

Refer to **Pricing Schedule B** on the order form for pricing information

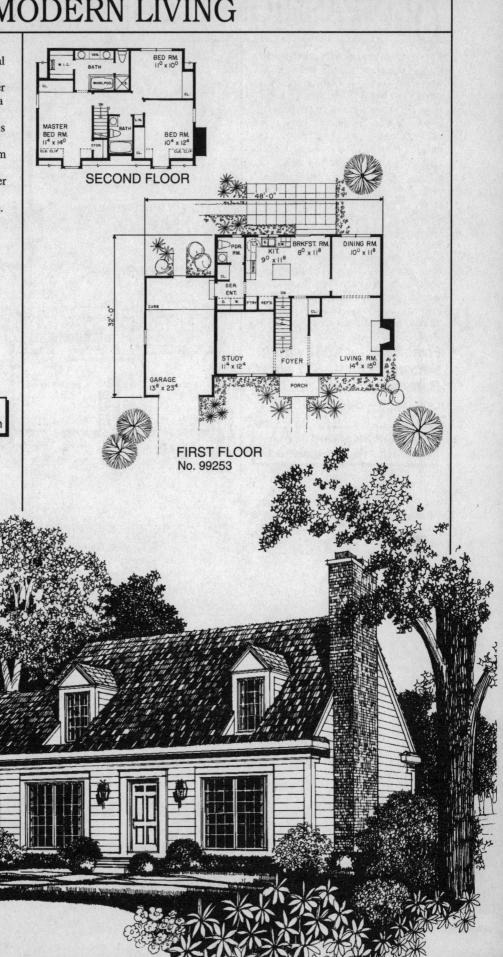

SECOND FLOOR

FIRST FLOOR
No. 99253

Design 93219

OLD-FASHIONED COUNTRY PORCH

The old-fashioned country porch on the front of this home warmly welcomes all who visit. As you enter the home, the warm glow of the fireplace in the living room encourages you to move further into the home. The dining room is close at hand for an elegant dinner party or an intimate evening. The U-shaped kitchen efficiently services both the formal dining room and the informal breakfast area. A first floor master suite ensures privacy for parents by sending the children to bed on the second floor. The master suite includes a luxurious master bath with a double vanity, walk-in closet, oval tub, and step-in shower. A convenient half-bath with a laundry center is located on the first floor. On the second floor the full hall bath is flanked by the two additional bedrooms. The second floor bedrooms are large and have ample closet space.

First floor — 1,057 sq. ft.
Second floor — 611 sq. ft.
Basement — 511 sq. ft.
Garage — 546 sq. ft.

Refer to **Pricing Schedule B** on the order form for pricing information

Total living area:
1,668 sq. ft.

SECOND FLOOR

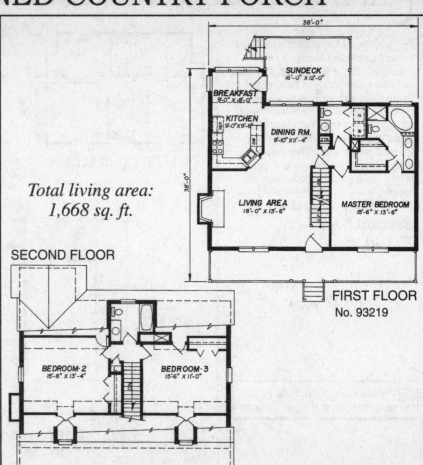

FIRST FLOOR
No. 93219

An
EXCLUSIVE DESIGN
By Jannis Vann & Associates, Inc.

Splendor and Distinction

The expansive kitchen in this home is sure to be a hub for activity. The cooktop island includes a convenient eating bar and a corner double sink looks out over the rear yard. The built-in pantry and planning desk add to its efficiency. The expansive family room is equipped with a built-in wetbar for convenience in serving your guests. The formal living room boasts a second fireplace and a view of the front yard. A bay window adds elegance to the formal dining room. The master suite is on the second floor and its private master bath will pamper the owner in luxury. Three additional bedrooms share a full hall bath. A balcony overlooks the family room and the foyer. No materials list available for this plan.

**First floor — 1,720 sq. ft.
Second floor —
1,305 sq. ft.
Basement — 1,720 sq. ft.
Garage — 768 sq. ft.**

*Total living area:
3,025 sq. ft.*

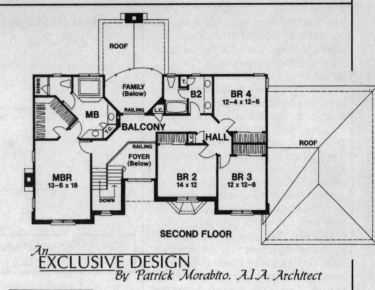

SECOND FLOOR

An
EXCLUSIVE DESIGN
By Patrick Morabito, A.I.A. Architect

No materials list available

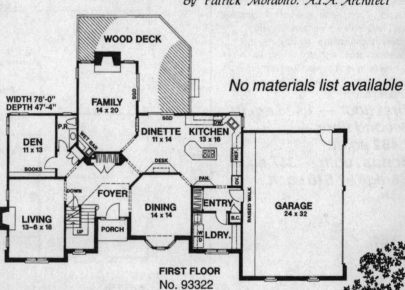

WIDTH 78'-0"
DEPTH 47'-4"

FIRST FLOOR
No. 93322

Refer to **Pricing Schedule E** on the order form for pricing information

IMPRESSIVE TWO-STORY FOYER

Design 24650

This beautiful home has a stucco and stone facade, accented by detailing around the multi-panned windows, and a stone arched covered entrance. The formal living room is directly to the right of the foyer. A bumped-out window provides a focal point and a view of the front yard. Entertaining is made easy by the open layout between the formal dining room and the formal living room. The gourmet of the family will find the kitchen efficient and convenient. An island work area, double sink with a garden window above, walk-in pantry and ample counter and storage space have been included in this well thought out kitchen. The sleeping quarters are located on the second floor. A luxurious master suite awaits the owner with a pampering, private bath and two walk-in closets. Three additional bedrooms share a full hall bath with a double vanity. Natural illumination streams into the commons area from two skylights. A bonus room is provided for your family's future needs. No materials list available for this plan.

First floor — 1,435 sq. ft.
Second floor — 1,462 sq. ft.
Bonus room — 347 sq. ft.
Garage — 616 sq. ft.

Total living area:
2,897 sq. ft.

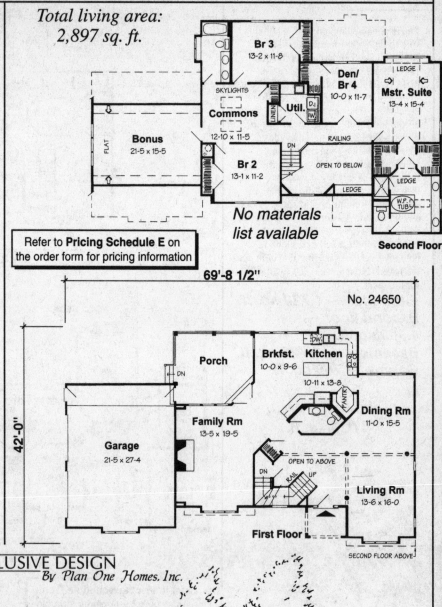

Refer to **Pricing Schedule E** on the order form for pricing information

No materials list available

Second Floor

First Floor

No. 24650

An EXCLUSIVE DESIGN
By *Plan One Homes, Inc.*

TWO-STORY FOYER ADDS ELEGANCE

As you enter this magnificent home the two-story entrance captures your attention. There is a cascading curved staircase directly in front of you. The foyer is flanked by the formal dining room and the formal living room, both enjoy the view of the front yard through large windows. The family room is enhanced by a fireplace and has access to a sundeck. A sunny breakfast area is directly off of the well-appointed kitchen. Upstairs, the master suite has a decorative ceiling and a large master bath. Three additonal bedrooms share the full hall bath. A bonus room is provided to accommodate your future needs. No materials list available for this plan.

Main floor — 1,277 sq. ft.
Second floor — 1,177 sq. ft.
Bonus room — 392 sq. ft.
Basement — 1,261 sq. ft.
Garage — 572 sq. ft.
Deck — 192 sq. ft.

Total living area:
2,454 sq. ft.

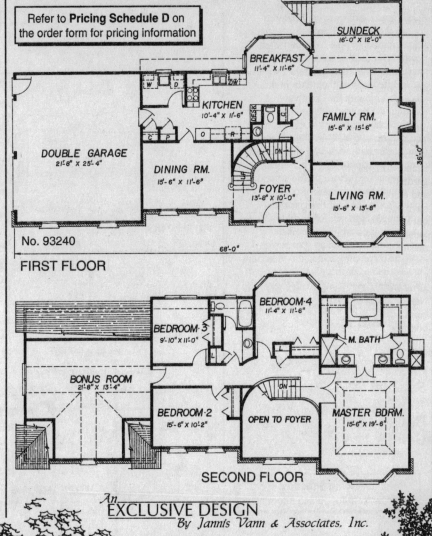

Refer to **Pricing Schedule D** on the order form for pricing information

SUNDECK 16'-0" X 12'-0"

BREAKFAST 11'-4" X 11'-6"

KITCHEN 10'-4" X 11'-6"

FAMILY RM. 15'-6" X 15'-6"

DOUBLE GARAGE 21'-8" X 25'-4"

DINING RM. 15'-6" X 11'-6"

FOYER 13'-8" X 10'-0"

LIVING RM. 15'-6" X 13'-6"

36'-0"

68'-0"

No. 93240

FIRST FLOOR

BEDROOM·4 11'-4" X 11'-6"

BEDROOM·3 9'-10" X 11'-0"

M. BATH

BONUS ROOM 21'-8" X 13'-4"

BEDROOM·2 15'-6" X 10'-2"

OPEN TO FOYER

MASTER BDRM. 15'-6" X 19'-6"

SECOND FLOOR

An EXCLUSIVE DESIGN
By Jannis Vann & Associates, Inc.

No materials list available

FIVE BEDROOM COLONIAL

The elegance of this five bedroom colonial classic design is reinforced by the symmetry of the front elevation with the arched windows and the three dormers. The interior offers a wealth of architectural excitement: in the living room with the open vaulted ceiling; the unique location on the first floor of the luxurious master bedroom suite, with two walk-in closets; and in the master bath with stall shower and step-up whirlpool spa. The other four bedrooms are located on the second floor with two convenient baths. Completing the first floor, is the impressive entrance foyer, family room, dining and living rooms, kitchen/dinette, laundry, breezeway and the three car garage. No materials list available for this plan.

First floor — 2,146 sq. ft.
Second floor — 1,176 sq. ft.

Total living area: 3,322 sq. ft.

Refer to **Pricing Schedule F** on the order form for pricing information

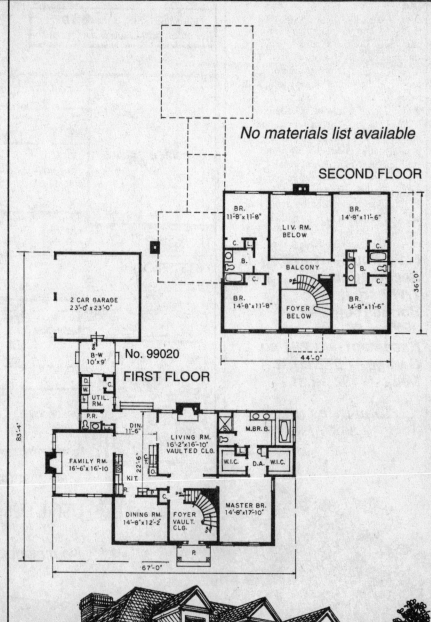

No materials list available

SECOND FLOOR

FIRST FLOOR

No. 99020

FOR A CONVENIENT LIFESTYLE

This home has been designed for convenience in today's lifestyle. The foyer leads straight to the family room, crowned by a vaulted ceiling and warmed by a fireplace flanked by bookshelves. The well-appointed kitchen is separated from the family room by the breakfast bar. An informal dinette flows from the kitchen, and the formal dining room is directly accessed. A convenient mudroom entrance from the garage into the laundry room, will keep tracked in dirt to a minimum. A private first floor master suite has a double door entrance, and includes a walk-in closet and a double vanity bath. Two additional bedrooms, on the second floor, share a full bath in the hallway. No materials list available for this plan.

First floor — 1,228 sq. ft.
Second floor — 483 sq. ft.

Total living area: 1,711 sq. ft.

Refer to **Pricing Schedule B** on the order form for pricing information

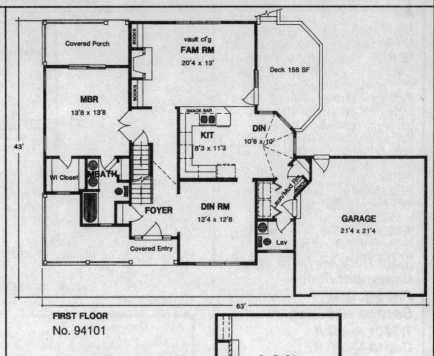

FIRST FLOOR
No. 94101

No materials list available

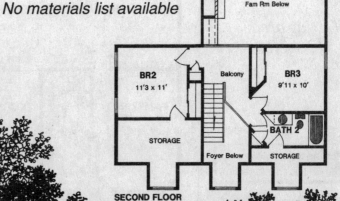

SECOND FLOOR

ENJOY THE VIEW

Here's a house that will take advantage of your location to create an irresistible view from the second floor. On the lower level, you'll find a bayed family room complete with a fireplace just off the foyer. But, the main living areas are upstairs. The L-shaped staircase brings you right into the living room. Bay windows, the open railing, and adjacent dining area with sliding glass doors to the sundeck give this area a spacious feeling. The family kitchen is large enough to accommodate a table for informal meals. Past the pantry and full bath, three bedrooms occupy the rear of the house, away from active areas and the noise of the street.

Main floor — 1,318 sq. ft.
Basement floor — 994 sq. ft.
Garage — 378 sq. ft.
Width — 40 ft.
Depth — 40 ft.

Total living area: 2,312 sq. ft.

Refer to **Pricing Schedule D** on the order form for pricing information

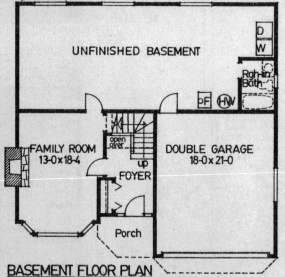

MAIN FLOOR PLAN

No. 90833

BASEMENT FLOOR PLAN

An **EXCLUSIVE DESIGN** *By Westhome Planners, Ltd.*

THREE FIREPLACES KEEP YOU WARM

Have you always wanted your own private getaway, where you could just kick off your shoes and relax? You'll find it in the luxurious master suite in this distinctive four-bedroom home. The built-in spa is a feature you'll welcome at the end of your day. And the fireplace, glass blocks, and skylights make this a sunny, warm retreat. On the main level, bay windows brighten the living room and nook. The kitchen, which features a cooktop island, is centrally located for convenient meal service to formal and informal dining rooms. This plan is available with a crawl space foundation only.

First floor — 1,207 sq. ft.
Second floor — 1,341 sq. ft.
Garage — 2-car

Total living area: 2,548 sq. ft.

Refer to **Pricing Schedule D** on the order form for pricing information

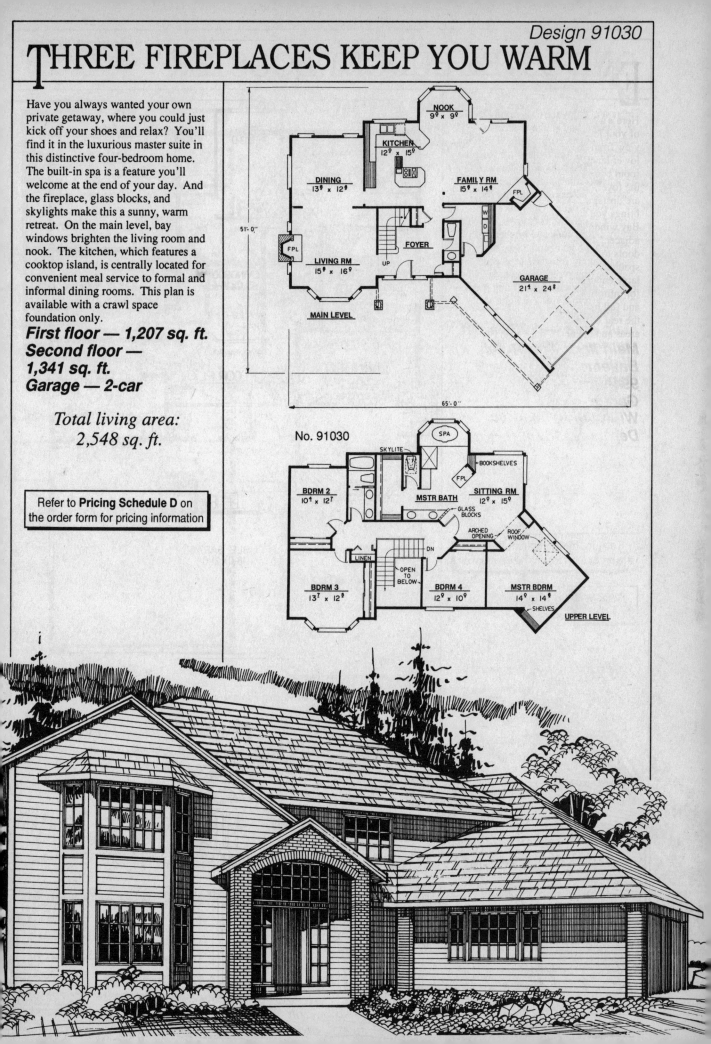

Design 90937

ONE-LEVEL BUDGET BOOSTER

Relax and enjoy the cost-saving advantages, and all the wonderful features, of this cozy ranch. From the central foyer, turn right to the sleeping wing. Tucked behind the garage away from active areas, three bedrooms boast easy access to the utility room and two full baths. Or, walk straight past the general storage areas into the family eating nook and kitchen with sliders to the rear patio. Step down from the entry into the fireplaced, sunken living room. Bay windows and a wide-open view of the dining room give this formal area a delightful, sunny atmosphere.

Main area — 1,238 sq. ft.
Garage — 399 sq. ft.
Width — 38'-0"
Depth — 52'-0"

Total living area:
1,238 sq. ft.

Refer to **Pricing Schedule A** on the order form for pricing information

PATIO

KITCHEN
dw
R
F

NOOK
18-6 x 9-0
5638 x 2743

W.I.C.

MBR
13-0 x 11-0
3962 x 3352

ENS.

Shwr.

P
brm
lin

DINING
9-6 x 10-0
2895 x 3048

BATH

BR 2
10-0 x 9-0
3048 x 2743

rail   dln
1-6" step

LIVINGROOM
12-0 x 16-6
3657 x 5029

dn
Foyer

Hall

W
D
F

BR 3
9-0 x 9-6
2743 x 2895

No. 90937

DOUBLE GARAGE

An
EXCLUSIVE DESIGN
By Westhome Planners, Ltd.

MULTIPLE LEVELS

Arched, bump-out windows lend a special elegance to the facade of this four-bedroom beauty. Entering the skylit foyer, you'll discover that those extra-large windows provide a wonderful unity of interior and exterior space. Extra touches combine to make this a special home: a built-in curio shelf, a sunken living room with a cozy fireplace, an eat-in kitchen for family meals, an extra bedroom on the family room level. And, with the bedroom wing a flight of stairs away from main living areas, you're assured of a restful bedtime atmosphere. This plan is available with a crawl space foundation only.

Main level — 1,398 sq. ft.
Lower level — 632 sq. ft.

Total living area:
2,030 sq. ft.

Refer to **Pricing Schedule C** on the order form for pricing information

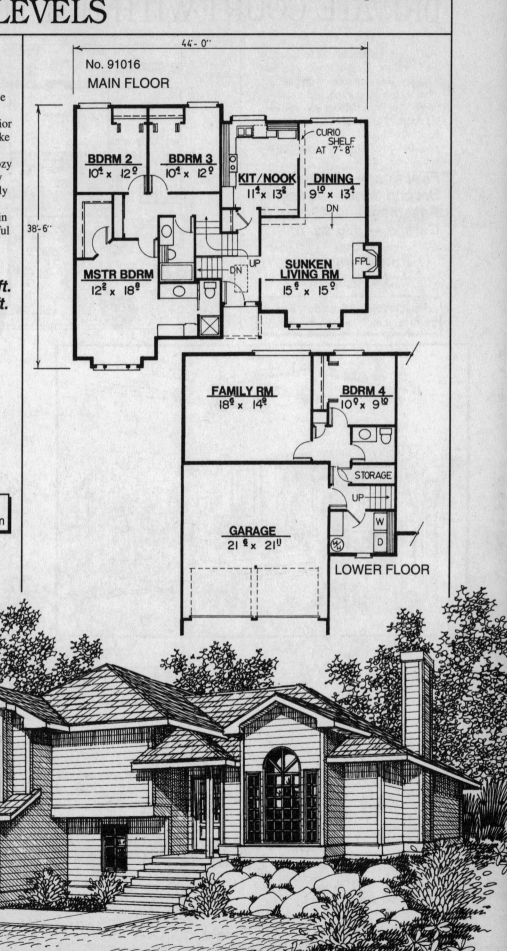

No. 91016
MAIN FLOOR

44'-0"

38'-6"

BDRM 2
10⁴ x 12⁹

BDRM 3
10⁴ x 12⁹

KIT/NOOK
11⁴ x 13²

DINING
9¹⁰ x 13⁴

CURIO SHELF AT 7'-8"

MSTR BDRM
12² x 18⁸

SUNKEN LIVING RM
15⁶ x 15⁹

FPL

FAMILY RM
18⁶ x 14⁹

BDRM 4
10⁰ x 9¹⁰

STORAGE

GARAGE
21⁶ x 21¹¹

LOWER FLOOR

PRIVATE COURT WITH HOT TUB

The luxury master suite is secluded on the first floor. Elegant touches include a library, morning room with built-ins, a bar with wine storage, and a sun porch with French doors into the dining room. The living room and foyer rise to the second floor which is comprised of three large bedrooms and two well-placed baths.

First floor — 2,486 sq. ft.
Second floor — 954 sq. ft.
Basement — 2,486 sq. ft.
Garage — 576 sq. ft.

Total living area:
3,440 sq. ft.

Refer to **Pricing Schedule F** on the order form for pricing information

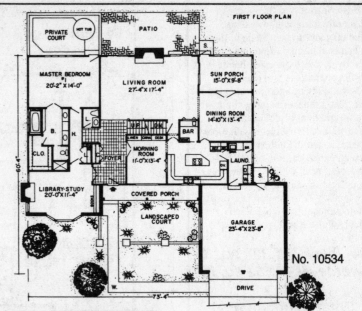

No. 10534

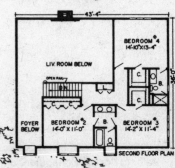

An
EXCLUSIVE DESIGN
By Karl Kreeger

BUILT-IN ENTERTAINMENT

Up-to-date features bring this center hall Colonial into the 20th century. The focus of the Early American living room is a heat-circulating fireplace, framed by decorative pilasters that support dropped beams. Both dining areas open to the rear terrace through sliding glass doors. The convenient mudroom provides access to the two-car garage. Four bedrooms, including the spacious master suite, and two baths occupy the second floor.

First floor — 1,094 sq. ft.
Second floor —
936 sq. ft.
Garage — 441 sq. ft.

Total living area:
2,030 sq. ft.

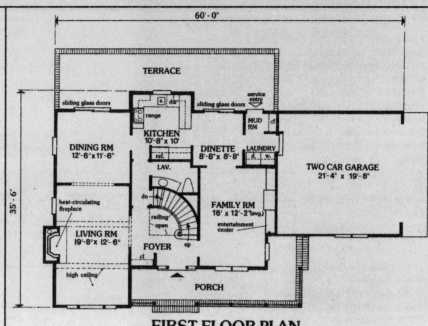

FIRST FLOOR PLAN

No. 90615

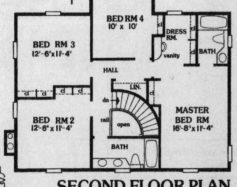

SECOND FLOOR PLAN

Refer to **Pricing Schedule C** on the order form for pricing information

Design 90684

WINDOW BOXES ADD ROMANCE

Practical yet pretty, this ranch home separates active and quiet areas for privacy when you want it. To the left, off the central foyer, you'll find a formal living and dining room combination that's just perfect for entertaining. The wing to the right of the foyer includes three spacious bedrooms and two full baths. Sunlight and warmth pervade the open, informal areas at the rear of the house, where the kitchen, dining bay, and family room enjoy the benefits of a large fireplace and an expansive glass wall overlooking the patio. When the kids come home after a day's play, you'll appreciate the convenient lavatory location just inside the back door. There's plenty of storage space in the garage, just past the mudroom off the kitchen.

Main area — 1,590 sq. ft.
Basement — 900 sq. ft.
Garage — 2-car

Total living area:
1,590 sq. ft.

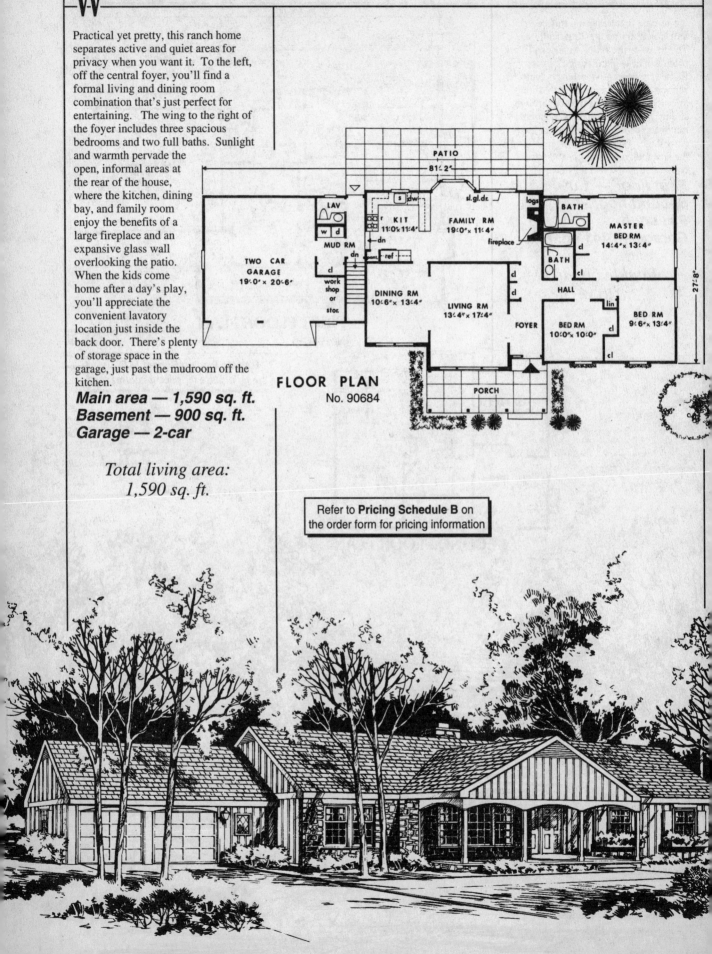

FLOOR PLAN
No. 90684

Refer to **Pricing Schedule B** on
the order form for pricing information

WATCH THE WORLD GO BY

Rain or shine, the wrap-around porch on this Colonial classic is a perfect spot to put up your feet and relax. But, if you want more privacy, retreat to the rear patio instead. Inside, the inviting atmosphere continues in the huge living room with fieldstone fireplace and the island kitchen that opens to the family room. A cozy sewing room and study with full bath flank main living areas. The central staircase off the foyer leads to a massive master suite that shares the upper floor with two ample bedrooms and a third full bath.

First floor — 1,463 sq. ft.
Second floor — 981 sq. ft.
Basement — 814 sq. ft.
Width — 59 ft.
Depth — 34 ft.

Total living area: 2,444 sq. ft.

An
EXCLUSIVE DESIGN
By Westhome Planners, Ltd.

Refer to **Pricing Schedule D** on the order form for pricing information

FIRST FLOOR
No. 90826

UTILITY
9-6x6-0
2895x1828

Lav.

SEWING
9-6x7-0
2895x2133

KITCHEN
11-0x12-3
3352x3733

DINING
13-0x12-3
3962x3733

FAMILY ROOM
13-0x10-0
3962x3048

PATIO

LIVINGROOM
13-0x25-3
3962x7696

STUDY/
GUEST RM.
9-6x11-0
2895x3352

Bath

FOYER

VERANDAH

WIDTH — 59'-0"
DEPTH — 34'-0"

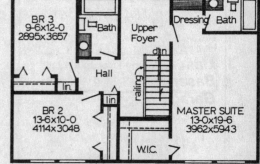

SECOND FLOOR

BR 3
9-6x12-0
2895x3657

Bath

Upper
Foyer

Dressing   Bath

Hall

BR 2
13-6x10-0
4114x3048

MASTER SUITE
13-0x19-6
3962x5943

W.I.C.

BAYS ADD SUNNY ALCOVES

You can reach every room in the house from the entry foyer of this convenient, one-level home. To the left, the quiet area includes two or three bedrooms, depending on your need for a den, office, sewing room, or exercise room. The ample master suite at the rear of the house features a walk-in closet, shower, and private spa tub. To the right off the entry, the Great room's massive fireplace, flanked by huge windows, warms the open living areas. The range island keeps the kitchen and living areas separate without isolating the cook. And, just off the sunny, bayed nook, a huge pantry will give you lots of storage space for those extra groceries. No materials list available for this plan. This plan is available with a crawl space foundation only.

Main area — 1,484 sq. ft.

Total living area: 1,484 sq. ft.

Refer to **Pricing Schedule A** on the order form for pricing information

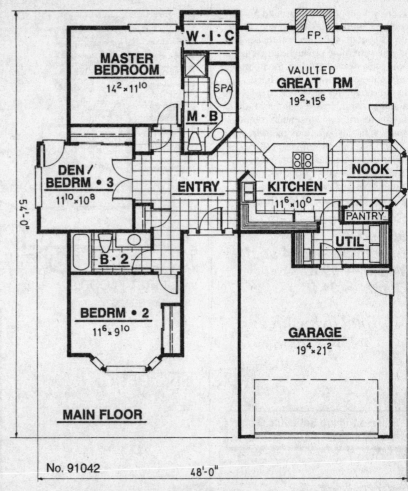

No. 91042   48'-0"

No materials list available

OPEN, SPACIOUS FEELING

Looking for just the right plan for that hillside lot? Here's a design that will fit a smaller lot with a front-to-back or a side-to-side slope. Vaulted ceilings and lots of glass brighten the living areas, arranged to afford a view to the street. The large kitchen and breakfast nook overlook a cozy family room, which opens out onto an attractive patio. Up a short flight of stairs are three roomy bedrooms and family bath. The master suite has its own bathroom, a wall of mirrored closets for dressing and a beautiful vaulted ceiling with clerestory windows overhead.

Lower floor — 1,118 sq. ft.
Upper floor — 688 sq. ft.
Unfinished basement — 380 sq. ft.
Garage — 430 sq. ft.
Width — 40'-0"
Depth — 37'-0"

Total living area: 1,806 sq. ft.

Refer to **Pricing Schedule C** on the order form for pricing information

An EXCLUSIVE DESIGN
By Westhome Planners, Ltd.

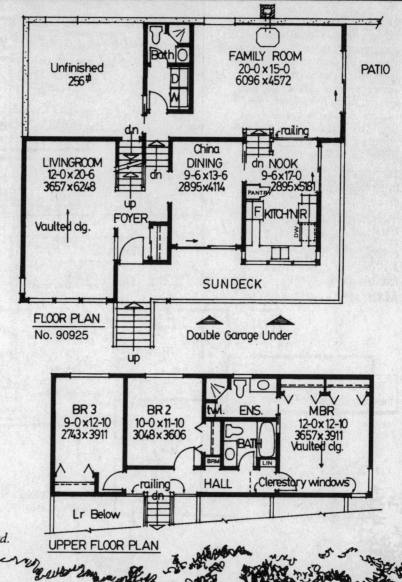

FLOOR PLAN No. 90925

Double Garage Under

UPPER FLOOR PLAN

CAREFREE CONTEMPORARY

This carefree ranch combines vertical siding with rows of tall windows for a contemporary flavor. A covered porch opens to the central foyer, flanked by the formal living and dining rooms. A corner fireplace adds intrigue to the elegant, sunny living room. You'll find another fireplace in the skylit family room at the rear of the house, where a greenhouse bay overlooking the terrace adds an outdoor feeling. Even the adjoining kitchen benefits from this cheerful, sun-washed atmosphere. A hallway to the right leads to the quiet area of the house. The two front bedrooms are served by the double-vanitied hall bath. The master suite boasts a private bath, a backyard view, and loads of closet space.

Main area — 1,597 sq. ft.
Total living area:
1,597 sq. ft.

Refer to **Pricing Schedule B** on the order form for pricing information

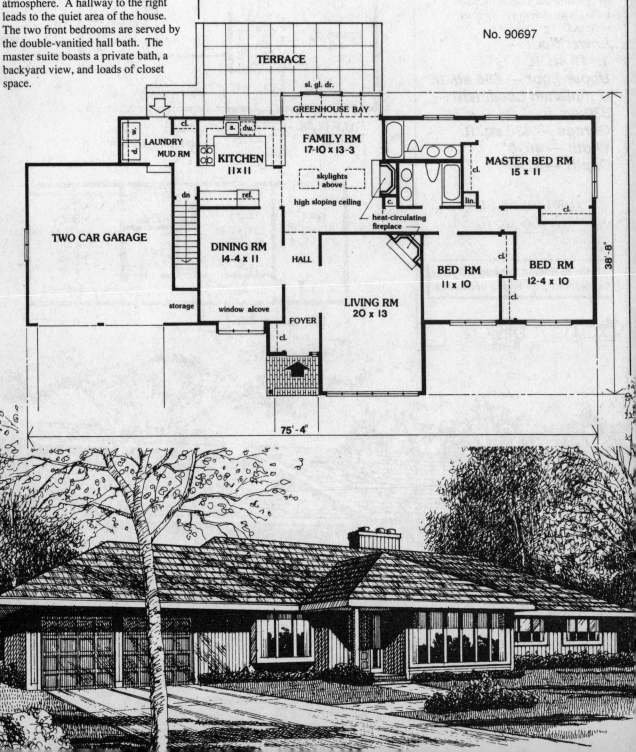

EASY LIVING DESIGN

All amenities of modern home planning have been incorporated into this plan. Perfect for vacation, year-round, or retirement, this house was designed with the handicapped in mind. The vaulted Great room, dining and kitchen areas create a feeling of spaciousness, while lending to a relaxed atmosphere. The kitchen, accented with angles, has an abundance of cabinets for storage and is enhanced by a tiled work island. A glass sliding door leads from the Great room areas to a unique triangular-shaped covered deck. The master bedroom has an ample sized wardrobe, a large covered private deck, and personal bath with double-sink vanity and tub bench. A non-handicapped master bath plan is also available. There are two secondary bedrooms that share a full bath.

Main area — 1,345 sq. ft.
Width — 47'-8"
Depth — 56'-0"

Total living area:
1,345 sq. ft.

Refer to **Pricing Schedule A** on the order form for pricing information

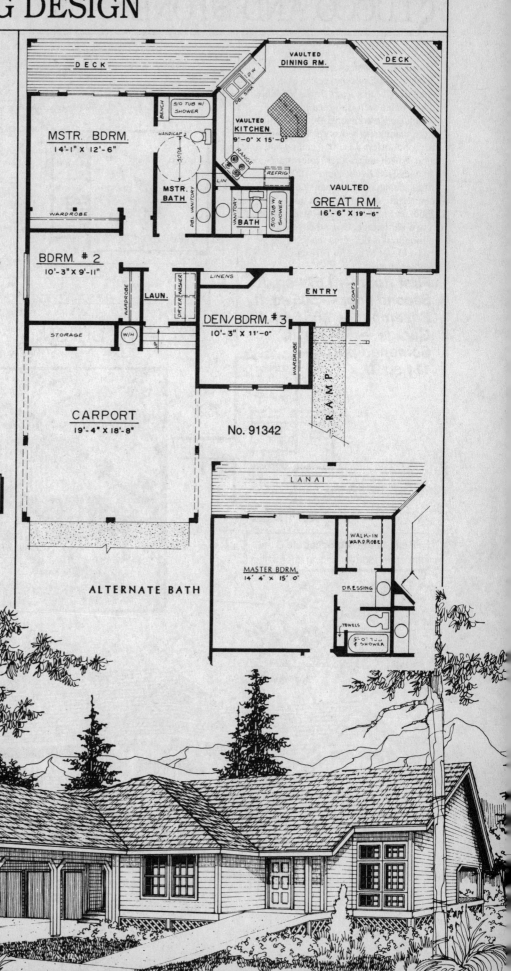

STUCCO AND STONE

This beautiful stucco and stone masonry Tudor design opens to a formal foyer that leads through double doors into a well-designed library which is also conveniently accessible from the master bedroom. The master bedroom offers a vaulted ceiling and a huge bath area. Other features are an oversized living room with a fireplace, an open kitchen and a connecting dining room. A utility room and half bath are located next to a two-car garage. One other select option in this design is the separate cedar closet to use for off-season clothes storage.

First floor — 1,671 sq. ft.
Second floor — 505 sq. ft.
Basement — 1,661 sq. ft.
Garage — 604 sq. ft.
Screened porch — 114 sq. ft.

No. 10555

An **EXCLUSIVE DESIGN** *By Karl Kreeger*

Total living area: 2,176 sq. ft.

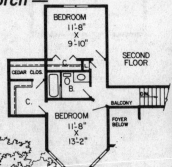

Refer to **Pricing Schedule C** on the order form for pricing information

TILED FOYER GREETS GUESTS

Make a wonderful first impression or return home to this massive, welcoming foyer and step right into the great room of this tastefully appointed design. The great room is enlarged by a wrap-around deck and highlighted by a fireplace, built-in bookcases and wet-bar. The first floor master suite is equally inviting with its spacious dressing area and separate bath. Adjacent to the central great room, the kitchen area has its own built-in desk, octagonal morning room and central island. The second floor includes three bedrooms linked by a balcony which overlooks the open foyer.

First floor — 2,419 sq. ft.
Second floor — 926 sq. ft.
Garage — 615 sq. ft.
Basement — 2,419 sq. ft.

Total living area:
3,345 sq. ft.

Refer to **Pricing Schedule F** on the order form for pricing information

No. 10501

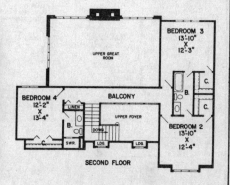

FIRST FLOOR

An EXCLUSIVE DESIGN *By Karl Kreeger*

SECOND FLOOR

Design 90012

MODEST TUDOR WITH A MASSIVE LOOK

Specifically designed to make its presence felt in any neighborhood, this stately Tudor home contains fewer square feet, and is more affordable, than one would imagine. Broken and steeply sloping roof lines, dormers, a large cantilevered bay, and an unique Gothic shaped entrance — as well as the charming stone, brick, and half-timber materials — all add keen interest to the exterior. The living-dining space is an open 34 foot area designed to be an impressive focal point; a large log-burning fireplace is centrally located on the far wall. The triple windows in the front allow for a grand view.

First floor — 1,078 sq. ft.
Second floor — 1,131 sq. ft.

Total living area: 2,209 sq. ft.

Refer to **Pricing Schedule D** on the order form for pricing information

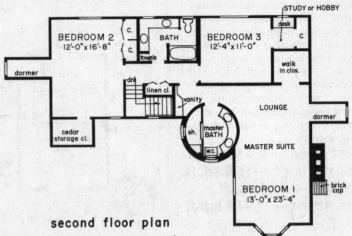

second floor plan

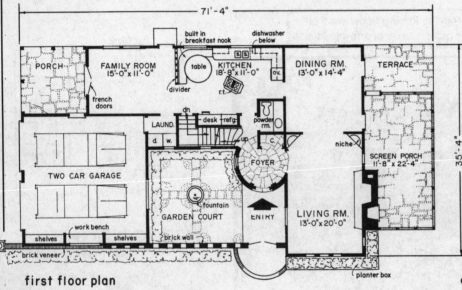

first floor plan
No. 90012

FORMAL BALANCE

Here's a magnificent example of classical design with a contemporary twist. The graceful columns that adorn the facade of this one-level beauty also separate interior spaces without walls. Combined with the half-round windows in the living room, they create an open, elegant feeling throughout formal areas. A bow window in the dining room overlooking the deck echoes the classic image. Kitchen and dinette share the open atmosphere, flowing together into a spacious unit that opens to the rear deck through sliding glass doors. The master suite enjoys a private corner of the deck, complete with hot-tub, double-vanitied bath, and ample closets. Two front-facing bedrooms across the hall share another full bath.

Main area — 1,476 sq. ft.
Basement — 1,361 sq. ft.
Mudroom/laundry — 102 sq. ft.
Garage — 548 sq. ft.

Total living area:
1,476 sq. ft.

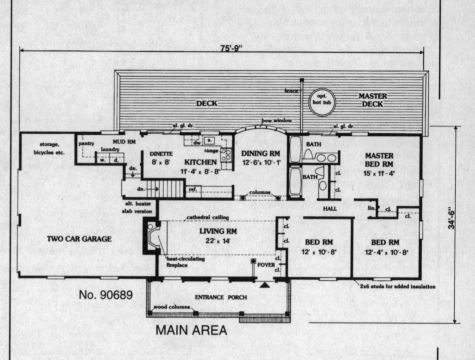

MAIN AREA

Refer to **Pricing Schedule A** on the order form for pricing information

MORNING ROOM ACCENTS

Tiled floors unify the dining and food preparation areas of this masterful design. Located off the well-organized kitchen is a morning room that's perfect for an elegant brunch or some private time before the day begins. Highlighted by a solarium, this octagonal room opens onto the centrally located living room that features built-in bookcases, a fireplace and a wetbar. The family room design employs more tile accents and opens onto the patio. The secluded master bedroom suite features a sunken tub, a small greenhouse for the plant enthusiast and roomy closets.

First floor — 2,466 sq. ft.
Garage — 482 sq. ft.

Total living area:
2,466 sq. ft.

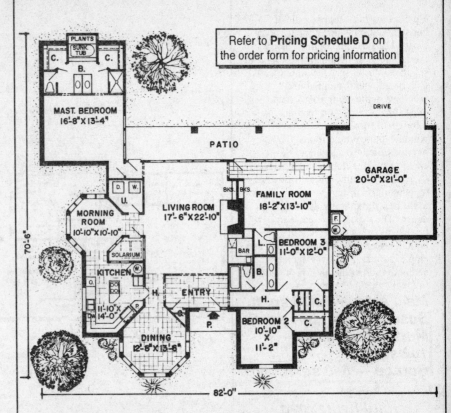

Refer to **Pricing Schedule D** on the order form for pricing information

No. 10445

ACCENT ON SPIRAL STAIRCASE

This roomy kitchen comes complete with a pantry and lots of cabinet space. The unique morning room is complemented with a large fireplace and an entry onto the patio for year 'round enjoyment. All four bedrooms are complete with full baths and walk-in closets.

First floor — 3,282 sq. ft.
Second floor — 956 sq. ft.
Basement — 3,235 sq. ft.
Garage — 936 sq. ft.

Total living area: 4,238 sq. ft.

An **EXCLUSIVE DESIGN** *By Karl Kreeger*

No. 10537

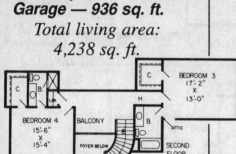

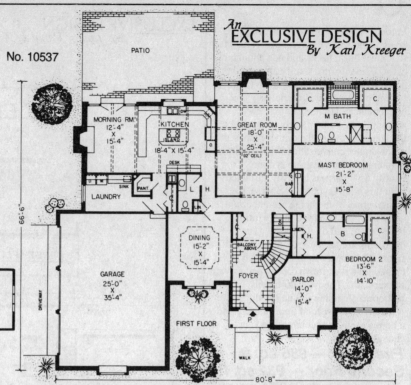

Refer to **Pricing Schedule F** on the order form for pricing information

Design 93216

CONVENIENCE WITH A TOUCH OF CLASS

An
EXCLUSIVE DESIGN
By Jannis Vann & Associates, Inc.

In today's busy world a family depends on efficiency and convenience. This plan will meet those needs and add a touch of class. The informal family areas of this home conveniently run together adding a feeling of space, added efficiency and convenience. Homework may be accomplished in the family room under the watchful eye of the dinner preparer. After-dinner conversations will continue uninterrupted as clean-up is done. Family togetherness is easily sustained with this open layout. Of course, the formal areas of the home are important and this plan includes a lovely formal living room and dining room. The bedrooms are all located on the second floor. The master suite has a touch of class with a decorative ceiling and private master bath. The two additional bedrooms share the full hall bath. There is a convenient second floor laundry and a bonus room to accommodate your changing needs.

First floor — 986 sq. ft.
Second floor — 932 sq. ft.
Bonus room — 274 sq. ft.
Basement — 882 sq. ft.
Garage — 532 sq. ft.

Total living area:
1,918 sq. ft.

Refer to **Pricing Schedule C** on the order form for pricing information

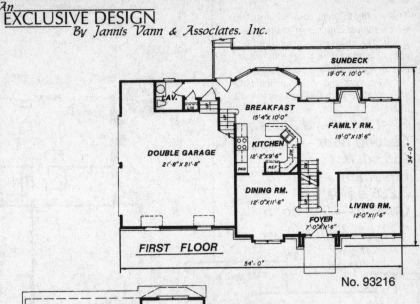

FIRST FLOOR

No. 93216

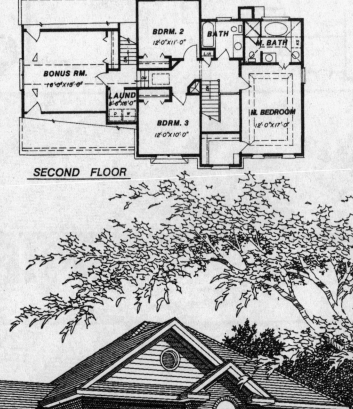

SECOND FLOOR

A LOT OF LIVING SPACE

There's a lot of living space in this four bedroom home with brick trim. Expansive windows in the vaulted living room allow for plenty of light, and the corner is the perfect place for a wood stove. The kitchen is generously sized and close to the garage for ease in unloading groceries. Two secondary bedrooms, one with a walk-in closet, share the main bath. There is a plant shelf above the staircase, which leads to the master suite and loft or optional bedrooms. The master suite bath features a skylight and walk-in closet. No materials list available for this plan.

First floor — 1,076 sq. ft.
Second floor — 449 sq. ft.

Total living area: 1,525 sq. ft.

Refer to **Pricing Schedule B** on the order form for pricing information

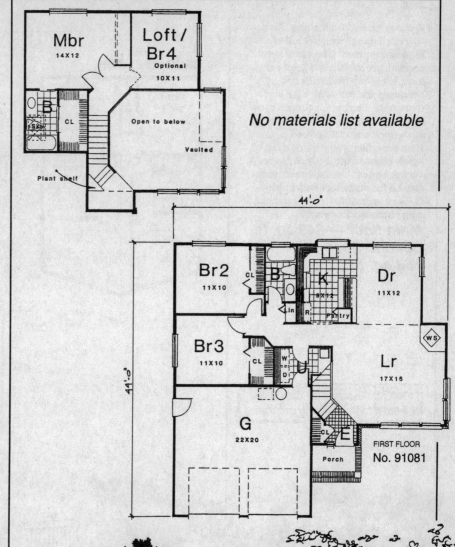

No materials list available

Mbr 14X12

Loft / Br4 Optional 10X11

B SKY CL

Open to below

Vaulted

Plant shelf

44'-0"

Br2 11X10 · CL · B · K 9X12 · Dr 11X12

ln R Pantry

Br3 11X10 · CL · W/D · Lr 17X15

WS

G 22X20 · CL · E

Porch

FIRST FLOOR
No. 91081

11'-0"

A CLASSY GLASSED FRONT

A classy glassed front graces this new A-framed design which is full of pleasant surprises. The use of shed dormers not only gives a great exterior look, but also provides the two bedrooms and bath with a full eight foot ceiling height. An attractive vaulted ceiling is visible from the rest of the roof, and one can look down from the railing to the living room below in the handy loft/study area. A very generous sized mudroom/ utility area on the main floor with nearby lavatory is great for family returning home from work or play.

**Main floor — 843 sq. ft.
Second floor —
768 sq. ft.**

*Total living area:
1,611 sq. ft.*

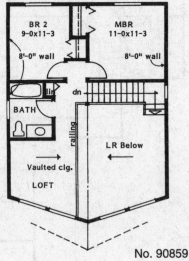

SECOND FLOOR

An
EXCLUSIVE DESIGN
By Westhome Planners. Ltd.

No. 90859

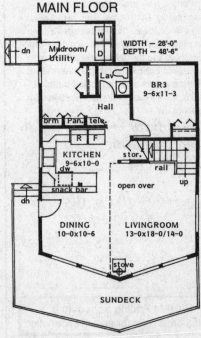

MAIN FLOOR

WIDTH — 28'-0"
DEPTH — 48'-6"

Refer to **Pricing Schedule B** on the order form for pricing information

A-FRAME UPDATE

Here's a superb home that truly defines the term "open space". You'll feel the spectacular spaciousness of this updated A-frame the moment you walk past the foyer and peek through the galley kitchen. Savor the view through the two-story glass walls in the fireplaced living/dining room surrounded by an outdoor deck. Look up at the towering ceilings crowned by an open loft. Even the bedrooms are exceptionally large. The master suite, including a private powder room, and a second bedroom lie at the rear of the first floor, as well as an adjoining full bath. The loft overlooking active areas shares the second floor with an expansive bedroom with its own private deck and full bath.

First floor — 1,086 sq. ft.
Second floor —
466 sq. ft.
Basement — 1,080 sq. ft.

Total living area:
1,552 sq. ft.

Refer to **Pricing Schedule B** on the order form for pricing information

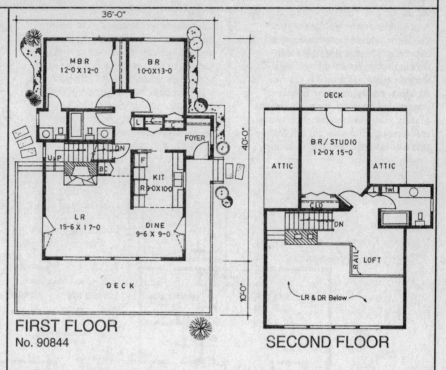

FIRST FLOOR
No. 90844

An
EXCLUSIVE DESIGN
By Westhome Planners, Ltd.

SECOND FLOOR

ALL THIS ON ONE LEVEL

A gracious feeling welcomes you inside the double entrance doors as you experience natural sky lights and flowing space enhanced by a high-sloped ceiling. Featured is the free-standing, heat-circulating fireplace surrounded by stone, to mantle height. Sliding glass doors connect to a large rear terrace. The adjacent informal space of kitchen, dinette and family room share an openness. The dinette has access to a private dining terrace and the laundry room leading to the garage, to the basement or to the side service entrance. The private bedroom wing contains two large bedrooms, a bath and a master suite off a short corridor. This suite consists of a generously-sized bedroom connecting to a bath with double sinks.

**Main living area —
1,629 sq. ft.
Laundry/mudroom —
107 sq. ft.
Garage — 424 sq. ft.
Basement — 1,457 sq. ft.**

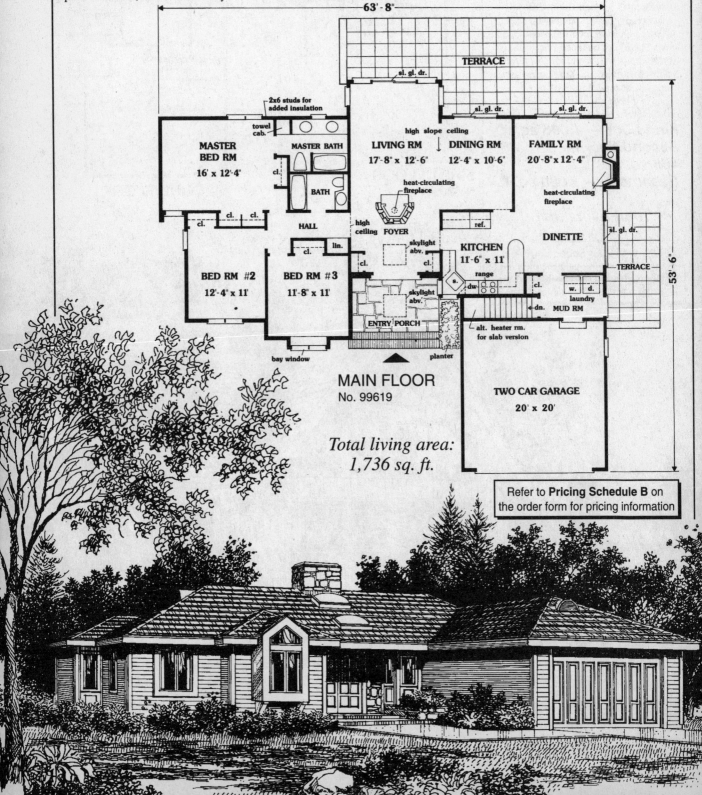

MAIN FLOOR
No. 99619

*Total living area:
1,736 sq. ft.*

Refer to **Pricing Schedule B** on the order form for pricing information

THREE BEDROOM TRADITIONAL CAPE

This three bedroom traditional Cape design, has a welcoming full-length country porch. Although this home is classified as small, it has a lot of potential for a growing family. The master suite has its own master bath with mirrored vanity, stall shower and step-up whirlpool spa. Upstairs the secondary bedrooms share a full bath. Completing the first floor is the U-shaped kitchen, the powder room, dining room and the living room with a log burning, brick faced fireplace. No materials list available for this plan.

First floor — 913 sq. ft.
Second floor —
581 sq. ft.

Total living area:
1,494 sq. ft.

Refer to **Pricing Schedule A** on the order form for pricing information

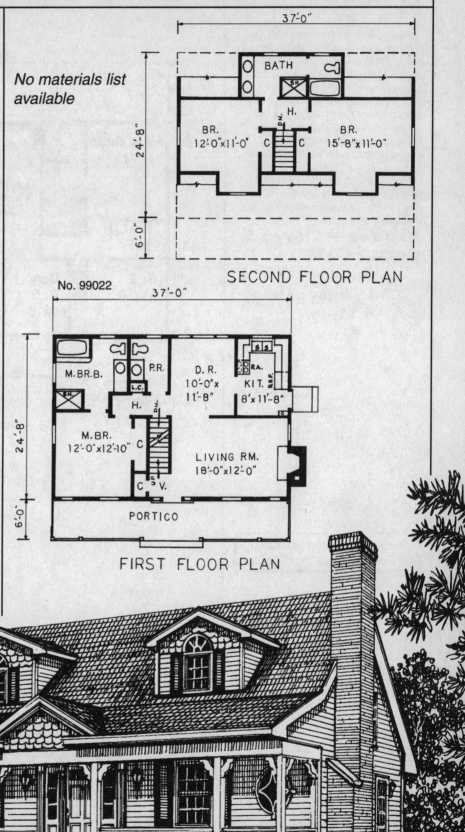

No materials list available

SECOND FLOOR PLAN

37'-0"
24'-8"
6'-0"

BATH
BR. 12'-0"x11'-0"
BR. 15'-8"x11'-0"
H.
DN.
C
C

FIRST FLOOR PLAN

No. 99022
37'-0"
24'-8"
6'-0"

M.BR.B.
P.R.
D. R. 10'-0"x 11'-8"
KIT. 8'x11'-8"
L.C.
H.
M.BR. 12'-0"x12'-10"
C
LIVING RM. 18'-0"x12'-0"
C
V.

PORTICO

Affordable Ranch

This simple-to-frame Ranch adds the right touches where they count the most. From the vaulted entry, with garage access, there is a view of the corner fireplace and the rear yard, which can be seen through the sliding glass doors of the vaulted living and dining rooms. The kitchen opens to the living areas and overlooks the covered corner patio which can easily be screened in. The three bedrooms include one with a double door den option, opening to the living room, and a full master bedroom with private full bath and walk-in closet.

Main area — 1,159 sq. ft
Garage — 2-car

Total living area:
1,159 sq. ft.

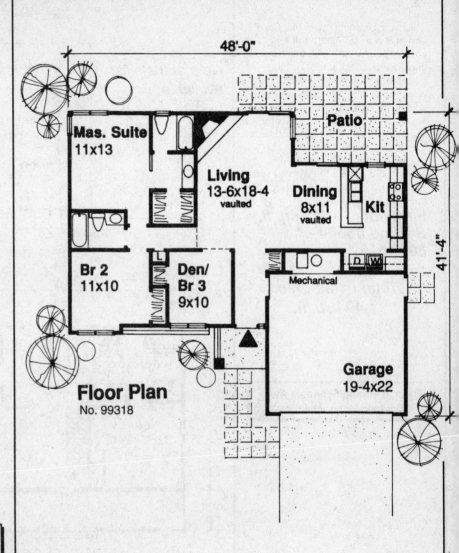

Floor Plan
No. 99318

NOSTALGIC CHARM

This home combines contemporary features such as dramatic vaulted ceilings, loft, well-equipped kitchen and energy efficiency. Outside, the nostalgic character is created by the covered front porch, curved arch and decorative support posts, lattice trim, divided sash and stone chimney accent. Inside, the vaulted foyer opens to the sunken living room with fireplace, vaulted ceiling with loft overlook, corner windows with transom glass above, and a focal point library alcove with quaint window seat.

Main floor — 744 sq. ft.
Upper floor — 833 sq. ft.
Garage — 2-car

Total living area:
1,577 sq. ft.

Refer to **Pricing Schedule B** on the order form for pricing information

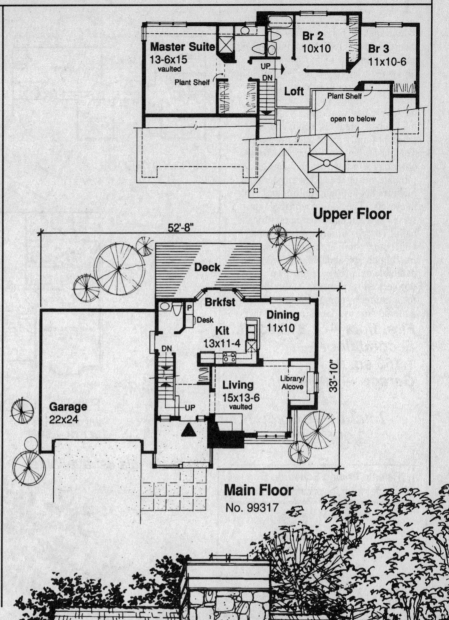

Upper Floor

Master Suite 13-6x15 vaulted · Plant Shelf · UP · DN · Br 2 10x10 · Br 3 11x10-6 · Loft · Plant Shelf · open to below

Main Floor
No. 99317

52'-8" · 33'-10"

Deck · Brkfst · Desk · P · Kit 13x11-4 · Dining 11x10 · Living 15x13-6 vaulted · Library/Alcove · DN · UP · Garage 22x24

TRADITIONAL ELEGANCE

Traditional in character, this eye-pleaser features twin bay windows and an angled garage. The foyer opens to the two-story living room beyond. The formal dining room is located on the front of the home and features one of the lovely bay windows. Nearby are the kitchen, breakfast room and adjacent family room with fireplace. The master bedroom is notable for the other bay window, which forms an intimate sitting area. The master bath includes his-and-her vanities and walk-in closets. The angled whirlpool tub serves as a dramatic focal point for the bath. Three bedrooms, a bath and a huge game room are located upstairs. In addition, expandable area is available over the garage. Two dormers allow plenty of natural light for a future, in-home office. No materials list available for this plan.

First floor — 1,832 sq. ft.
Second floor —
1,163 sq. ft.
Garage — 591 sq. ft.

Total living area:
2,995 sq. ft.

Refer to **Pricing Schedule E** on the order form for pricing information

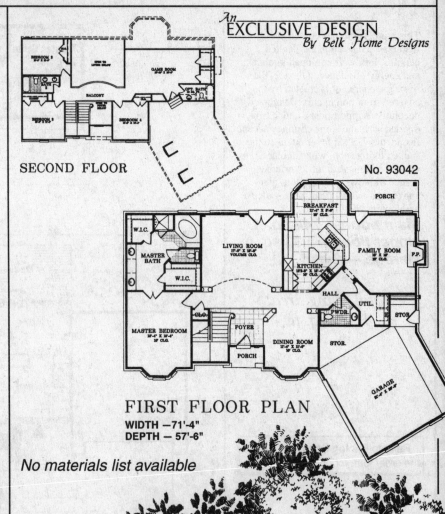

An EXCLUSIVE DESIGN
By Belk Home Designs

SECOND FLOOR

No. 93042

FIRST FLOOR PLAN
WIDTH —71'-4"
DEPTH — 57'-6"

No materials list available

FOR AN INFORMAL LIFESTYLE

You'll find daily living relaxed and comfortable in this stylish plan. Both the Great room and the kitchen/dining room of this home are accented by vaulted ceilings. In addition to having a conveniently arranged L-shaped food preparation center, the dining area overlooks the deck through sliding glass doors. The Great room incorporates all adjacent floor space and is highlighted by the corner placement of the fireplace. Two bedrooms are secluded from the living areas and feature individual access to the full bath. The master bedroom also includes a separate vanity in the dressing area.

Main area — 988 sq. ft.
Basement — 988 sq. ft.
Garage — 400 sq. ft.

Total living area:
988 sq. ft.

Refer to **Pricing Schedule A** on the order form for pricing information

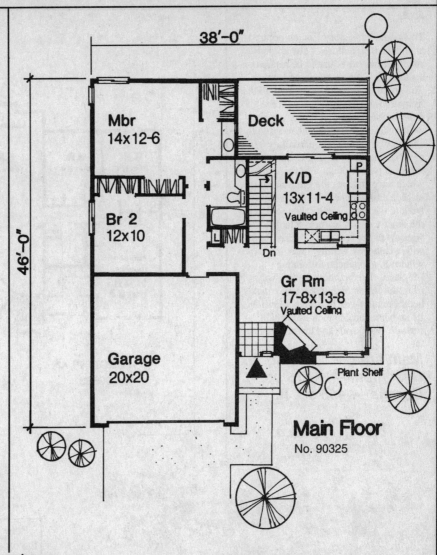

38'-0"

46'-0"

Mbr
14x12-6

Deck

Br 2
12x10

K/D
13x11-4
Vaulted Ceiling

Dn

Gr Rm
17-8x13-8
Vaulted Ceiling

Garage
20x20

Plant Shelf

Main Floor
No. 90325

ANGLED CONTEMPORARY

This angled one story Contemporary is abundant with features. The angled shape allows the house to be rotated on a site to give the optimum orientation. The spacious foyer opens widely to the living room which merges with the dining room. The combined space, each distinguishable, is enhanced with sliding glass doors to a partially covered terrace. Moving to the informal part of the house, the space which encompasses the family room, kitchen and dinette flows from the front to the rear. The kitchen separates the dinette which features a large window in the rear and a family room with a cathedral ceiling, large windows, and a heat-circulating fireplace. The bedroom wing, away from the action, features a large master bedroom also with a cathedral ceiling. Its lavish bathroom includes a stall shower, two basins and a whirlpool tub.

Main area — 1,798 sq. ft.
Basement — 1,715 sq. ft.
Garage — 456 sq. ft.

Total living area:
1,798 sq. ft.

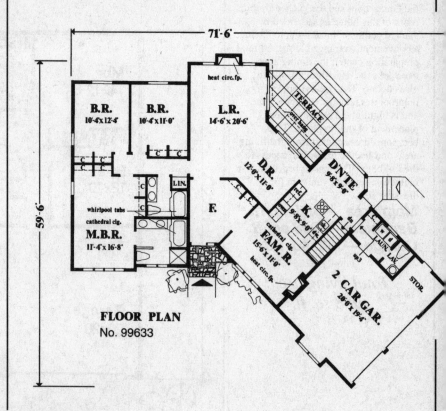

FLOOR PLAN
No. 99633

Refer to **Pricing Schedule B** on the order form for pricing information

OUTDOOR EXCITEMENT

Here's one-level living with an exciting outdoor feeling. The drama begins in the vaulted-foyer, flooded with natural light by an arched window high overhead. Look into the sunken living room for a sweeping view of the decks, backyard, and formal dining room that adjoins. Step past the open staircase to a comfortable, informal area that includes an efficient kitchen with built-in pantry, a sunny breakfast nook, and a sunken, fireplaced family room with sliders to the deck. Even the bedrooms, tucked down a hallway off the foyer for privacy, enjoy a cheerful atmosphere. Both front bedrooms, which share a hall bath, feature built-in desks with a view. And the master suite is a delight, with its private deck and luxurious bath.

Main area — 1,870 sq. ft.
Garage — 2-car

Total living area:
1,870 sq. ft.

Refer to **Pricing Schedule C** on the order form for pricing information

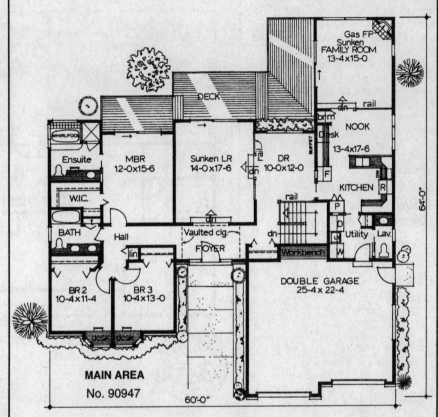

Gas FP
Sunken
FAMILY ROOM
13-4x15-0

DECK

NOOK
13-4x17-6

MBR
12-0x15-6

Sunken LR
14-0x17-6

DR
10-0x12-0

Ensuite

WHIRLPOOL

W.I.C.

KITCHEN

BATH

Hall

Vaulted clg.

FOYER

Utility   Lav.

Workbench

BR 2
10-4x11-4

BR 3
10-4x13-0

DOUBLE GARAGE
25-4 x 22-4

64'-0"

60'-0"

MAIN AREA
No. 90947

An
EXCLUSIVE DESIGN
By Westhome Planners. Ltd.

CAREFREE CONVENIENCE

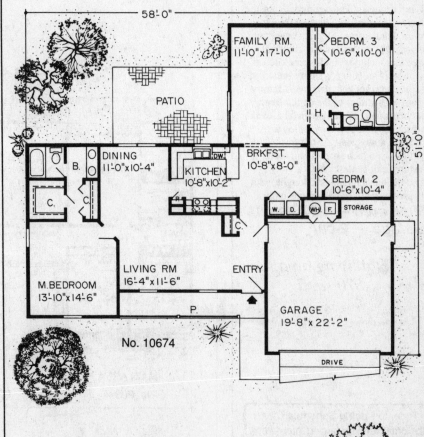

Design 10674

One-level living is a breeze in this attractive, three bedroom beauty designed with your budget in mind. The covered porch adds a romantic touch to the clapboard facade. Step through the front door into a huge living room. Active areas surrounding a spacious patio at the rear of the house are served by a centrally-located galley kitchen. Eat in the formal dining room, or the handy breakfast room that adjoins the huge family room. A short hall leads to a handy full bath and two bedrooms. The master suite, tucked off the living room, features double closets and vanities for early-morning convenience.

Main living area —
1,600 sq. ft.
Garage — 465 sq. ft.

Total living area:
1,600 sq. ft.

Refer to **Pricing Schedule B** on the order form for pricing information

No. 10674

PLAN YIELDS LOTS OF LIVING SPACE

The sloped ceilings of this well-designed home's living and dining rooms, plus the central, open stairway, create a spacious, inviting living area. The efficient, U-shaped kitchen is well located with access to the dining room, the laundry area and the lavatory. It has direct access outside too, so bringing in the groceries is less of a chore. The first floor bedroom has double closets and a private bath. The two second floor bedrooms share a bath on the upstairs hall where two large linen closets are located. Each bedroom has ample closet space.

First floor — 872 sq. ft.
Second floor — 483 sq. ft.

Total living area:
1,355 sq. ft.

Refer to **Pricing Schedule A** on the order form for pricing information

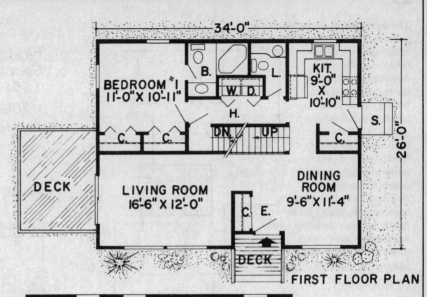

FIRST FLOOR PLAN

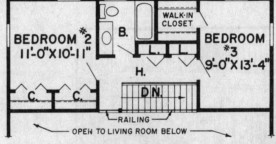

SECOND FLOOR PLAN

No. 10519

DESIGNED FOR ENTERTAINING

Design 10587

The double doors of the vaulted entry are just a hint of the graceful touches in this three-bedroom home. Curves soften the stairway, deck, and the huge bar that runs between the formal and informal dining areas. Skylights, bay, and bump-out windows flood every room with light. And when the sun goes down, you can keep things cozy with fireplaces in the family and sunken living rooms. For a quiet retreat, sneak upstairs to the deck off the master bedroom suite.

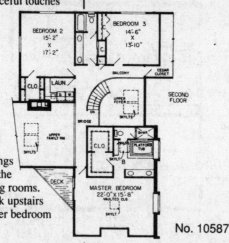

No. 10587

First floor — 2,036 sq. ft.
Second floor —
1,554 sq. ft.
Garage — 533 sq. ft.
Total living area:
3,590 sq. ft.

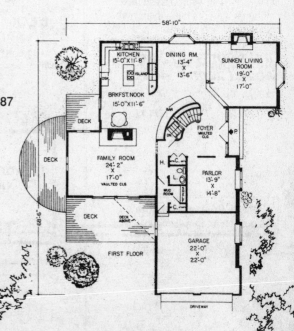

Refer to **Pricing Schedule F** on the order form for pricing information

RUSTIC COMFORT AND CHARM

Hanging plants would make for a magnificent entrance to this charming home. Walk into the fireplaced living room brightened by a wonderful picture window. The kitchen and dining area are separated by a counter island featuring double sinks. In the hallway, toward the bedrooms, is a linen closet and full bath. The master bedroom features its own private bath and double closets. The two other bedrooms have good-sized closets, keeping clutter to a minimum. Many windows throughout this home lighten up each room, creating a warm cozy atmosphere. Please indicate slab, crawl space or basement foundation when ordering.

Main area — 1,146 sq. ft.

Total living area: 1,146 sq. ft.

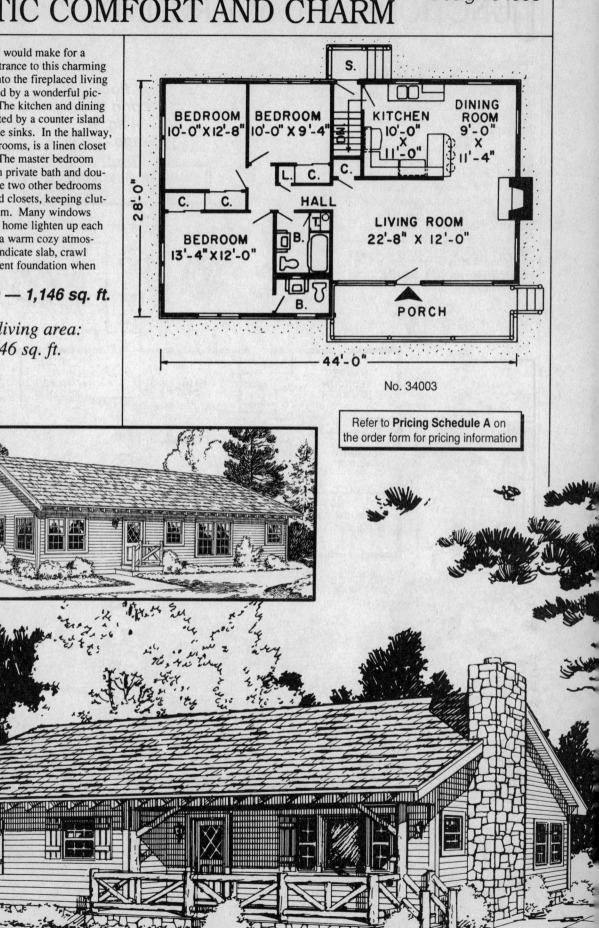

BEDROOM 10'-0" X 12'-8"

BEDROOM 10'-0" X 9'-4"

KITCHEN 10'-0" X 11'-0"

DINING ROOM 9'-0" X 11'-4"

S.

L. C.

C.

C.

C.

HALL

BEDROOM 13'-4" X 12'-0"

B.

T.

B.

LIVING ROOM 22'-8" X 12'-0"

PORCH

28'-0"

44'-0"

No. 34003

FUNCTIONAL FAMILY ROOM

Creating the focal point in the family room is a heat circulating fireplace, encased in masonry and faced with cut stone. Bookshelves, a T.V. shelf and wood storage area fit into the stone flanking the fireplace. The family room flows through an eating bar to the kitchen. A utility room is handily tucked around the corner behind the kitchen and has access to both the double garage and the outdoors. Secluded on the other side of the family room are three bedrooms, a bath and master bedroom suite.

First floor —1,954 sq. ft.
Garage — 431 sq. ft.

Total living area:
1,954 sq. ft.

Refer to **Pricing Schedule C** on the order form for pricing information

No. 1064

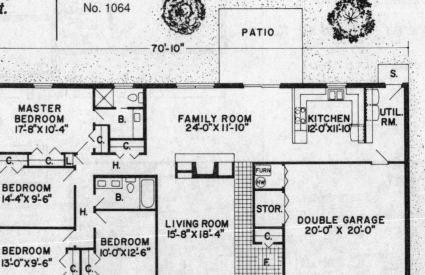

TRADITIONAL ENERGY-SAVER

Design 20071

Take advantage of a southern exposure and save on energy costs in this beautiful family Tudor. Heat is stored in the floor of the sun room, adjoining the living and breakfast rooms. When the sun goes down, close the French doors and light a fire in the massive fireplace. State-of-the-art energy saving is not the only modern convenience in this house. You'll love the balcony overlooking the soaring two-story foyer and living room. In addition to providing great views, the balcony links the upstairs bedrooms. You're sure to enjoy the island kitchen, centrally located between formal and informal dining rooms. And, you'll never want to leave the luxurious master suite, with its double vanities and step-up whirlpool.

First floor — 2,186 sq. ft.
Second floor — 983 sq. ft.
Basement — 2,186 sq. ft.
Garage — 704 sq. ft.

Total living area: 3,169 sq. ft.

Refer to **Pricing Schedule E** on the order form for pricing information

No. 20071

An **EXCLUSIVE DESIGN** *By Karl Kreeger*

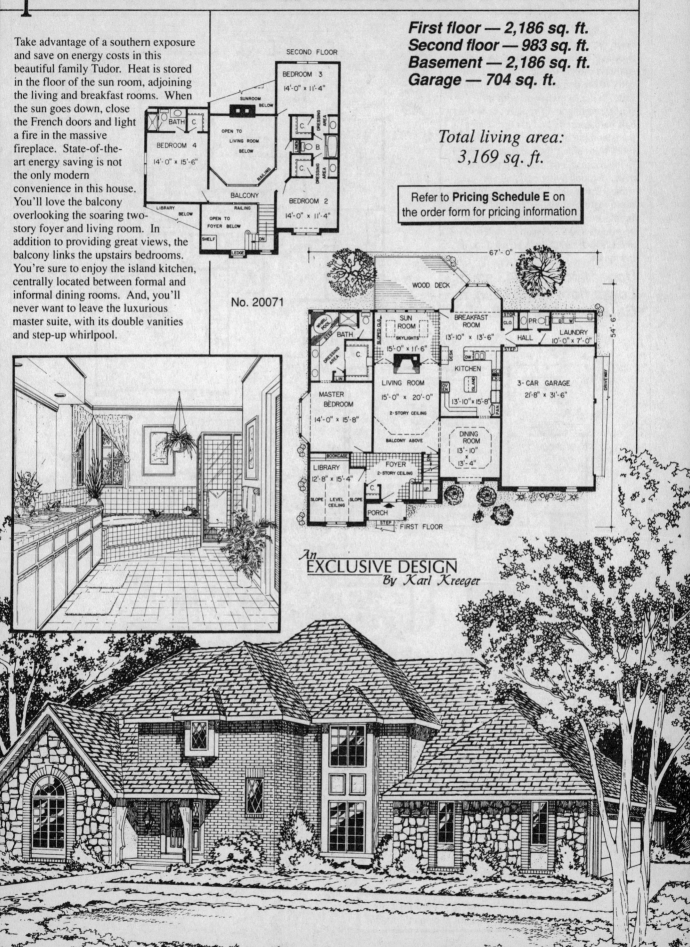

Design 10595

PERFECT FOR A HILLSIDE

From the road, the appearance of this two-level home is deceiving. A central staircase directs traffic from the front entry to the den and master bedroom suite, to the living room, with its sloping ceiling and fireplace, or to the half bath, laundry and garage. Enter the island kitchen and formal dining room from either the breakfast or the living rooms. Two screened porches make outdoor living easy, rain or shine. Downstairs, the huge recreation room features a kitchenette and fireplace for entertaining. Two more bedrooms and a full bath complete this level, which could even be used for in-law quarters.

Upper floor — 1,643 sq. ft.
Lower floor — 1,297 sq. ft.
Garage — 528 sq. ft.

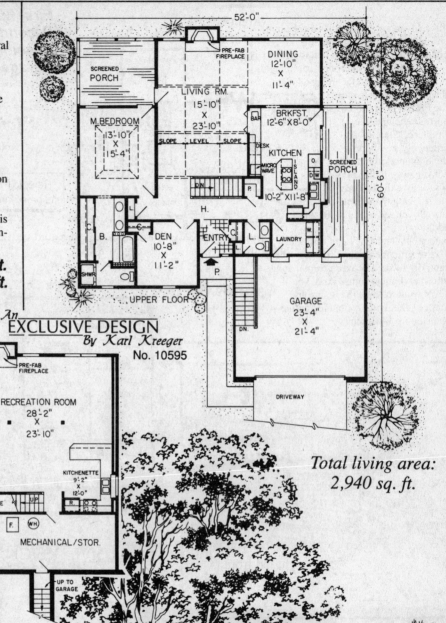

An EXCLUSIVE DESIGN *By Karl Kreeger*
No. 10595

Total living area:
2,940 sq. ft.

Refer to **Pricing Schedule E** on the order form for pricing information

Ignoring Copyright Laws Can Be A $1,000,000 Mistake

Recent changes in the US copyright laws allow for statutory penalties of up to **$100,000** per incident for copyright infringement involving any of the copyrighted plans found in this publication. The law can be confusing. So, for your own protection, take the time to understand what you can and cannot do when it comes to home plans.

——— What You Cannot Do ———

You Cannot Duplicate Home Plans

Purchasing a set of blueprints and making additional sets by reproducing the original is *illegal*. If you need multiple sets of a particular home plan, then you must purchase them.

You Cannot Copy Any Part of a Home Plan to Create Another

Creating your own plan by copying even part of a home design found in this publication is called "creating a derivative work" and is *illegal* unless you have permission to do so.

You Cannot Build a Home Without a License

You must have specific permission or license to build a home from a copyrighted design, even if the finished home has been changed from the original plan. It is *illegal* to build one of the homes found in this publication without a license.

What Garlinghouse Offers

Home Plan Blueprint Package

By purchasing a single or multiple set package of blueprints from Garlinghouse, you not only receive the physical blueprint documents necessary for construction, but you are also granted a license to build one, and only one, home. You can also make any changes to our design that you wish, as long as these changes are made directly on the blueprints purchased from Garlinghouse and no additional copies are made.

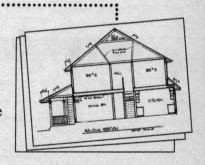

Home Plan Vellums

By purchasing vellums for one of our home plans, you receive the same construction drawings found in the blueprints, but printed on vellum paper. Vellums can be erased and are perfect for making design changes. They are also semi-transparent making them easy to duplicate. But most importantly, the purchase of home plan vellums comes with a broader license that allows you to make changes to the design (ie, create a hand drawn or CAD derivative work), to make an unlimited number of copies of the plan, and to build up to three homes from the plan.

License To Build Additional Homes

With the purchase of a blueprint package or vellums you automatically receive a license to build one home or three homes, respectively. If you want to build more homes than you are licensed to build through your purchase of a plan, then additional licenses may be purchased at reasonable costs from Garlinghouse. Inquire for more information.

You've Picked Your Dream Home!

You can already see it standing on your lot... you can see yourselves in your new home... enjoying family, entertaining guests, celebrating holidays. All that remains ahead are the details. That's where we can help. Whether you plan to build-it-yourself, be your own contractor, or hand your plans over to an outside contractor, your Garlinghouse blueprints provide the perfect beginning for putting yourself in your dream home right away.

We even make it simple for you to make professional design modifications. We can also provide a materials list for greater economy.

My grandfather, L.F. Garlinghouse, started a tradition of quality when he founded this company in 1907. For over 85 years, homeowners and builders have relied on us for accurate, complete, professional blueprints. Our plans help you get results fast... and save money, too! These pages will give you all the information you need to order. So get started now... I know you'll love your new Garlinghouse home!

Sincerely,

TYPICAL WALL SECTIONS

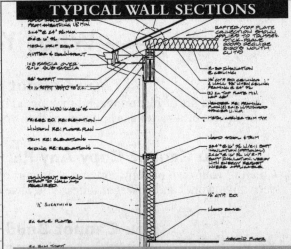

Detailed views of your exterior walls, as though sliced from top to bottom. These drawings clarify exterior wall construction insulation, flooring, and roofing details. Depending on your specific geography and climate, your home will be built with either 2x4 or 2x6 exterior walls. Most professional contractors can easily adapt plans for either requirement.

KITCHEN & BATH CABINET DETAILS

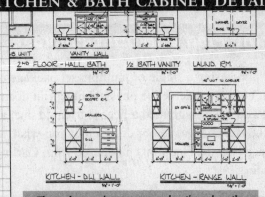

These plans or, in some cases, elevations show the specific details and placement of the cabinets in your kitchen and bathrooms as applicable. Customizing these areas is simpler beginning with these details. Kitchen and bath cabinet details are available for most plans featured in our collection.

EXTERIOR ELEVATIONS

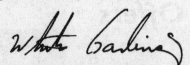

Exact scale views of the front, rear and both sides of your home, showing exterior materials, details, and all necessary measurements.

DETAILED FLOOR PLANS

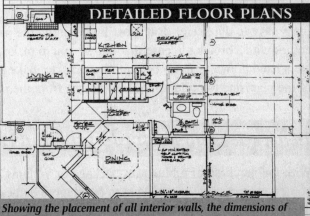

Showing the placement of all interior walls, the dimensions of rooms, doors, windows, stairways, and other details.

ke Your Dream Come True!

or home designs by respected professionals.

FIREPLACE DETAILS

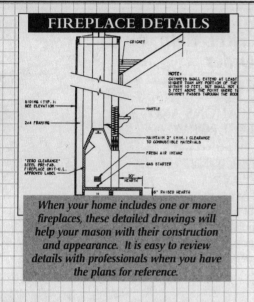

When your home includes one or more fireplaces, these detailed drawings will help your mason with their construction and appearance. It is easy to review details with professionals when you have the plans for reference.

TYPICAL CROSS SECTION

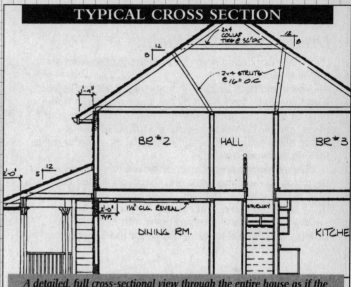

A detailed, full cross-sectional view through the entire house as if the house was cut from top to bottom. This elevation allows a contractor to better understand the interconnections of the construction components.

FOUNDATION PLAN

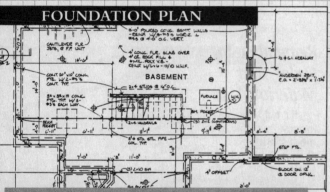

With footings and all load-bearing points applicable to your home, including all necessary notation and dimensions. The type of foundation supplied varies from home to home. Local conditions and practices will determine whether a basement, crawlspace or a slab is best for you. Your professional contractor can easily make the necessary adaption.

SCHEMATIC ELECTRICAL LAYOUTS

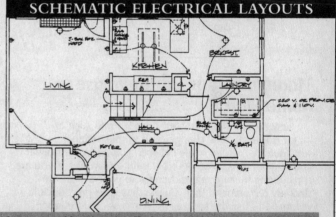

The suggested locations for all of your switches, outlets and fixtures are indicated on these drawings. They are practical as they are, but they are also a solid taking-off point for any personal adaptions.

ROOF PLAN

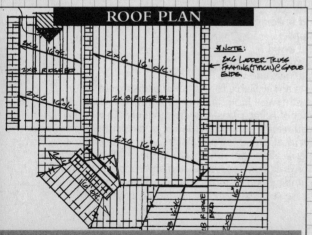

All information necessary to construct the roof for your home is included. Many blueprints contain framing plans showing all of the roof elements, so you'll know how these details look and fit together.

STAIR DETAILS

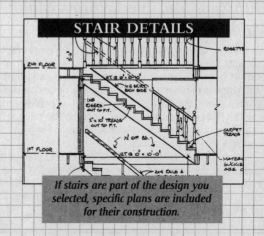

If stairs are part of the design you selected, specific plans are included for their construction.

GARLINGHOUSE OPTIONS & EXTRAS
MAKE THE DREAM TRULY YOURS.

Reversed Plans Can Make Your Dream Home Just Right!

"That's our dream home... if only the garage were on the other side!"

You could have exactly the home you want by flipping it end-for-end. Check it out by holding your dream home page of this book up to a mirror. Then simply order your plans "reversed". We'll send you one full set of mirror-image plans (with the writing backwards) as a master guide for you and your builder.

The remaining sets of your order will come as shown in this book so the dimensions and specifications are easily read on the job site... but they will be specially stamped "REVERSED" so there is no construction confusion.

We can only send reversed plans with multiple-set orders. But, there is no extra charge for this service.

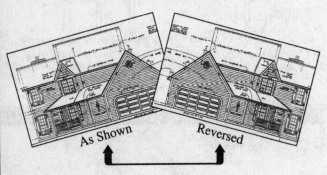

As Shown   Reversed

Modifying Your Garlinghouse Home Plan

Easy modifications to your dream home such as minor non-structural changes and simple material substitutions, can be made between you and your builder and marked directly on your blueprints. However, if you are considering making major changes to your design, we strongly recommend that you purchase our reproducible vellums and use the services of a professional designer or architect. Modifications are not available for plan numbers 90,000 and above. For additional information call us at 1-203-343-5977.

Our Reproducible Vellums Make Modifications Easier

With a vellum copy of our plans, a design professional can alter the drawings just the way you want, then you can print as many copies of the modified plans as you need. And, since you have already started with our complete detailed plans, the cost of those expensive professional services will be significantly less. Refer to the price schedule for vellum costs. Call for vellum availability for plan numbers 90,000 and above.

Reproducible vellum copies of our home plans are only sold under the terms of a license agreement that you will receive with your order. Should you not agree to the terms, then the vellums may be returned unopened for a full refund.

Yours FREE With Your Order

FREE
SPECIFICATIONS AND CONTRACT FORM

provides the perfect way for you and your builder to agree on the exact materials to use in building and finishing your home before you start construction. A must for homeowner's peace of mind.

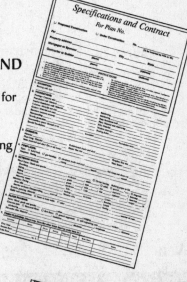

Remember To Order Your Materials List

It'll help you save money. Available at a modest additional charge, the Materials List gives the quantity, dimensions, and specifications for the major materials needed to build your home. You will get faster, more accurate bids from your contractors and building suppliers — and avoid paying for unused materials and waste. Materials Lists are available for all home plans except as otherwise indicated, but can only be ordered with a set of home plans. Due to differences in regional requirements and homeowner or builder preferences... electrical, plumbing and heating/air conditioning equipment specifications are not designed specifically for each plan. However, detailed typical prints of residential electrical, plumbing and construction guidelines can be provided. Please see next page for additional information.

Questions?

Call our customer service number at 1-203-343-5977.

How Many Sets Of Plans Will You Need?

The Standard 8-Set Construction Package

Our experience shows that you'll speed every step of construction and avoid costly building errors by ordering enough sets to go around. Each tradesperson wants a set — the general contractor and all subcontractors; foundation, electrical, plumbing, heating/air conditioning, drywall, finish carpenters, and cabinet shop. Don't forget your lending institution, building department and, of course, a set for yourself.

The Minimum 5-Set Construction Package

If you're comfortable with arduous follow-up, this package can save you a few dollars by giving you the option of passing down plan sets as work progresses. You might have enough copies to go around if work goes exactly as scheduled and no plans are lost or damaged. But for only $40 more, the 8-set package eliminates these worries.

The Single-Set Decision-Maker Package

We offer this set so you can study the blueprints to plan your dream home in detail. But remember... one set is never enough to build your home... and they're copyrighted.

New Plan Details For The Home Builder

Because local codes and requirements vary greatly, we recommend that you obtain drawings and bids from licensed contractors to do your mechanical plans. However, if you want to know more about techniques — and deal more confidently with subcontractors — we offer these remarkably useful detail sheets. Each is an excellent tool that will enhance your understanding of these technical subjects.

Residential Construction Details

Eight sheets that cover the essentials of stick-built residential home construction. Details foundation options - poured concrete basement, concrete block, or monolithic concrete slab. Shows all aspects of floor, wall, and roof framing. Provides details for roof dormers, eaves, and skylights. Conforms to requirements of Uniform Building code or BOCA code. Includes a quick index.

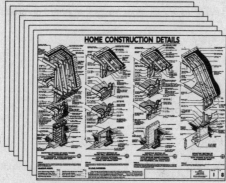

$14.95 per set

Residential Plumbing Details

Nine sheets packed with information detailing pipe connection methods, fittings, and sizes. Shows sump–pump and water softener hookups, and septic system construction. Conforms to requirements of National Plumbing Code. Color coded with a glossary of terms and quick index.

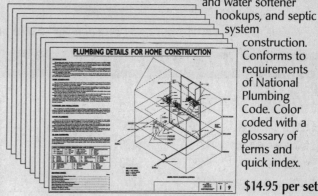

$14.95 per set

Residential Electrical Details

Nine sheets that cover all aspects of residential wiring, from simple switch wiring to the complexities of three-phase and service entrance connection. Explains service load calculations and distribution panel wiring. Shows you how to create a floor-plan wiring diagram. Conforms to requirements of National Electrical Code. Color coded with a glossary of terms and a quick index.

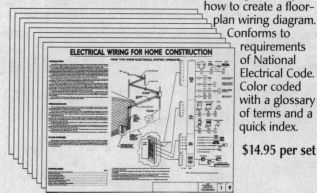

$14.95 per set

Important Shipping Information

Your order is processed immediately. Allow 10 working days from our receipt of your order for normal ground delivery. Save time with your credit card and our "800" number. Our delivery service must have a street address or Rural Route Box number — never a post office box. Use a work address if no one is home during the day.

Orders being shipped to Alaska, Hawaii, APO, FPO or Post Office Boxes must go via First Class Mail. Please include the proper postage.

Only Certified bank checks and money orders are accepted and must be payable in U.S. currency. For speed, we ship international orders Air Parcel Post. Please refer to the chart for the correct shipping cost.

An important note:

All plans are drawn to conform to one or more of the industry's major national building standards. However, due to the variety of local building regulations, your plan may need to be modified to comply with local requirements — snow loads, energy loads, seismic zones, etc. Do check them fully and consult your local building officials.

A few states require that all building plans used be drawn by an architect registered in that state. While having your plans reviewed and stamped by such an architect may be prudent, laws requiring non-conforming plans like ours to be completely redrawn forces you to unnecessarily pay very large fees. If your state has such a law, we strongly recommend you contact your state representative to protest.

Please submit all Canadian plan orders to:
Garlinghouse Company
20 Cedar Street North, Kitchener, Ontario N2H 2W8
Canadian Customers Only: 1-800-561-4169/Fax #: 1-519-743-1282
Customer Service #: 1-519-743-4169

ORDER TOLL FREE— 1-800-235-5700
Monday-Friday 8:00 a.m. to 5:00 p.m. Eastern Time
or FAX your Credit Card order to 1-203-343-5984
All foreign residents call 1-203-343-5977

Please have ready: **1. Your credit card number   2. The plan number   3. The order code number ⇨ H5NH1**

GARLINGHOUSE BLUEPRINT PRICE CODE SCHEDULE:
Additional sets with original order $25

PRICE CODE	A	B	C	D	E	F	G	H
8 SETS OF SAME PLAN	$330	$350	$375	$400	$430	$470	$510	$555
5 SETS OF SAME PLAN	$280	$300	$325	$350	$380	$420	$460	$505
1 SINGLE SET OF PLANS	$210	$230	$255	$280	$310	$350	$390	$435
VELLUMS	$420	$440	$465	$490	$520	$560	$600	$645
MATERIALS LIST	$25	$25	$30	$30	$35	$40	$40	$45

DOMESTIC SHIPPING*	1-2 Sets	3+ Sets
UPS/RPS Ground Service	$6.50	$8.50
First Class Mail	$8.00	$11.00
2-Day Express	$16.00	$20.00
Overnight Express	$26.00	$30.00

INTERNATIONAL SHIPPING	1-2 Sets	3+ Sets
Canada	**$11.00**	**$15.50**
All Other Nations	$40.00	$52.00

Plan Numbers 90,000 & Above For Domestic Shipping — Standard Express 3-5 Days -- $20.00

Canadian Orders and Shipping: To our friends in Canada, we have a plan design affiliate in Kitchener, Ontario. This relationship will help you avoid the delays and charges associated with shipments from the United States. Moreover, our affiliate is familiar with the building requirements in your community and country. We prefer payments in U.S. Currency. If you, however, are sending Canadian funds please add 40% to the prices of the plans and shipping fees.

— Blueprint Order Form —
GARLINGHOUSE

Order Code No. **H5NH1**

Plan No._____
❑ As Shown   ❑ Reversed *(mult. set pkgs. only)*

	Each	Amount
8 set pkg.		$
5 set pkg.		$
1 set pkg. (no reverses)		$
_____ (qty.) Add'l. sets @		$
Vellums		$
Materials List (with plan order only)		$
Residential Builder Plans		
_____ set(s) Construction	@ $14.95	$
_____ set(s) Plumbing	@ $14.95	$
_____ set(s) Electrical	@ $14.95	$
Shipping		$
Subtotal		$
Sales Tax (CT residents add 6% sales tax, KS residents add 6.15% sales tax) (Not required for other states)		$
Total Amount Enclosed		**$**

Prices guaranteed until 8-15-96
Payment must be made in U.S. funds
Foreign Mail Orders: Certified bank checks in U.S. funds only

Credit Card Information
Charge To: ❑ Visa   ❑ Mastercard

Card # |_|_|_|_|_|_|_|_|_|_|_|_|_|_|_|_|

Signature _____   Exp. _____/_____

Send your check, money order or credit card information to:
(No C.O.D.'s Please)
Please Submit all United States & Other Nations plan orders to:
Garlinghouse Company
P.O. Box 1717
Middletown, CT 06457

Please Submit all Canadian plan orders to:
Garlinghouse Company
20 Cedar Street North
Kitchener, Ontario N2H 2W8

Bill To: (address must be as it appears on credit card statement)

Name_____

Address_____

City/State_____ Zip_____

Daytime Phone (_____) _____

Ship To (if different from Bill to):

Name_____

Address_____

City/State_____ Zip_____